Creating Africa in America

CONTEMPORARY ETHNOGRAPHY

Kirin Narayan and Paul Stoller, Series Editors

A complete list of books in the series is available from the publisher.

Creating Africa in America

Translocal Identity in an Emerging World City

JACQUELINE COPELAND-CARSON

PENN

University of Pennsylvania Press

Philadelphia

10 9 8 7 6 5 4 3 2 1

Published by
University of Pennsylvania Press
Philadelphia, Pennsylvania 19104-4011

Library of Congress Cataloging-in-Publication Data
Copeland-Carson, Jacqueline.
   Creating Africa in America : translocal identity in an emerging world city / Jacqueline
Copeland-Carson.
      p. cm.—(Contemporary ethnography)
   Includes bibliographical references (p.   ) and index.
   ISBN 0-8122-3790-0 (alk. paper)—ISBN 0-8122-1876-0 (pbk. alk. paper)
   1. African Americans—Minnesota—Minneapolis—Social conditions. 2. African
Americans—Minnesota—Minneapolis—Ethnic identity. 3. African Americans—Services
for—Minnesota—Minneapolis. 4. Cultural Wellness Center (Minneapolis, Minn.)
5. Community life—Minnesota—Minneapolis. 6. Minneapolis (Minn.)—Social conditions.
7. African Americans—Social conditions—Case studies. 8. African Americans—Ethnic
identity—Case studies. 9. Community life—United States—Case studies. 10. African
diaspora—Case studies. I. Title. II. Series.
F614.M59N44 2004
305.896'073776579—dc22   2003070544

For Patricia Copeland, Jurene Jones, and Virginia Aiken, three family ancestors who continue to inspire and sustain me

Contents

viii   Contents

On Life Betwixt and Between

My deceased grandmother, who was originally from South Carolina and moved to Philadelphia in her forties, was at least of partial Gullah heritage. An unschooled farmer who, as family legend has it, delivered her six babies on her own without the aid of doctor or midwife, she taught herself to read by memorizing the Bible. Grandma Aiken had a battery of sayings that could have filled a "good book" of her own. The family's youngsters rarely knew *exactly* what Grandma was talking about. When I'd ask my mother to interpret what she was saying, she would just look down and, while shaking her head, say, "Chile, that's just that old country Geechee English; don't pay too much mind to it." But I paid attention anyway and the meanings of many of her mysterious sayings have slowly revealed themselves to me over the years—I think once I had enough life experience to fully relate to what she was saying. Every time I saw her she would say to me with a hug and with earnest certainty, "How's my lil' school teacher?!" Eventually, Grandma's nickname for me became School Teacher. I remember being initially a little perplexed about why she would call a six-year-old "School Teacher." Over time I intuitively came to understand that for Grandma, who was largely denied opportunity because of Jim Crow, this was an act of aspiration and faith that my future might realize her deferred dreams.

I continue to be driven by the visions of this woman who survived and accomplished much in conditions that I can barely imagine. In part because of her, and even though I didn't grow up in the most privileged of circumstances, I always believed I could write books that people might read and maybe find in some way interesting. I wrote this book in large part to honor my deceased grandmother's hopes for my generation. For me she represents the Black women who have nurtured and inspired me and who created many "firsts"—big and small—that have made African Americans' astounding survival as a people possible in America.[1] I stand in their shadow and spirit, trying to make myself worthy of their sacrifice. This book is as much their creation as it is mine and is dedicated to them.

Grandma Aiken left me with a particular saying that has been a running motif of my life and this book. Frequently, when I would ask her how she was doing, she would say that she was "betwixt and between." As a young woman I came to understand that what Grandma meant was that she wasn't feeling bad; she wasn't feeling good; she was just existing some place between happiness and resignation—a general state of many people's lives. Technically, the term, derived from Old English, means a midway position—neither one thing nor the other. But I think that Grandma was also making a kind of existential statement—an expression of a condition of feeling out of sync for some reason that she could not quite explain.

Black people in America have long written about this condition of betwixt-and-betweenness that W. E. B. Du Bois called double consciousness: a disjointed identity, partially imposed by racism—the "two-ness" of living between Whiteness and Blackness, Africanness and Americanness—always seeing oneself through another's vision, never feeling quite whole. With the global flow of people and ideas in the contemporary world, this feeling of disjuncture—of being betwixt and between—as Grandma would say—is increasingly common for many people. In many ways this book is the most current iteration of my longstanding personal effort to weave together the seemingly disconnected threads that have shaped the many cultural worlds in which I live: Black; White; nonprofit; corporate America; Nigeria; Philadelphia, Pennsylvania; Minneapolis, Minnesota; and many others.

This book tells the story of the Cultural Wellness Center (CWC), a Minneapolis (Minnesota) nonprofit organization that attempts to create new approaches to build "African" community to reduce feelings of alienation, for Black people and many others living through the most rapid demographic changes in this region's history. The CWC teaches that many of the lifestyle-related illnesses, such as diabetes and hypertension, that disproportionately affect persons of African descent are in fact a result of warring identities literally inside the bodies of people of color and others as they attempt to assimilate into mainstream society. The CWC offers a complex array of programs to help people create a more integrated identity and more healthful lifestyles to support it.

I was drawn to do this ethnographic case study for several reasons. The theoretical, applied, and methodological reasons are presented in great detail in this book's main sections. But there are personal reasons as well. I began my training as an Africanist and anthropologist largely because I also felt this sense of betwixt-and-betweenness. I was living in some no-(wo)man's-land between the tough Philadelphia neighborhood where I grew up and Georgetown University, trying to define my place in the world and how I could contribute to it. I grew up in an urban community that was challenged by many social issues such as poverty and drug abuse, while it also had strong institutions, including churches, mosques, drill and step teams, block clubs—all created by Black people. There were also the people in the community that the youth would call the "old heads"—people who were thought to have wisdom about a particular aspect of life or Black history—particularly African Americans' relationship to Africa. These peo-

ple and institutions held together the sometimes tattered but still whole social fabric of our community.

I was amazed once I went off to study anthropology as an undergraduate
and graduate student that ethnographies featuring these people and institutions were rarely written. The picture of Black urban communities often
presented in many 1970s and 1980s ethnographies did not represent the
inner-city community that I or my family and friends knew. There was
much written about our social problems. Studies of the functional aspects
of our communities were somehow often presented as distorted versions of
normative, that is White, social structures. Social problems were certainly
one aspect of many ghettos with concentrated poverty. But the pimp and
wino approach to much urban ethnography had the unpleasant side effect
of pathologizing Black urban communities and blinding the field to the assets that also existed in them. I felt stuck betwixt and between the one-sided
picture of Black life that was prominent in many academic—and media—
accounts and my actual experience of it. I decided at that point that there
were sufficient ethnographies about "what's wrong with us." I hoped to one
day support and write about the longstanding, homegrown efforts, many in
the nonprofit sector, to address these social issues—what I call the "glass is
half full" approach to African diasporan ethnography in the United States.
Much of what I present in this book will seem like common sense to people who have worked on such grassroots social efforts or who grew up in
Black inner-city communities like those of Philadelphia. The CWC is not
representative of all nonprofit sector work involving Black people and, in
fact, this agency works with a multicultural constituency. But it does provide a glimpse into this largely unrecognized aspect of Black cultural life
and will hopefully provoke the interest of a broader academic and popular
audience into the historical importance of Black America's self-help traditions that have existed since the colonial period.

As many Africanists and Americanists know, throughout America's history, African American culture grew from the intermingling of the cultures
and traditions of various African peoples and others who come to this
country. I have personally been part of the contemporary flow of these exchanges between Africans and African Americans and my experiences have
informed my interest in how people in the African diaspora—and diasporas in general—create identities and communities. In the early 1980s I lived
in Nigeria as an exchange student, and I was constantly surprised by the impact of Black American culture—from the arts to standards of beauty—on
contemporary life in Nigeria's cities, towns, and villages. The ensuing cultural interchange has happened at the level of family and many other social institutions. Although this intermixing is recognized as an historical
fact, fine-grained ethnographic studies of African immigrants to the United
States and their relations with African Americans are few. Studies of the
impact of Black American culture on West African culture are also few

and far between. In addition to contributing to social science theory, particularly in anthropology, the process of researching and writing this book also has been an illuminating personal experience. I now better understand how trends in the global economy have influenced my own journey as a Black woman through Africa's diaspora. I am most thankful to the CWC for enabling me to learn much more about myself and my family history than I had ever anticipated when I started this project.

During the fieldwork for this book I was having new personal struggles with betwixt-and-betweenness. After finishing all of my doctoral course requirements, for almost five years I served as a vice president of the Philadelphia Foundation. My job was to help build community in some of the most depressed inner-city neighborhoods in the region; to create coalitions among nonprofits, government agencies, and businesses to strengthen these areas; and to make grants to support the various projects that emerged from these efforts. For me it was a perfect job—a rare opportunity to practice community ethnography and to make a real difference in the city that had nurtured me as a youth. I kept current with new developments in the field because anthropological theories and models were important sources of innovation in my social sector work. But, like many scholars who work professionally, I felt lost between full practice and full scholarship. I was a closeted anthropologist; I was not able, at the time, to integrate the two sides of my persona as an anthropologist—practitioner and theoretician. Ethnography in an applied setting, as presented in this book, is a natural outgrowth of my work in the nonprofit sector. A personal lesson learned is that many of the cultural trends and issues that anthropologists study are indeed created in this intermediate space between government and private enterprise. Nonprofit sector ethnography provides a tool to practice anthropology while making new contributions to culture theory. In many ways this book is a coming out for me as a cultural anthropologist who is now comfortable with a dual identity as a practitioner and scholar.

In 1995 I moved to Minnesota to join my husband where he had taken a new job. Although I have lived in at least half the world, my stays in other countries and communities were generally temporary. The culture that supported me in Philadelphia was not apparent in Minnesota. Since my culture was no longer at my doorstep, I had to seek it out and develop a social network through which I could express it with other people.

During this period, to my absolute shock and surprise, Minnesota's African immigrant community began to grow by leaps and bounds. By the late 1990s, the state had more Somalis than any other place in the country, as well as Ethiopians and other Africans from many countries—many of whom were refugees escaping the wars and civil unrest affecting their homelands. I certainly did not expect to find many African immigrants in one of the most frigid parts of the country, where winter often lasts from

October to May. All of sudden, it seemed to me, African groceries started opening up. I could now easily buy a powdered pounded yam mix, plantains and other foods that had become a regular part of my diet after living in Nigeria. Slowly but surely, African restaurants, tailor shops, and social service agencies began to appear. At the same time, I kept running into African American professionals who had recently relocated to Minnesota, which has one of the highest concentrations of Fortune 500 companies in the United States and, at the time, one of the lowest unemployment rates. I later learned from the 2000 Census and other statistical studies that I cite in this book that in the 1990s, Minnesota also had a large influx of African Americans from other cities—poor and middle-class—who arrived here for opportunities in the region's vibrant economy. In fact, as I later discovered, the recent census also showed that Minnesota has the most diverse Black population in the United States in terms of ethnic and national origin. My personal sense that America's Black diaspora was converging in the Twin Cities was validated by the statistics, and I was living through these demographic changes. The process of writing this book helped me understand why these changes were occurring and what they meant for contemporary global cultural dynamics.

Like most ethnography, this piece of scholarship also contains shards of the ethnographer's personal life. Throughout this book the reader will see that I recognize these influences and address them in my scholarly analysis. In other words, in current anthropological parlance, I attempt to be "reflexive"—to put myself as ethnographer in the story and attempt to self-consciously control for ways in which my personal biases might influence the research setting and my interpretation of it. This preface serves in part as an additional personal disclosure. However, it is also a commentary on the particular challenges that the field of anthropology sometimes presents for people of color, women, and others who do "native anthropology," that is, ethnography in their own country or community of origin applying reflexive approaches. Until writing this book, I felt caught between two competing but often implicit claims of reflexive ethnography. On the one hand, the field maintains that such an approach is legitimate and even necessary for contemporary ethnography. On the other hand, scholars who use reflexive approaches, especially when doing native anthropology, can be seen as less objective. This book presents key fieldwork encounters and other personal perspectives that may have affected collection and interpretation of the ethnographic data. But this book is an ethnography, not a memoir or diary. I keep community voices dominant and my voice is evident to the extent it may have influenced the research context. I present diverse perspectives on the CWC's work and include verbatim statements of people during CWC meetings and programs to give the reader an authentic sense of the dynamic culture-building processes taking place there. At the same time I try to protect the identities of the persons with whom I

worked. This is particularly important because the leadership and participants were wary of being subjected to studies that had no clear benefit to
their community. Thus, pseudonyms are used throughout and I avoid providing personal detail about participants' lives that would easily identify
them and their opinions here in the local community.

Some might find the CWC's mission and programs controversial. For example, some Africanists might find its notions of Africa romanticized. Anthropologists might take issue with its notions of race and culture. Those
with little experience in grassroots Black community efforts might deem
their ideas Afrocentric. But cultural anthropologists specialize in documenting human cultural creativity. Thus, the CWC's work is by definition
worthy of study, even if its views may be disagreeable to some scholars. As
an individual, I do not necessarily agree with all CWC doctrines and to
write an unbiased case study does not require that I do so. However, as a
cultural anthropologist I recognize one of the field's basic tenets: people's
beliefs are culturally true for them, and we are charged to study them
regardless of our own beliefs—personal or scholarly.

I have had numerous guides and supporters on this stage of my diasporan journey. Although the interpretation of these experiences is mine, survival through this sojourn would not have been possible without them.
First, I must recognize the support and encouragement of Paul Stoller
and Peter Agree, my two editors at the University of Pennsylvania Press. I
appreciate their ability to see in this case study a story worthy of being told.

I must also acknowledge the excellent training and support that I have
received from many people for many years from the Department of Anthropology at the University of Pennsylvania. Sandra Barnes, in particular,
has been an indefatigable advocate and mentor. Her openness to my exploration of unconventional topics in Africanist anthropology has been
critical to my development. Her steadfast support through the sometimes
unpredictable twists and turns of my diasporan journey has been above and
beyond the call of duty.

Igor Kopytoff's steady support and exemplary training in the history of
anthropology as well as classical approaches in Africanist anthropology
have also made important contributions to my development. His consistent
reminder to study the classics and friendly debates about postmodern theory have influenced the eclectic blending of old and new theory in this
study's interpretation of transnational cultural processes in the Twin Cities
African diaspora. I am also grateful for Peggy Sanday's encouragement to
publish the study and her public-interest anthropology perspective.

Classes by Arjun Appadurai, now at the New School for Social Research,
and Kris Hardin provided invaluable explorations of issues in ethnohistory,
ethnoaesthetics, and the anthropology of complexity which are evident
throughout this study. Finally, Gwendolyn Mikell of Georgetown University

and Elliot Skinner of Columbia University have provided appreciated encouragement and advice since my undergraduate days.

The Bush Foundation's Leadership Fellowship Program (1997–1998)
provided funding for this study. Its support enabled me to take a much-
needed leave of absence from practicing anthropology to conduct the primary research for this study. I am especially thankful to John Archabal,
Martha Lee, and Charlene Edwards of the foundation for their feedback
and support. While on this leave of absence I was a fellow at the Roy
Wilkins Center at the University of Minnesota's Humphrey Institute. The
center's current and former staff—Professor Samuel L. Myers, Jr., director;
Judy Leahy; Mary Lou Garza; and Julia Blount—provided not only an academic home base in Minnesota but constant encouragement. I would especially like to thank Julia, who helped me solve the mysteries of word
processing.

I must also recognize two agencies where I had professional experiences
that helped to sensitize me to the potential of the nonprofit and philanthropic sector to inform contemporary issues in anthropology: the
Philadelphia Foundation and the OMG Center. My sincere thanks to Car-
rolle Devonish, formerly president of the foundation, and Tom Burns and
Gerri Spilka of the OMG Center for Collaborative Learning, who provided
me with practical forums to cultivate some of the approaches to nonprofit
sector ethnography used in this study.

I cannot express enough appreciation to the staff, participants, and volunteers of the Cultural Wellness Center, where I based the ethnographic
research for this study. Their bold and unconventional approach to issues
of health and wellness and their capacity to build concrete consensus
around a wide range of potentially volatile community issues are inspiring.
I am thankful for their collaboration and hopeful that the concepts presented in this study are in some way useful to their work.

Finally, I must recognize my extended network of family and friends who
have been a bedrock of support through what has been one of the most
challenging undertakings of my life. A special thanks to my husband, Emmett D. Carson, and my thirteen-year-old daughter, Yetunde, for tolerating
my often arcane dinner conversation digressions about "deterritorializa-
tion" and "transnational scapes of global cultural flow." Emmett, thank you
for staying the course in this journey and believing in me. The unflinching
belief of my sister and brother, Parthenia and Aaron, in my aspirations was
a constant source of strength and inspiration. Also, special thanks to my
mother, Willette Copeland, whose sacrifices, high expectations, and constant faith always inspired me to dream, even when I've lived nightmares.

Although I have had the good fortune of unwavering support and advice
throughout this process, the study ultimately represents my interpretations
of the issues. It does not necessarily reflect the perspectives of the numer-

ous people and institutions who have in some way supported this project. Nor does its analysis in any way constitute an evaluation of the effectiveness of the CWC, which is its subject. The findings and conclusions are primarily designed to inform issues in anthropology and not the decisions of current or prospective CWC funders.

I have emerged from this process affirmed in my identity as an anthropologist practitioner-scholar—a bridge between two sides of social life upon which our field is ultimately based. This space between theory and application, called public anthropology by some, is fertile ground for those of us who want to inform our discipline's theory building while building community. I am most indebted to the Cultural Wellness Center for showing me a path out of the betwixt-and-betweenness of the practice-versus-theory divide.

Prologue to a Diasporan Journey

Suddenly a woman, who seemed African American, stood up in the middle of a moderated session at a daylong conference called "Understanding African Refugees in Our Community." Dressed in a West African factory-print head tie with bubba and wrapper, her emotionally charged plea suggests the debates about African diasporan identity occurring in Minnesota, which, according to the 2000 Census has the most diverse Black population in the nation: "If you want to build bridges, then look at me as African. When you look at me, you see the spirit of Africa. Look at me as an African; I am not here by choice. Politically, I'm African American; but in my soul and spirit, I'm African."[1]

After her statement, there was an uncomfortable silence across the diverse audience comprised mostly of African immigrants, and White and Black Americans. Before her declaration, the three-hundred-person audience of community activists, foundation staff, and public servants was having a polite discussion. The session moderator was the director of a Washington, D.C. based African immigrant advocacy organization who was also a Zimbabwean immigrant. The theme of his speech was the need for various African immigrant groups to "build bridges" with African American civil rights groups, as both African immigrants and African Americans are affected by racial discrimination. After the stunned silence, a heated exchange ensued prompted by a question from an African American grant maker about how foundations should address factionalism in the Twin Cities' African immigrant community. An Ethiopian immigrant and locally well-known community activist argued for recognizing the various factions and funding nonprofit organizations to support them: "You can't expect people to suddenly come to America and forget!" The African American foundation grant maker argued that factions could not be accepted: "In America, we should require that you serve everyone—regardless of clan or tribe—we should apply the same standard."

The Twin Cities have recently become a crossroads in the global flow of people, ideas, symbols, and capital that increased immigration to the United States has produced. Attracted largely by the metropolitan region's strong economy, the region has the largest Somali, Hmong, and urban Native American populations in the United States. It also has growing numbers of Chicano, Latino, and Russian immigrants as well as a sizable Tibetan community.[2] The region's profound demographic changes have even caught the attention of the national media. Within the past few years, the *New York Times, Washington Post,* and *Wall Street Journal* have all had prominent front-page articles on these profound demographic changes.

The Stockholm of America, this city of lutefisk and liberals has long boasted a tradition of generous social programs and enlightened views on American race relations. But for all the proudly progressive attitudes, only a tiny percentage of blacks actually lived in Minnesota, a place where a mixed marriage once meant the union of a Swede and a Norwegian.

That monochromatic fabric has been changing swiftly. Migration of Blacks, especially those in poverty, has been stronger in the Minneapolis and St. Paul area than in any other urban center in the North. And other groups, especially Hmong, Somalis and Ethiopians, most of them refugees brought to Minnesota by religious groups, have become a growing part of the city's ethnic mix.

The demographic changes in the land of Lake Wobegone[3] are a striking illustration of the ethnic and racial shift that is remaking the nation. And the new mix, particularly the growth among poor blacks from Chicago, is testing the mettle of Minnesota liberalism and changing the texture of the political debate, as civic leaders grapple with issues of race, class, and crime that most other big American cities were forced to confront long ago.[4]

Leaving aside the article's implied equation of increased racial diversity with crime and a more general sense of social chaos and danger, this excerpt provides a good overall sense of the issues of race, poverty, and diversity, which are very much at the forefront of Twin Cities public discourse and politics.[5] Concurrent with the increasing settlement of African-born and African American peoples in the Twin Cities, there have been increasing racial disparities on a range of socioeconomic indicators. Despite the relative economic vitality of the region, until the post-September 11 economic downturn, the Twin Cities had been suffering from a critical shortage of skilled labor. Unemployment rates were below the national average—about 2 percent—but many newcomers did not have the skills necessary to fill the plentiful open positions that paid competitive livable wages. Although there was a low overall unemployment rate, the unemployment rate was much higher for people of color.[6] According to recent census data, four out of every ten African Americans in urban Minnesota live in poverty. This is the highest rate among the nation's twenty-five largest cities. As a result of these and other socioeconomic factors, including segregation, there is an increasing concentration of poverty in the Twin

Cities that is especially affecting communities of color (powell 1999:1; Harrison and Weinberg 1992).[7]

Local social service agencies and the business community, including the many multinational corporations that have Twin Cities headquarters (e.g., 3M and General Mills), have attempted to adjust to the profoundly increased cultural diversity of their customers and workers through the promotion of cultural sensitivity training, specialized employee recruitment efforts, and support of job training and other community development initiatives sponsored by their corporate philanthropy programs. This relatively well-off community is now grappling with perceived convergences of race, class, and poverty that other cities began to confront years ago. Counterbalancing this intensifying concentration of poverty is Minnesota's vibrant nonprofit and philanthropic sector. The state is generally recognized as having one of the highest levels of philanthropy; innovative, nonprofit activism; and civic participation in the United States.[8]

The Twin Cities, and by extension many of its most diverse neighborhoods, are fast becoming translocalities in Appadurai's (1996:192) sense of the term. The region, while certainly not on the scale of a New York City or London, is emerging as a world city at the nexus of a global flow of people, ideas, and resources. Everyday social life is at once local and global.

This study examines how a neighborhood-based nonprofit attempts to create a sense of locality in a place where residents may have community affiliations that crosscut the globe.[9] In this book, my forum for exploring how Africans and Americans are addressing the cultural implications of these changing demographics is the Cultural Wellness Center (CWC). The CWC is a community-based, Minneapolis nonprofit that is deliberately attempting to create a shared sense of community across the diverse new and native-born ethnic groups that now inhabit the Twin Cities metropolitan region.

Exploration of Minnesota's active construction of new African identities is my most recent leg is an almost twenty-year journey as a practitioner-scholar in the nonprofit sector. During this time, mostly in Nigeria and several North American cities, I have had vexing encounters that blur the lines between what would be considered African and American, or European. In many ways this work is a meditation on the multiple intellectual and personal epiphanies I had along the way. It chronicles the experiences of Twin Cities residents who shared with me their transformative insights as they struggled to adjust to American society on their own cultural terms. It represents a new phase of my understanding of the impact of the global flow of culture through African peoples.[10] It is next to impossible to understand contemporary Africa outside of this flow, and the influences manifest themselves in ways that anthropologists are just beginning to acknowledge and understand. Not only are African peoples mixing the constituent parts

of cultures, such as American music, dance, and aesthetics and other influences, to create new practices and identities; this creativity also occurs at
a metacultural level. The very theories and models of identity such as culture, race, and ethnicity employed by anthropologists and other social scientists are often also being studied and deliberately reconstructed by
everyday African people in this culture-building enterprise.

One of my first experiences of the impact of global cultural dynamics on
Africa was as an undergraduate student in African studies at Georgetown
University in the early 1980s. I did my first anthropological study from 1982
to 1983 as an exchange student at Ọbáfémi Awólọ́wọ̀ University in Ilé Ifẹ̀,
Nigeria.[11] The study concerned the Aladura Church, a religious revitalization movement that began in Nigeria (see Peel 1968). My most striking experience doing this research was learning that the Aladura Movement had
been transplanted to the United States by Yorùbá immigrants. Indeed,
Washington, D.C. had, at the time, become an important center for the
Aladura Movement, drawing together African American, Caribbean, Nigerian, and other West African adherents. I completed my fieldwork for my
senior thesis in African studies on the Aladura Movement not in Nigeria
but in Washington, D.C. at an Aladura church founded by a Yorùbá man
and his Gullah wife from South Carolina.

My experience in Nigeria, as well as early career experiences in community development efforts back in the United States, led to an interest in the
ways in which academic anthropology could be applied to nonprofit sector
issues and to the ethnographic research opportunities presented by the
community development field. My next African study that underscored the
importance of global cultural forces to African societies was ethnoaesthetic
research on contemporary Yorùbá architecture in Ilé-Ifẹ̀. In my anthropology and urban planning master's theses I presented an alternative conceptual model and research method for understanding how contemporary
sociocultural, class, and identity issues were reflected in Yorùbá housing design. An important lesson in how transnational cultural flows influence
local cultural production was the evolution of the "Brazilian" house, introduced to Nigeria by repatriated Brazilian slaves in the nineteenth century,
as the prototype of the "modern" Yorùbá house (Vlach 1984, 1986). This
Nigerian project further sensitized me to the limitations of conventional
categories such as "traditional" and "modern," as well as notions such as
"ethnicity," "history," and even "culture" itself, for capturing the nuances of
indigenous cultural dynamics.

My exploration of indigenous models for conceptualizing sociocultural
complexity was enhanced by the emerging critical anthropology literature
(Said 1978; Fabian 1983; Hobsbawm and Ranger 1983; Marcus and Fisher
1999). In particular, Said's notion of orientalism (1978); Cohn's studies of
the role of the British census on the construction of South Asian identities
(1987a); Fabian's analysis of the impact of conventional anthropology

(1983); comparative studies of historicity; and various analyses of the limits of essentially Western models of nation, ethnicity, and culture (see Barth 1984 and 1989; Depres 1984; Worsley 1984; Harvey 1989; Fardon 1987; Moore 1987; Handler 1988; Appadurai 1990) were instrumental in my still evolving eclectic blend of conventional and critical perspectives in both academic and applied anthropology.

During this period, I became particularly interested in the Nupe of central Nigeria, who were key intermediaries in trans-Saharan trade with the medieval and late nineteenth-century West African forest kingdoms and who built an expansive empire lasting from about the sixteenth century until the British conquest. Additionally, since Nadel's (1942) classic work, there had been little anthropological attention paid to Nupe history and culture. It seemed to me that the study of indigenous Nupe models for organizing and managing cultural diversity would be a base from which to initiate an ongoing original contribution to the field. I decided to do an ethnohistorical study of Nupe identity formation focused on the medieval through early colonial period. In preparation for fieldwork I spent almost a year working with a Nupe immigrant living in Philadelphia who tutored me in the language, using a Nupe grammar guide and dictionary devised by an early twentieth-century British missionary (Banfield 1969). I defined my research problem as an effort to reconstruct indigenous models for the organization of cultural diversity and their transformation through the contemporary period. After completing my Ilé-Ifẹ̀ fieldwork for my master's theses, I started preliminary fieldwork for this project and was based at the University of Ìlọrin in the summer and fall of 1988 for several months. During this period, I collected and reviewed primary historical records archived in Kaduna and conducted exploratory ethnohistorical interviews in several Nupe villages and towns. This fieldwork was a watershed in my understanding of ethnohistory and identity formation.

Alhaji Aliyu Idress, a scholar of Nupe history then at the University of Ìlọrin and a member of the Nupe royal family, was my guide and interpreter during this visit. Among the several Nupe towns, villages, and cities we visited was Patigi, which prior to the British conquest was an important, cosmopolitan trading center. In Patigi, I interviewed a group of chiefs about the process of a ze Nupe, that is, becoming Nupe. I was particularly interested in following up a notion raised in Nadel's ethnography that there were "hyphenated" Nupe—people who had emigrated to the Nupe empire from other mostly western Africa polities and were described as Fulani-Nupe, Yorùbá-Nupe, Hausa-Nupe, and so on.

After an astonished and extended commentary on my physical appearance—the shadings of my skin color (which was described as "very black like Hausas"); my facial features, particularly my nose (which was described as "Fulani"); whether my original people were actually "real Nupe" or actually Yorùbá or Fulani; and promising me that "if I found out that my ancestors were Nupe I could return"—one chief explained the *a ze Nupe* process to me this way:

NUPE CHIEF   Daughter, let me help you understand. You know in America, they call you "Negro."

JCC   Yes, that is an old term, but that is a term that some people still use.

NUPE CHIEF   Now, Daughter, why do you think they call you Negro?

[Uncomfortable silence.]

NUPE CHIEF   Well let me tell you. Now you think that you are American. They think you are something else and the other people—the Europeans—are really American. *That's* how it is with us. Those people that come from outside, they can become Nupe—speak the language and everything—but they are not *real Nupe*!! Just like you are not a *real American*!!

I was too shocked by the chief's unexpectedly insightful analysis of contemporary North American identity politics to present the various possible standard counterpoints to such arguments: America—except for native peoples—was a country of immigrants, so I was as American as anyone else, and so forth. However, for a relatively new initiate to ethnography, this encounter offered several critical and practical lessons that fundamentally influence this study's orientation toward African diasporan identity formation.

Indigenous notions of identity are not easily disaggregated from the influence of contemporary sociopolitical issues, derived from both local and translocal sources. Instead of reconstructing the historical facts that contributed to the development of the *a ze Nupe* process, I was actually studying a component of Nupe historicity—the way in which Nupe people conceptualize and remember history based on the convergence of historical events, cultural, and sociopolitical factors. It was difficult to extract an indigenous Nupe model for conceptualizing diversity from the chief's apparent exposure. I learned later that this exposure to North American notions of identity was largely gained from foreign newspapers, television, and reports of local people who had traveled and lived abroad. Nupe models developed within a transnational cultural flow.

It also became clear, through many incidents similar to the above encounter, that I—and people's preconceptions and understanding of my own identity as a "Black" person or a person of some sort of African descent—was an unavoidable part of the research context. Whether the notions of the historical connections between Africa and African Americans were considered real, imagined, or invented, the issue was one of active debate whenever I entered a conversation, despite my earnest efforts to keep the group interview focused on "*Nupe* issues of identity." Nupe perspectives on my identity and how it influenced the research context were also ethnographic facts that had to be addressed. If I approached this task self-consciously and explicitly (the move to reflexivity and critical analysis of native anthropology were just beginning in the field), the typical debates about my own identity in African diasporan research contexts could add important dimensions to the ethnographic data. On the other hand, if I hid this dimension through the various stylistic artifices possible in ethnographic writing (for example, assumption of the socially neutral, omniscient ethnographer role), I would be contorting the ethnographic data to screen out personally discomforting aspects of the contemporary sociopolitical environment and my perceived role in it.

Yet another experience during this same fieldwork period, this time in Ilé-Ifè, Nigeria, underscored the importance of transnational cultural flows through the African diaspora in shaping contemporary African identity. I had my hair braided in Ilé-Ifè before traveling to my Ìlọrin base for ethnographic site visits to several Nupe villages and towns. The style that I had was not one with which the Ife-Yorùbá hair braider was familiar. It was a style popular among professional African American women in Philadelphia. It involved braiding the hair into cornrows off the face and arranging the resulting cascade of hair that fell to the back of the head into what was known in Philadelphia as a "French twist." A friend from Ilé-Ifè and I talked the braider through adaptations of a classic Yorùbá style to get this Philadelphia-derived, French-twisted design. Well, when I returned from Ìlọrin to Ilé-Ifè en route to Lagos for my return to Philadelphia, I was surprised to learn that the painted barbershop sign outside the beautician's parlor where I had had my hair braided now included the style that the braider created, but it was called the "Sade"—a common Yorùbá female name. When questioning the braider, who was also the shop's proprietor, about it, she said that several people had subsequently asked her for the style, so she had it added to the barbershop board. She also said that it reminded her of the hairstyle of a London-based rhythm and blues and jazz singer, who is still popular both in the United States and Europe, named "Sade." The singer also, incidentally, has a Yorùbá father and an English mother. When I returned to Philadelphia, I noticed that many of the braiders that I and my African American friends used were either relatively recent immigrants from Africa or the Caribbean, or native-born African Americans who had adapted some styles imported from Africa. After talking to many of these women, I discovered that in the late 1980s and early 1990s, in several cities in the United States, with Washington, D.C., New York, Los Angeles, and Chicago most prominent among them, mostly African American braiders who were also licensed beauticians, concerned about allegedly unfair and increasing competition from home-based braiders, were leading efforts to create curricula, training programs, and standards for licensing braiders through cosmetology review boards. Many of these home-based braiders, who were not licensed but were making up to $300 per person for the more elaborate styles, were African immigrant and largely low-income African American women working in the informal economy. To more fully explore this issue, through an internship and later consultancy at the Smithsonian Institution's Program in African American Culture (National Museum of American History and Culture), I conducted an ethnographic study of the aesthetics of the African braiding industry in Washington, D.C., particularly as it related to contemporary African diasporan women's identity formation. This study not only emphasized the transnational exchange of symbols and images through the contemporary African diaspora but also hinted at what appeared to be the increasing commodification of these images in the contemporary global economy.

Thus, whether I was studying the Aladura religious movement, Nupe historicity, Yorùbá ethnoaesthetics and architecture, or identity politics and economics of African diasporan hairdressing, it became clear that a transnational approach is increasingly necessary to fully understand contemporary African and American cultural experience. This book builds on recent advances in culture theory, African diasporan studies as well as approaches from African diasporan ethnoaesthetics, ethnohistory, literary criticism, and religion (see Soyinka 1976, 1984; Gates 1984, 1988; Apter 1991, 1992; Mintz and Price 1992; Gilroy 1993; Murphy 1994; Chambers 1996). It represents the findings of a twenty-eight-month ethnographic study of the CWC's work to mobilize the region's small but relatively diverse and growing African American, African immigrant, and Afro-Caribbean immigrant residents to promote a notion of a shared "African" culture.[12]

With this ethnographic examination of African diasporan cultural dynamics in the Twin Cities, Minnesota, my academic and professional study of African identity formation has come full circle, expanding from its initial focus on such processes in West Africa to include a more global perspective, including the African diaspora as manifested in the United States. The CWC story about creating and promoting a transnational sense of African identity provides ethnographic insights into how people are creating notions of culture, identity, and place in the context of the global cultural interchanges that characterize contemporary urban America.

The research applies the longstanding anthropological study of indigenous African ethnicity to redress the relative neglect by the field, and immigration studies in general, of identity formation processes in North America's African diaspora. It also extends widely influential ethnographic and ethnohistorical studies in Africanist anthropology (e.g., Kopytoff 1981, 1988; Peel 1983; Comaroff 1985; Barnes 1986; M. Jackson 1986, 1989; Fardon 1988) to the study of the African diaspora in the United States. It attempts to connect these partially disconnected streams of African and African diasporan studies to provide an expanded theoretical pool for interpreting the polyvalent cultural flows that have historically informed and continue to connect Africa and the Americas—from Nigeria's nineteenth-century "Brazilian" architecture to variations on the African-derived religions in today's New York City (Barnes 1997). It sees the historical and contemporary cultural interchanges of the African diaspora—and diasporas in general—as providing important case studies that contribute to anthropology's current effort to understand global cultural formations. In addition to contributing to the movement toward research-driven ethnography in applied settings (Sanday 1976, 1998b; Ahmed and Shore 1995; Reed 1997), the study particularly informs the field's just emerging interest in the ethnography of the nonprofit sector, particularly the development of nongovernmental organizations (NGOs) (Escobar 1991, 1995; Ferguson 1994; Weisgrau 1997; W. F. Fisher 1997).

I attempt to apply and combine modified versions of what some scholars consider outmoded constructs—for example, "culture," "thick ethnographic description," and social network perspectives—with contemporary processual and reflexive approaches that look at the transnational flow of images and symbols, the construction of identity, and discourses on culture, race, gender, and hegemony, and with a self-consciousness of my sociopolitical role and impact as a native ethnographer.

As fieldwork progressed, it became evident that the intimate issues of health and wellness at the core of the CWC's community-building agenda focus on the body as a vehicle and agent for cultural recall and revitalization. A more sensual approach to ethnography than is typical in ethnography of immigrant experiences and ethnicity was required. In constructing African identity, CWC was very much attempting to create a different way of conceptualizing, sensing, and reconnecting what they call the "mind/body/spirit divide." The spoken word was critical for expressing and knowing the African reality the CWC was attempting to create. However, a methodology that privileges the written or spoken word over other ways of knowing would misconstrue a critical dimension of the CWC's mission. Therefore, an explicit effort is made to accommodate multiple modes of expression—the sounds, smells, and rhythms that comprise the aesthetics of the CWC's identity formation process.

Drawing on current approaches in sensorial anthropology and embodiment theory (see Howes 1991; M. Jackson 1983, 1989; Stoller 1989, 1987, 1996), the study is sensitive to the various ways the CWC's "African" leadership combines dialogical, visual, tactile, olfactory, gustatory, and oral modes of sensing, knowing and expressing reality—their lived, embodied experience of Africanness.[13] I attempt to present what the CWC's "African" leadership calls the "African way of seeing and knowing the world." In an effort to convey the intimate, lived, embodied experience of CWC participants I cite at length class and support group conversations as well as staff meetings, without any specific participant attribution. To fully comprehend and convey the insider's point of view on cultural wellness and identity formation required more than ethnographic interviewing and detached participation in meetings. I sometimes engaged in a rather rigorous—and physically challenging—form of intensive participant observation involving classes, staff and volunteer planning sessions, community meetings, and special events. This gave me multiple points of view on experiences of participants as well as a sense of the physical sensations they felt as something the CWC leadership considered to be a core component in the transformative identity formation process.

Special attention is given to the way participants felt about the CWC's spatial environment—its smell, design, decor, and ambiance—all of which figured prominently in interviews and comments. Photographs (see Appendix B), most of which were taken by a CWC participant and part-time teacher who also happened to be a professional photographer, aid this effort to depict the comprehensive, affective sense of Africanness that many participants felt was conveyed by the CWC's space.

Firm boundaries between African and African American are increasingly difficult to sustain with the accelerating global flow of peoples and cultures across continents. I hope that this ethnographic study of contemporary African diasporan identity formation in the North American nongovernmental sector contributes to the field's ongoing journey to help theory and practice catch up to this important piece of African peoples' cultural reality.

This book is divided into three major sections with chapters that document the CWC's strategies to create embodied African culture and community. The prologue and Part I, Reimagining North America's African Diaspora, set the personal, theoretical, methodological, ethnographic, political, and demographic context for the study. Part II, Across Diasporan Space/Time, considers the question: Who is "African" in a world of global cultural flows, meanings, and connections? I present the CWC participants' sometimes conflicting theories of African identity and the leadership's attempts to organize them into a coherent theory and practice of African healing and culture. I show how the CWC's cultural wellness discourse on African identity is an indirect form of resistance to dominant notions of race, class, and culture. Part III, Creating "Africa": A State of Mind/Body/Spirit, asks the question: How does the CWC promote embodiment of African identity, community, and culture? Specifically, I examine how various support group meetings and movement classes work to transform the CWC's concepts of diversity into a visceral experience of African wellness and healing that displace territory as the locus of African culture and community. The epilogue to this journey through the Twin Cities African diaspora presents how the context has changed in the post-September 11 period. I also discuss how the CWC case, and the community-based non-profit sector more generally, might inform theory and practice in our discipline.

Part I
Reimagining North America's African Diaspora

> . . . as anthropology increasingly abandons the idea that cultures can be treated as integrated wholes . . . we would do well to look at those African American communities that . . . defined themselves in neodiffusionist terms as nations apart, diasporas, and transnational communities, long before postcolonial theory made it fashionable to recognize that many non-African communities do so as well.
>
> —J. Lorand Matory, "Revisiting the African Diaspora"

"Africa" in Minnesota

The Cultural Wellness Center (CWC) was located on the major commercial strip of the Powderhorn neighborhood, a key crossroads in the Twin Cities' changing demographic landscape.[1] At one time, this busy intersection was a major commercial corridor in midtown Minneapolis. The corridor declined significantly over the past five years as major businesses, for example, a large Sears department store, left the area. No longer called "midtown" Minneapolis in the media, to the chagrin of local activists who emphasized the neighborhood's notable cultural and socioeconomic assets, the area was popularly referred to as the "inner city." In the media, the area was, unfortunately, known for its growing violent crime rate and drug trade, although many economic development projects were under way to revitalize it. Local merchants organized with nonprofits to create a business association that promoted the area's development. There were plans to redevelop the Sears site, several major business and health care facilities anchored the neighborhood's economy, and there were a growing number of small businesses, including several that were Asian, Chicano, Latino, or African immigrant owned.

Across the street from the CWC was the Lagos International Market and an African music shop. Farther down the block was a Somali recording studio that also sold Somali music and was becoming a community meeting place. Several shops down was an African bookstore owned by a Kenyan immigrant. In an office across from the CWC on the second floor of a drug store was the Association for Hmong Women, which used the CWC's space for community meetings, youth gatherings, and folk dance classes. There was a Mexican restaurant and an Indian curry house on the same block. About a half block from the CWC's offices was Ingebretsen's, a well-known store established in the neighborhood for about eighty years, specializing in Scandinavian foods and handicrafts.[2] A couple of blocks up from this store on the same boulevard were various specialty shops patronized by an international clientele including Latino Catholics, African people of various backgrounds (immigrants from different countries as well as American-born), as well as an interethnic group of White American Wiccans, that is, witches, many of whom identified themselves as feminists reconnecting with the lost healing traditions of pre-Christian Europe.

When I first started working in Powderhorn, this daily comingling of aromas—curry, tortillas, and lutefisk—with the sounds of West African high life and Tejano gave this corner of Minneapolis a disorienting, out-of-place, surreal flavor not found in the region until very recently. This is the story of a translocal nonprofit's effort to create a sense of place—a sense of home—for the many different peoples living in the Twin Cities and its African diaspora.

The CWC was actually located in a bank building owned and operated by a nonprofit housing developer. There were no outdoor signs identifying the center. In fact, the only outdoor signs were those of the bank. Unless you were observant enough to notice the distinctive colorful curtains and large picture windows, one might not even know the CWC was inside.

As you walked into the bank building, you entered double doors into a hallway. On one side there was the bank—a rather small neighborhood branch—distinguished by very large and colorful papier-maché masks suspended from the bank ceiling and made by a local community arts group just a block away from the CWC.[3] As you proceeded down the corridor, you would sometimes notice the aroma of sage or jasmine incense burning from the offices of the CWC, an unusual combination of smells for a bank building. Off the corridor there was an 8½" by 11" sign marking the CWC's entrance.

The smell of incense intensified once you opened the CWC's doors. On a typical day, there was an intoxicating blend of smells that one does not usually experience when visiting nonprofit offices and certainly not bank offices. Sage, jasmine, or other incense intermingled with the aromas of red beans and rice and cornbread cooking in a very homey kitchen at the back of the CWC between the formal conference room and the Invisible College where many classes and other large meetings were held.[4]

The reception area was adorned with African sculpture and textiles (see photographs in Appendix B), on loan from an African art gallery owned by an Ethiopian woman who was an active CWC supporter, and a shrine to European women killed during the witch burnings in medieval Europe. The reception desk had a glassless storefront window design with a ledge from which a long piece of bright yellow, purple, and red handwoven silk kente cloth from Ghana was hung. On the ledge were various small African sculptures, some from South Asia, and above the ledge were several ornate Guru masks. The office was usually very dim and there were typically scented or unscented candles burning on the reception area ledge and throughout the room giving the front reception area a calming ambience. Behind the ledge was a standard office desk used by the administrative assistant, a computer, printer, fax machine, and photocopier.

The rather large reception area was set up like a living room, with a comfortable sofa and two side chairs. Large and small vases with fragrant dried flowers or candles adorned the cocktail table and open spaces. Surrounding the reception area were small offices where the full-time staff worked. Children of all ages were often in the reception area, and their joyous drone could also be heard during meetings; children even sometimes came to adult classes. They were welcome, and the staff, particularly African leaders, often graciously integrated the babies, especially, into the meetings, by carrying and bouncing them in their arms, even occasionally directing baby talk to them as they facilitated meeting discussion. Meeting participants did not seem disturbed or irritated by the integration of children into official activities, as it seemed to be a part of CWC culture.

Connected to the reception area was a small corridor with two additional offices on either side. One was sublet by a Somali women's organization. Two were called meditation rooms. Both could be used for meditation, but one was more like a counseling room with an easy chair, a wooden, hand-carved West African stool, and a kitchen chair upholstered in black vinyl with white cowry shell symbols. The walls had various African trade bead necklaces with African basketry strewn on a corner table. The other meditation room had indoor/outdoor carpet and several pillows. The fourth room stored exercise equipment.

Framing the entire reception area and down the main corridor was a black-and-white photo exhibit of the people of Powderhorn taken by a professional photographer when the CWC was still in its pilot phase. Forming a border around the three sides of the wall were magnificent photographs of Hmong, Chicano, Latino, White, and African or African American residents of Powderhorn at play and work.

Proceeding to the Invisible College room down the corridor, one went through the kitchen and met a large painting done by Powderhorn children as a special project representing the various people of Powderhorn working together on several neighborhood projects. One side of the Invisible College was lined by long picture windows which allowed passersby to look inside and CWC participants to look out. Sheer white curtains hung from the windows. In front of them were tables filled with plants; there were also large pots of plants and flowers on the floor in front of the window.

On the other side of the Invisible College and through a transparent glass door was a large open exercise and dance room. Many of what the CWC called bodywork classes, like Capoeira, an Afro-Brazilian martial arts form, were held here. In addition to a photo exhibit on Ghanaian medicine, prepared and donated by a European medical doctor and CWC participant chronicling his recent experience studying indigenous medicine, there was a large piece of kente cloth hanging from a corner in the ceiling draped to the new, shiny parquet dance floor. There was also a poster board report on the African origins of Capoeira done by a twelve-year-old student who participated in the African Science Academy, designed to help children of African descent learn about contributions of Africans to science. Rolled up in the corner was floor padding that was used to protect the floor when special events were held.

This large room could hold up to about one hundred people, and it was transformed in many creative ways for a variety of uses. Community groups and foundations frequently rented this room for large meetings. For example, the neighborhood chamber of commerce organized its annual meeting with the community arts group that decorated the room with bright red and blue fabrics and reproductions of Turkish rugs. The visitors left these curtains behind, and during the day they reflected subtle hints of red and blue onto the parquet floors and bright white walls of the room. Tai Chi, African Soul Movement, Yoga, Capoeira, and all of the other group classes that include physical movement were held in this room.

From the Invisible College, one could often see participants practicing many of these activities through the large sliding glass picture windows connecting this teaching and planning room to the exercise room. The Invisible College had conference tables which were creatively arranged for the wide range of activities sponsored by the CWC. When the CWC held a jazz fundraiser, the tables were arranged café style and the track lighting was dimmed. With the incense and scented candles burning, the room took on the ambience of an intimate jazz club. The room also had large African masks in shades of brown, beige, red, and black earth that dominated the neutrally colored wall space around them.

The Invisible College led to the CWC's kitchen, where many meals for meetings and special events were prepared. The two were separated by two large white wooden partitions from which were hung fabrics of many traditions, including a green and yellow African tie-dye and a tapestry with Celtic symbols. The kitchen was recently constructed and had all new appliances. It always seemed to be in use. Between the kitchen and another conference area was a large table, a small computer station, another entrance to the receptionist's desk area, a photocopier, and a basket of children's toys. On the walls were two large displays of Malian mud cloth with African basketry and pottery on the window ledges.

The combination of African artifacts with material culture from various communities in its offices was a critical component of the CWC's effort to create a surrogate sensorial experience of a modern African home that was accessible to all its participants. The space was designed to actively symbolize a new, revitalized "African" culture with a sort of cultural chameleon aesthetic that could successfully adjust to its surroundings, representing itself in different ways as necessary, while retaining some defined fundamental core.

This research describes how this nonprofit organization's programs and spatial aesthetics interfaced to create an alternative to what it saw as mainstream and Afrocentric approaches to African identity issues, and presents the general lessons it offers for the study of transnational cultural phenomena and public interest anthropology. I see the CWC as a translocal nonprofit in Appadurai's (1996) sense of the term, because although its facilities are based in one particular locality, in this case Minneapolis' Powderhorn neighborhood, its work has ramifications across several national boundaries. It is one of several key agents in managing the transnational flow of images and networks of peoples to and from the Twin Cities. I examine what its agenda and activities can tell us about how contemporary African identities are being built. I also explore how we might reform conventional approaches to the study of African diasporan culture in North America to include not only immigrants but also American-born peoples of African descent such as African Americans and Afro-Caribbeans.

From the perspective of African diasporan history in the United States, the CWC's work is not unusual, even though voluntary or nonprofit sector activity has not traditionally been a focus for either Africanist or African Americanist anthropological study. Starting with the formation of African American churches and mutual aid societies in seventeenth century America through the 1960s civil rights and contemporary nongovernmental organizations like TransAfrica Forum, the African diasporan nonprofit sector has been a critical, albeit little studied, forum for people of African descent in the Americas to create new identities and, in some cases, transnational ones. Much of African American cultural production occurs in this independent or third sector as it is sometimes called in the literature. Many of these grassroots initiatives became bases for political action, the historical role of the African American church as well as various pan-African movements being among the most poignant examples.

The African diasporan nonprofit sector, from colonial times in the United States to the present, has much to teach us about how locality, that is, a sense of place or community, and identity are created in conditions of globalization. Afrocentricity is just one of several sometimes conflicting ideologies (for example, variants of pan-Africanism and African diaspora approaches) that have emerged, largely through the collaboration of academics and grassroots activists, to reconcile African Americans' relationship to Africa—what W. E. B. Du Bois so aptly called the persistent "double-consciousness" of "black folks" in the Americas (see Du Bois 1903/1990).[5]

Pan-Africanist scholars as early as Du Bois (e.g., 1939, 1990) attempted to define the diaspora as a model for African and African American cultural dynamics. These earlier conceptions of the African diaspora conceived of it as the cultural aggregate of individuals of African descent; the term was used to refer to persons of African descent living outside the African continent as a result of transatlantic slavery and resulting international oppression and racial terror (Padmore 1956; Drake 1982). For various reasons, despite the longstanding scholarly study of African peoples in the Americas as part of a transnational diaspora, a critical discourse on this model only recently became part of the anthropological mainstream (Appiah 1992; Gilroy 1993; Clifford 1994; Harrison and Harrison 1998; Holtzman and Foner 1999).

In this study, the term "African diaspora" does not refer to any one of the particular current models (e.g., Appiah 1992; Gilroy 1993; Clifford 1994; Harrison and Harrison 1998). Following Sanchez (1997:61), the term "African diasporan identity" as used in this study applies to a group of people linked by their collective social memory of common historical experiences (for example, slavery, racial terror, migration) as well as some aspects of common African ancestry, whether "imagined," acknowledged, or denied. Instead of presuming that African diasporan identity is necessarily rooted in geography, "race," or a predetermined notion of culture, this study presents its composition and dynamics as a research problem to be studied.

Even though the scale and intensity of global cultural interchange has accelerated in the contemporary period for America's African diaspora, these processes are centuries old and begin with the transatlantic slave trade. There are several reasons that despite the prevalence of African diasporan identity formation projects and initiatives in North America's nonprofit sector, they, and African American cultural production more generally, have until recently received little attention from the discipline of anthropology.

Generally, the complexity of African diasporan cultural dynamics in the New World relegated African American anthropology to a minor role in the discipline. Conventional, place-based notions of culture do not accommodate the complexity of the African American cultural experience.[6] Anthropology's primary focus, in the nineteenth through mid-twentieth centuries, on smaller-scale societies diverted attention from more heterogeneous communities or intercontinental cultural processes. In this context, United States African Americans did not seem exotic enough to warrant serious anthropological attention. Also, because of the historical role of slavery and the contemporary context of racism, studying U.S. African American culture was an inherently political proposition. Thus, even Sidney Mintz (1970:14), a pioneering theorist and ethnographer of the African diaspora in the tradition of Melville Herskovits, acknowledged that the unequal racial power relations and relative cultural familiarity of U.S. African Americans caused him and other African Americanists to study the corresponding African diasporas of the Caribbean and South America and to avoid North America. Although there is increasing recognition of the contributions of African Americans, for example, W. E. B. Du Bois and Zora Neale Hurston, until recently their role in the early formative stages of the discipline has not been fully acknowledged (see Muller

1992; Harrison 1995; Harrison and Harrison 1998; Sanday 1998a). The cumulative effect of these factors has been the field's relative marginalization of the anthropology of African American cultural processes.

By default and neglect, until the 1970s and 1980s, race became a surrogate for culture in the study of African American identity. During this period, with a few notable exceptions (e.g., Hannerz 1969; Stack 1975), African American cultural dynamics received very little serious attention. The core debates centered on whether African Americans truly possessed a distinctive culture or only pathological adjustments to ghetto poverty (e.g., Frazier 1939; Glazer and Moynihan 1965; Lewis 1966; Liebow 1967). The ghetto focus was a comparison of African American families to white middle-class norms, and its emphasis on social problems had the unintended effect of supporting variations of Lewis's "culture of poverty" theory as a way of describing African American cultural dynamics. The culture of poverty theory also tended to underplay the active role of racism and unequal employment opportunities as factors in producing poverty and supported genetic explanations of African American culture (see Valentine 1968 and Stack 1975 for critiques of the culture of poverty thesis).

The field of anthropology is just beginning serious study of the African immigrant experience in North America (see Stoller 2002). Unfortunately, immigration studies are generally not very helpful in understanding the new immigration or its African variations. Conventionally, North American immigration studies primarily focused on European origins (Gans 1962; Gordon 1964; Anderson 1974; Handlin 1974; Greene 1975; Lopata 1976) and neglected the study of the African diaspora in North America. Immigration studies were dominated by models of ethnicity and assimilation inherent in the "melting pot" theory (Glazer and Moynihan 1965). As noted by several contemporary theorists (e.g., McDaniel 1995), the melting pot theory did not fully take into account some of the unique aspects of race and racism in the African immigrant experience. Any study of African immigrant identity formation needs to address not only ethnicity but also the social reality of North America's system of racial stratification and African immigrants' reaction to it. Recent immigration studies expand the conventional assimilationist "melting pot" theory to accommodate the ways ethnicity and race interface and constrain African immigrant identity formation in North America (Alba 1990; Waters 1990; McDaniel 1995; Sanchez 1997).

Scholars are outlining how various groups, particularly immigrants of African descent, negotiate the United States system of racial classification. Omi and Winant (1986:75) define racialization as a process whereby "previously racially undefined groups" are situated within a prevailing racial order. Sanchez (1997:54) notes that immigrants of African descent, in particular, are directly confronted with this system of racial classification; they are often assigned a racialized status as "Black" or "African American," on the basis of visible and/or suspected African ancestry, without regard to their particular cultural or political histories. In response, so-called Black immigrants and their descendants may negotiate their identity within certain parameters of choice: they may adhere to a binational identity (e.g., "Jamerican"[7]); or they may align themselves locally with the African American community and globally with the international African diaspora by identifying as Black (see Bryce-Laporte 1972a; Butcher 1994; Foner 1987; Reid 1939; Waters 1990; Woldemikael 1989a, 1989b).

Drawing on exciting new conceptual models that are beginning to emerge as anthropologists address the complexity of contemporary cultural experience (e.g., Massefoli 1996; Ortner 1997b), immigration studies are also now beginning to accommodate the complex transnational interactions that inform contemporary African immigration to North America. For example, Stoller (1996, 2002) chronicles the economic and political impact of a Harlem-based association of native-born African American vendors and transnational African immigrant traders from Niger, Senegal, and the Gambia working in the informal sector (also see MacGaffey 2000). This study seeks to add to anthropology's very early efforts to understand the lives of African immigrants in America and to examine more closely how identity is being defined and expressed. It elaborates these efforts by expanding upon their primary focus on conflict and competition among various African diasporan groups (for example, African refugees or immigrants versus U.S. born Black Americans) by also examining explicit efforts to promote cooperation and build more inclusive identities between these communities.

Instead of dismissing the CWC's work as Afrocentric and, therefore, not worthy of serious academic analysis, as a scholar of cultural dynamics I proceed from the assumption that any act of human cultural creativity is a legitimate area of academic study. I reject the notion sometimes proposed in the study of African American culture that diasporan variants of culture which are self-consciously or deliberately created are somehow less authentic than other types of putatively more spontaneous types of cultural production (Herskovits 1937, 1941, 1966, 1971; Herskovits and Herskovits 1934; Herskovits and Herskovits 1936; Apter 1991).[8] The unintended and outmoded implication of such approaches is that African Americans, unlike any other grouping of people on the planet, somehow do not have culture per se but instead have surrogates such as race or style (see Hebdige 1979). The CWC and groups like them are engaged in the type of culture-making activity that numerous recent studies over the past twenty years or so (see Bourdieu 1977; Giddens 1979; Hobsbawm and Ranger 1983; Gupta and Ferguson 1997a) now recognize as implicit in all societies, not just diasporan variants (see also Brandon 1993; Mudimbe 1994; and Barnes 1997 for other examples of African diasporan "culture-making"). There is no reason that African Americans or any other group should be seen as exceptions to what is increasingly recognized as a universal human practice. Following Gupta and Ferguson (1997b:4), instead of taking the notion "African" as a given, I start from the position that all "associations of place, people, and culture are social and historical creations, not natural facts. . . . Whatever associations of place and culture may exist must be taken as problems for anthropological research rather than the given ground that one takes as a point of departure." I accept the CWC's notions of African identity and culture as "true" for its adherents even though their ideas may seem unconventional or misplaced in some academic circles or differ from my own personal views. The study's essential question is this: How do the people at the CWC who call themselves "African" create, define, express, experience, and promulgate this cultural category?

2

Ethnographic Grounding

As noted by Lamphere (1992:7), there are some important differences between earlier phases of immigration to the United States (before 1924) and current immigration. A 1965 amendment to the Immigration and Nationality Act abolished country-by-country quotas that made it difficult for anyone but North Europeans to emigrate to the United States. Subsequent changes in immigration law, intensifying global economic restructuring, and political strife in their countries of origin have increased dramatically the numbers of immigrants and refugees from non-European countries, mostly Asian and Latin American, with smaller numbers of Black Caribbeans and Africans (Lamphere 1992:7). Furthermore, the class composition of immigrants has substantially changed. Earlier in the twentieth century, immigrants were mostly of peasant or working-class backgrounds. Since 1965, immigrants have included substantial numbers of middle- and even upper-class people with professional or entrepreneurial backgrounds, as well as those from rural and working classes (Portes and Rumbaut 1990). With these changes, anti-immigrant sentiments have also increased (Lamphere 1992:14).

For example, in 1986 the Immigration Reform and Control Act (IRCA) was passed to control and contain illegal immigration, primarily through employer sanctions against hiring undocumented workers (Bean et al. 1989:25). Another indication of anti-immigration and anti-immigrant attitudes includes the passage of "English-only" legislation in states with large Spanish-speaking populations, including Arizona, Florida, California, and Colorado (see Castro 1989). The post-September 11 restrictions on immigration and civil liberty while ostensibly designed to prevent terrorism, also seem to be having the effect of exacerbating this preexisting xenophobic trend. While these sentiments are certainly not new in American history, current trends provide an important part of the context for the present analysis of African/African American identity formation.

The diversity of America's contemporary African diaspora even further complicates what it means to be both American and of African heritage, providing the context for intense debate and innovative production of new identities among newcomers and native-born groups in Minnesota. The state is now home to the highest concentration of Somalis in the United States and to sizeable and growing Ethiopian, Liberian, Nigerian, and Sudanese communities, as well as other African immigrant groups.[1] The number of African immigrants living in the Twin Cities is expected to grow. According to the U.S. Committee for Refugees, because limits on the numbers of African immigrants allowed to enter the country have been raised, there will be dramatic increases in the number of African immigrants to the United States when already established newcomers attempt to reunite their families. An estimated 12,000 were projected to arrive in 1999 alone and more than 25,000 were expected in 2003. However, government restrictions on emigration to the United States in the post-September 11 period may curtail the number of African immigrants. In addition to its growing Somali population, Minnesota also has a sizable Ethiopian and growing Sudanese and Kenyan populations (see Holtzmann and Foner 1999 for an ethnography of Minnesota's Sudanese immigrants). The numbers of West Africans living in Minnesota is smaller, but significant, with about 750 Liberian families as well as almost 1,000 Yorùbá, Igbo, and Hausa families, mostly from Nigeria. Also attracted by economic opportunities and the comparatively high quality of life in the Twin Cities, the number of African American and other native-born people of color, particularly those living in poverty and migrating from other Midwestern cities such as Chicago and Gary, Indiana, has also increased in the past two decades (Minnesota Advocates for Human Rights 1998). During the 1980s, the "minority" population rose to 21 percent children of color public school enrollment; and students spoke some seventy languages. These demographic changes were a sociocultural shock for an urban area that as recently as 1970 was 93 percent white.

The specific translocality which is the focus of this study is the culturally diverse, largely low-income Powderhorn community of Minneapolis. Powderhorn is a microcosm of the broader demographic patterns now found in Minnesota. The largest of Minneapolis's eleven planning districts, Powderhorn has eight neighborhoods, six of which have significant poverty rates. Despite its high rate of poverty, Powderhorn retains some economic assets such as vibrant business and nonprofit sectors and relatively high numbers of owner-occupied single-family homes. Incorporated in 1887, Powderhorn has traditionally been a "launching pad" for new immigrant and native-born arrivals to the Twin Cities. As noted in a recent study of Powderhorn's history and culture (Larson and Azzahir 1995:13), this very diverse community is perceived by many Twin Cities residents as having an activist culture and community institutions and a strong "feminist culture . . . with wide acceptance of non-western health practices, new age spiritualists, acupuncturists, and homeopaths."

Defining its mission as "unleashing the power of citizens to heal themselves," the CWC attempted to use what it called "cultural health practices" to deliberately build a shared sense of identity among the native-born and immigrant groups that comprise Powderhorn's 51,000 residents, including Whites, Blacks, Native Americans, Asians, and Latinos of diverse backgrounds.

The CWC's mission operated simultaneously at two levels.[2] It attempted to build community *among* these groups, while providing programs to cultivate shared identity and networks *within* the various groups that made up its Powderhorn constituent base. The CWC had three core program divisions which provided support groups, health counseling, and classes to develop the body (often called "bodywork" classes) to accomplish its community-building goals: the Health Institute, the Invisible College, and Core Member Activities.[3] The Health Institute provided services to help individual members better manage their relationship with mainstream medical practitioners and sponsored research and evaluation studies to document the CWC's model. The Invisible College conducted educational and support group activities for a wide segment of the CWC's constituency, including patients and medical doctors, to help them understand the interface between health and culture and regenerate these connections in their personal and community lives. Core Member Activities included basic member services considered fundamental to cultural wellness, including, for example, health self-assessments, introductory courses in cultural health issues, and nutritional and exercise classes.

Although the CWC's underlying program philosophy will be discussed in much greater detail later in this study, it maintained that to build healthy pluralistic communities, people must be reconnected to their specific cultural traditions. Thus, reflecting its dual mission, the three CWC program divisions also operated at two levels. There were general classes which would be of interest to any constituent, for example, health self-assessments, relaxation techniques, and a farmer's market. And there were constituent-specific classes, for example, parenting classes for African Americans, leadership classes for women, Hmong dance, English as a Second Language classes for Chicanos and Latinos, European traditional healing, or cultural health sessions for medical doctors.[4]

Two subtle philosophical distinctions also characterized the CWC mission. Its general mission and programs applied to all participants, regardless of ethnocultural, educational, or occupational background. At the same time, according to the CWC's African leadership, its cultural wellness mission, although universal, had an essentially African base. Therefore, "African" at the CWC was construed as both an ethnocultural category referring to people of African descent, *and* a universal cultural wellness philosophy and way of life that could be adopted by anyone regardless of their background.[5]

A thorough study of the CWC's mission, program tracks, and profound constituent diversity was not feasible in the context of this two-year study.

This study focuses on the CWC's role in the construction of African diasporan diversity in the Twin Cities. Given my training as an Africanist and my ethnographic research experiences in African communities in Nigeria and African diasporan ones in the United States, an African diasporan focus seems appropriate. This focus in no way implies that I consider the CWC's African constituents more important than other participants. Nor does it imply, as indicated by the many general and culturally specific services available to its non-African participants (see Table A6 in Appendix A), that this nonprofit organization only has African programs. The African diasporan focus is driven by the need to delineate a manageable focus for a two-year ethnographic research project, my own training, and my related interest in African diasporan studies issues. Interrelations between CWC Africans and other participants are studied to the extent that it helps to inform African diversity dynamics.

The CWC was formed in 1997 as a spin-off of a foundation-funded demonstration project called here the Cultural Health Initiative (CHI).[6] The healthcare foundation supported the CHI for two years (from 1995 to 1996) as an experiment to see if a grassroots approach to health care could reverse the high incidences of infant deaths, hypertension, diabetes, homicide, and other lifestyle-related ailments that plague this community. CHI convened several community-based committees called "Citizen Health Action Teams," or CHATs, which met during this formative stage to design a community-based health center. CHATs focused on both culturally specific issues—for example, defining an African philosophy for health and wellness—and general concerns such as defining a healthy person and community. CHATs represented the diversity of the CWC's Powderhorn constituency. The goal of these CHAT meetings was to design a health center in which all Powderhorn people felt some sense of ownership. Although staff and volunteers elaborated and refined programs during this research, these formative CHAT proceedings defined all of the cultural wellness approaches described and analyzed in this study, including the CWC's mission, its program design, spatial philosophy and layout, and what it called "the people theory," a grassroots model of health and wellness, as well as related program principles and strategies.

In addition to describing the official program and mission of the CWC, this study also uses ethnographic methods to explicate the underlying folk theories of health, wellness, and identity that inform the CWC's public discourse. While the CWC was a grassroots organization, its mission and programs, of course, evolved within a broader set of power relations. This study describes how the wider sociopolitical climate and CWC African diversity dynamics mutually inform each other.

As a comparatively new and relatively small-budget nonprofit organization, the CWC had a full-time, all female staff of only six people and ten to fifteen part-time instructors (mostly women with about five men) who taught specialty classes (for example, African dance and other classes featured in this study) on either a pro bono or contractual basis. Staff positions included an executive director, a medical director (who was also a physician), an office manager, two cultural healers (who were also licensed social workers), and an administrative assistant (who was also a cultural healer).[7] As is typical of tax-exempt nonprofit organizations, the CWC had a volunteer board which set program policy. The CWC also housed self-help groups from various communities, for example, a Laotian women's support group, which had sources of funding independent of the CWC but, in exchange for helping to pay rent and other expenses, may have utilized office equipment, participated in other CWC programs, and/or received general CWC administrative services such as accounting and fiscal agency for foundation grants.[8] Augmenting the capacity of its full-time staff, board, and part-time instructors was a large network of special-project volunteers from the community, for example, members of CHATs, medical doctors, and other professionals who were members of advisory committees, such as an evaluation committee and a health and wellness policy committee. These committees also shaped CWC program direction. The staff, board, and volunteers reflected the ethnocultural diversity of the Powderhorn community where the CWC was based. Although the majority of board and special-project volunteers were women, there were significant numbers of men working in these capacities.[9] Thus, the CWC, through its volunteer network, had an effective reach and capacity that extended far beyond its small staff.[10]

Anthropologists have been criticized for focusing their studies on disenfranchised populations and exhorted to "study up," that is, include those who hold power in their research for a more complete understanding of the formation and operation of sociopolitical and cultural systems (Weatherford 1985; Herzfeld 1987). It became evident early in the research that although the CWC focused on the Powderhorn planning district, which included several of the poorest neighborhoods in the Twin Cities region, it worked across a diverse social network that brought together, in sometimes very direct ways, some of the metropolitan area's poorest residents with the region's most powerful people, who included foundation funders, wealthy donors, politicians, and public servants. As I better understood the socioeconomic background of the CWC's African participants, it became clear that although they were working with low-income constituents, the leadership which organized and implemented CWC programs and related efforts would probably be classified by most people as middle class.

One of the many challenges of this study was that I initially set out to understand the broader dynamics of identity and community formation among people of African descent, inclusive of diverse class backgrounds. However, including a broad sample of class backgrounds, particularly among African immigrants, proved difficult. The most active CWC participants tended to be well-educated people who were fluent in both their native language (often in addition to at least one other African and/or European language) and English. They tended to be more established immigrants who had some post-secondary education, professional careers, and had lived in the United States for at least five years. However, there seemed to be more class variation among African American participants than their African counterparts. For example, several African American participants in the CWC's network held very prominent leadership positions in either the public, corporate, or nonprofit sectors. I did not meet any African participants who held such positions. This was probably a function of their status as relative newcomers. The average age of African and African American participants was about thirty-six, with a range from the early twenties to late sixties. A conscientious effort was made to include intergenerational diversity in the research.

As will become evident in the presentation of the ethnographic data, the CWC's leadership often acted as intermediaries or agents—cultural, linguistic, and socioeconomic—for people of African descent (immigrant and United States-born) of lesser financial means, education, international exposure, or experience negotiating American institutions. For example, several of the CWC African immigrant leaders who shared their migration stories and opinions about African identity formation acted as volunteer interpreters and providers of various social services to people from their community. They helped people with fewer resources and less knowledge of American society navigate the various bureaucracies they needed to understand for survival: for example, by helping with a job interview, working with the U.S. Immigration and Naturalization Service to arrange for emigration of relatives; accompanying them on doctors appointments; or working as a liaison with attorneys, social workers, schools, and so forth. Indeed, in many instances African immigrants saw this kind of support as their personal responsibility. This same role of cultural or bureaucratic intermediary was also prevalent among African American CWC leaders with both African immigrants and lower-income African Americans.

Most CWC leaders of African descent, at the staff, board, and special-project levels, were women. While I cannot offer any conclusive statements about why this was the case, it did seem that part of the CWC's ideology was that identity and community building—defined by the CWC as working to strengthen connections to heritage—was "women's work," the actual term often used by the CWC leadership. Therefore, partly by design, across all constituent groups, the CWC leadership and most active participants tended to be mostly, though not exclusively, female. Several active African and European male participants took special note of the many occasions where they were among only a few men in CWC workshops, classes, or other activities.

The CWC was not part of any national initiative. Although the CWC was one of about six local nonprofits working to explicitly promote some version of pan-African identity, such groups were not part of a broader, organized movement. In the context of the Twin Cities' vibrant and relatively large nonprofit sector, the CWC, as a new organization, had a relatively low profile. Groups like the CWC represent a highly creative, local response to global cultural dynamics in the Twin Cities.[11]

Given the unique work and particular sociodemographic background of the CWC's African and African American network, it was not possible to make conclusive generalizations about an identity or community formation process that applied to the Twin Cities metropolitan region's entire African diasporan population. Nonetheless, the CWC provided an important lens on the region's broader identity dynamics. With the limitations and contours of the "sample population" in mind, the CWC's diverse African and African American network, its strong support from the philanthropic and public sectors, and its location in one of the most ethnically diverse and immigrant-populated neighborhoods in the region made the CWC an ideal institutional and ethnic crossroads for case study. The CWC was a mediating institution—a space that brought together African people across various class, ethnic, and political divides to experiment with a particular approach to building pluralistic ethnocultural identities. So, this research does not so much study *up* as study *across* the diverse African ethnicities that comprise part of the CWC's constituent base. It examines how the CWC, particularly its predominantly middle-class African and African American and female leadership, worked across the Twin Cities' power and ethnic structure (and national boundaries) to promote a shared sense of African community.

It became evident from the earliest phases of the research that the term "African" was a key issue for debate among the CWC's African and African American constituency. To emphasize participant self-definitions of identity, the term "African" is often used in quotes in this study to underscore the culturally contentious and contextual meanings of the term. In describing various events and conversations in the course of fieldwork, there is also a deliberate effort to use ethnic classificatory terms that the participants themselves use, with explanation where necessary. So, for example, the reader will find, in some instances, the term "African born in America" used by many CWC participants to refer to what some people might describe as "African American" or "Black American." Another term, "continental African," is used by African Americans, who define themselves as "African" or "Africans born in America" to refer to a person of African heritage born in Africa but living outside Africa, in this case, in the United States.

The use of the self-defined ethnic terms gives a truer sense of the internal dynamics of identity formation than forcing CWC participant labels into those that I might personally prefer or that are more common in academic discourse. Indeed, the terms themselves are part of what is being posited and debated as various CWC participants create a shared sense of "African culture" among people of diverse origins and backgrounds. By the end of Part II, the tenor of CWC identity formation terminology is established, and I generally discard the quotation marks around the term "African," although I continue to use self-identified ethnic labels with explanation where necessary.

Ideally, an anthropological study of any transnational cultural formation, including a diaspora, would involve "multi-site ethnography" (Marcus 1995)—in this study, ethnography in the various places in which the CWC's work was somehow manifest. Unfortunately, such a geographically wide-ranging ethnography was not feasible in the context of this study. An alternative strategy that I used for this study was to track the perceptions, life histories, and social relations of key agents involved in the creation and maintenance of transnational networks as they live and work in a given translocal site. With increased global mobility and cultural interchange, networks—and not places—may provide an important part of the social glue that holds "community" and other collectivities together (Sullivan 1996). Thus, I saw the CWC as a key point of connection—a linking mechanism—in a larger and more complex transnational flow of meaning, images, and symbols connecting various people to places in the African diaspora. Although based in one place, the CWC represented and shed light on a cross section of the micro- and macro-level sociopolitical factors that impact African diasporan identity formation in the Twin Cities and in networks beyond them.[12] This strategy, while providing for an intense study of the CWC's African diasporan networks, does have its limitations as a transnational ethnography. The findings do not provide for definitive generalizations about African and African American relations in either the Twin Cities or the United States. Instead the study is a point of departure to contribute to anthropology's efforts to define the contemporary theoretical and methodological grounds of intercontinental cultural production.

The field research for this study was carried out in an applied setting. Although relatively new and small, the CWC was an innovative, high-profile nonprofit funded by several large foundations as part of an effort to promote new approaches to addressing the increasing concentration of poverty in the Twin Cities urban neighborhoods and the disproportionately high levels of physical health problems, for example, diabetes, high blood pressure, and high infant mortality rates, in these areas.[13] Because of its deliberate and planned efforts to promote a pan-African sense of identity and social relations among Twin Cities' Africans and African Americans, the CWC was an ideal forum for studying translocal cultural processes. Since the research was in an applied setting and was not a foundation- or government-sponsored evaluation, the CWC was not required to participate in this study. Furthermore, the CWC's staff and board of directors were committed to a "participatory research policy." As explained to me, the CWC would only engage in research projects where the benefits to its work were clear, CWC constituents were in some way included in research design, and the researcher "helped out" in setting up meetings or taking minutes and was able to apply what she or he learned to his or her own personal growth and health. The participatory and applied research setting provided unique access to CWC's culture-building work. Participants' reactions and my personal reactions to the sometimes unexpected implications of a participatory research strategy are included in the study as ethnographic data and are fundamental to understanding the CWC's identity formation process.

Key CWC staff and volunteers were involved in every phase of the research design and implementation. The overall research design as presented here was negotiated to ensure that the goals and methods complemented the CWC's interests and philosophy of working with the community. CWC staff and participants reviewed and commented on interview guides, suggesting questions they thought might better address the study's key issues. Periodic research reports were provided to the CWC executive director and medical director and to health and wellness committee representatives. I held regular briefings with key CWC African staff, and reported on my general interpretations (while maintaining a confidentiality policy) about what I was learning in various CWC contexts, sessions, committee meetings, and so forth. These briefings provided regular opportunities for me to enrich the study by including participant reactions to my interpretations as research data.

As has been noted by several anthropologists, participatory research has its own set of unique challenges and opportunities. These were compounded here by the dual expectations in the CWC's participatory research policy that participants be involved in the research design and that I make efforts to apply my research to my personal life. Many of the ensuing challenges and opportunities could not have been anticipated because they emerged as the fieldwork evolved. Situations occurred in which I had to set boundaries about the nature and extent of my participation in a specific context to maintain the always (at some level) sociopolitical balance between "insider" and "outsider" perspectives. I established some practical participatory research rules. For example, while I would occasionally take meeting minutes or volunteer to make reminder calls to participants about meetings, I reached an understanding with the CWC leadership that I would not act as a CWC staff person, promote a particular point of view, or encourage a participant to take a particular action. Also, we eventually agreed that while this study would include CWC participant perspectives on African diasporan identity, it could not promote or advocate particular participants' points of view. Staff members understood that my role as an anthropologist was not to reduce these views to one perspective, for exam-ple, that of the CWC leadership, but to put together the broader story of CWC African identity formation from the feedback of participants of vari-ous ethnic backgrounds, social positions, and opinions. The resulting study is my interpretation of these processes. It is not in any way an evaluation or social impact assessment of the effectiveness of the CWC's work. In many instances, certain situations and their resolution enriched my understand-ing of the divergent perspectives among the CWC's participants and are in-cluded in this study.

There was a mutually beneficial convergence of interests between the academic goals of my research and the CWC's activist agenda. The CWC staff was interested in learning how one could document, describe, and ex-plain the effort to define and build community in tangible terms. Given the CWC's pluralistic constituent base and mission of creating community out of diversity through health care, the complementarity with theoretical in-terests in anthropology was not surprising. Groups like the CWC are close to the pulse of contemporary translocal cultural dynamics. Yet it is difficult to describe such "soft" community development approaches to funders and practitioners who are more accustomed to a "hard" nuts-and-bolts empha-sis on housing or job development programs. Through this study, the CWC hoped to be able to use anthropology's emerging models to provide a vocabulary that better explained their work to others.

The study's participatory research approach was complicated and en-riched in unexpected ways by the fact that I was also a "native anthropolo-gist." Although, in keeping with current anthropological practice, I was aware of the sociopolitically contingent nature of ethnography, I did not begin the study by defining or problematizing my role as a "native ethnog-rapher." However, once the fieldwork began, the CWC's interest in build-ing a shared sense of African identity to embrace the diversity of the Twin Cities' African peoples, combined with the research's participatory nature, quickly highlighted my position as a native ethnographer. I was not only a member of the culture being studied but I was also a participant in various other professional and academic networks and cultures, several of which overlapped with the CWC's work. Many of the features of my life—being an educated African American female with complex personal, academic, and professional experiences in the African diaspora; being a native Philadel-phian and a relative newcomer to the Twin Cities struggling to establish this place as "home"; being a mother and wife balancing family and career; being a former foundation executive and community development pro-gram evaluator—were in many ways reflected in the struggles, debates, and triumphs of the diverse people and institutions that used and supported the CWC.

Like any ethnographer, I recognized that as cultural creatures, we all have perspectives drawn from our personal lives—academic and professional experiences that color our ability to fully represent the diverse views and dynamism of the participants of the cultures we study. The quality of our work is largely influenced by our ability to keep distinct the perspectives of the "insider" and "outsider" and make systematic, self-conscious, and documented efforts to understand how these points of view mutually influence each other in the research process. Throughout my fieldwork, analysis, and writing, I made explicit attempts to understand and document how my own cultural, political, and other perspectives influenced the research design and findings. My primary strategy for accomplishing this was to include in the research as diverse a representation of African diasporan constituents as possible, and to make explicit in the narrative my personal perceptions, how I attempted to control for them, and how these efforts influenced the research context, wherever relevant. For me, the participatory fieldwork context required that I explicitly recognize my multiple sociopolitical roles—including that of a native ethnographer—and practice, at some level, what is now called reflexive ethnography (see Clifford 1988). My hope was that the inclusion of a diversity of perspectives as well as explicit inclusion of myself in my roles as both participant and observer deepened my analysis of CWC efforts to create African community, while avoiding the kind of self-centered, personal diary type of ethnography that sometimes characterizes reflexive ethnographic approaches.

Part II

Across Diasporan Space/Time: Who Is "African" in a Global Ecumene?

African Americans' ancestry is African whether they like it, know it, or recognize it or not. Culture has to do with ancestry—blood origins—not nationality—that's where you happen to be living.

—Akin, a "continental African" and Yorùbá man born in Nigeria, active CWC participant and leader

Some people are really into the African stuff and because their ancestors are African, they say that "Africa is my home"—even though they might be from the southside of Chicago . . . My ancestors are African, but Africa is not my home. I'm American too—a black American—and I want my due here.

—Mavis, an "African American" and active CWC participant

"Three Parts African":
Blood, Heart, Skin, and Memory

The CWC's "African born in America" leadership, in other words, African Americans, had a three-part definition of who was African. According to a key CWC "African" leader who was a locally well-known African American activist, an African was a person who was "black in skin color or race; has an ancestry that ties them to the continent of Africa; and has an African spiritual identity, meaning that you identify with the intellectual tradition that you are part of creation. Do you view the world as interconnected, or do you have an objective, technological view of the world? Who was African cannot be defined by one of these traits in isolation from the others. "It's a matter of a both and—not an either or."[1]

At the most fundamental level, in the CWC's three-part framework, an "African" was anyone who was "Black." "Blackness" and "Africanness" were often used interchangeably, although they were not necessarily synonymous. From the perspective of the CWC leadership, if one was "Black,"[2] one was also "African," regardless of whether a person self-identified and/or self-described an African heritage as a primary and defining component of his or her ancestry or identity. In the words of an African American CWC leader, "Either you're born African, or you are not."[3] Here the notion of "Blackness" was more than just phenotypical features, particularly skin color. "Blackness" also included a sense of cultural principles and memory which happened to be manifested, in part, through skin color. For example, Nefertiti, the African Soul Movement (dance) teacher, who was also a very active CWC participant, explained to me that "Africans in America were taken from the land. Continental Africans had the land taken from them. Until we can take the land back, our grounding as Africans is in our way of thinking, our history, our symbols, our principles. If we want to be whole, it can't be about geography. Although I was not born there [in Africa], there are things that I do that are African and it has to be counted—I keep them through the vibrations of skin and memory."[4]

For many African American CWC participants who defined themselves as "Africans born in America," an African cultural memory was retained in the body through the skin. This sort of skin-absorbed, retained memory—not skin color alone—constituted "Blackness."

The CWC had an ongoing class called Old Ways of Parenting for Young African American Parents. The class functioned like a support group and was facilitated by a key CWC "African born in America" leader. The topic for one session was a discussion and analysis of the ways that mothers, grandmothers, or other senior women in their families influenced the participants' parenting styles. A friendly debate developed around whether certain parenting practices were "genetic" or "genealogical"—inherited through biology, or learned from observing the practices of one's mothers and grandmothers. Someone in the class, a regular and active participant, mentioned that the discussion represented the classic nature/nurture debate. Several of the women maintained that most behavioral traits, including "memory, talent, mental/psychological disorders, spirit, attitude, stress, and mannerisms" were genetic—according to one participant—"inherited through the skin."[5]

Despite the inclusion of "Blackness," partially indicated by skin color, as a component of Africanness, the CWC leadership's theory of African identity was not easily explained as exclusively biological or racial. In fact, several CWC "African born in America" participants were very adamant and vocal about their rejection of the term "black" as a racial category. For example, Sandra, an "African born in America" who was in her forties, explained it this way:

I've gotten to the point where I'm not offended by the term "Black." I like Black, actually, because I went through this whole, "I'm Black and I'm proud" thing. So, I actually like Black, but I'm trying to teach my children "African" because there are so many negative things—even though their dad says "Black"—I just want them to know that there are so many negative things that are out there in the media connected with the word "Black," that they hopefully don't internalize the negative affects that come from that. I think those things were put there on purpose to denigrate us . . . I just think that the reality is, in a global sense, that Africans still refer to ourselves as being Black. So I think in that sense it's OK . . . I view myself as Black. I'm not so sensitive about it. There was a time when I was kind of more with the African, but I've softened that more.[6]

Sandra was also a licensed social worker who worked in the Minneapolis public school system. Originally from Mississippi's Delta area, she had lived in Minnesota for almost two decades. An impassioned community advocate, she had also lived for a time in Thailand. She was married to a man who was born in Somalia and had very interesting insights on intercultural issues in African American and African communities.

Sandra had also been involved in a grassroots Black study and community action group called Asili, which in Swahili means root or foundation.

Founded in about 1987 and disbanded in 1992, the group explored participants' African heritage. Although the group was open to both men and women, women seemed to be the most active of the almost one hundred participants. A respected African American university professor and community activist, whom Sandra described as their griot, mentored the group. Asili could be seen as a precursor to several of the African-centered nonprofits that emerged during the mid-1990s.

One technique I used to further elicit insider perspectives on African identity was to explicitly ask some key participants to review and comment on various versions of guides used to facilitate ethnographic and life history interviewing. Sandra, the same participant cited above, went through an early version of an interview guide and changed every lowercase "b" to an uppercase "B" in the term "black." When I asked her why this was important to her, she said, "Black is more than skin color. It's a group of people with a spiritual base."[7] Elaine, another CWC participant who described herself as African or African American, depending on the context, explained why she thought that skin color was not the primary indicator of who was "African":

This country is still divided by skin color. And it's not just White people. It's affected us. My father—God rest his soul—was jet black—like Nat King Cole. My mother was light like a Lena Horne. Now my great-grandmother, who raised me, did not want my mother to marry my father because he was dark. We are divided along the color line. We are some of the worst offenders. So, some people say "black" and they say "ugly." They say "black" and they say "stupid." "Black" is always seen as denoting something negative. But when I say "Black," I'm using it as a category for a group of people—not for skin color. Because you can have light skin and still be Black and African . . . Being African is about the way you think—not just about what you espouse but where you stand and what you do . . .

So, you know there are people who are mixed—they might have a Black mama and a White daddy but if they think like a African, they can be African; after all they need some way to define their identity. But to me they're still African even if they don't accept it . . . You know, even if they [White society] gives them probationary White status, it's only for a while and they need to have some place where they are accepted.[8]

Elaine, who was in her fifties, was a prominent attorney and health care professional who was an executive at a public agency. She was also a leader in several professional African American women's social clubs.

For Elaine, a person was also "African" by virtue of having African ancestors, not only because of having phenotypical characteristics that may be described as "Black." According to CWC "African born in America" leadership, along with race, skin color, or bloodline, the second component of who was "African" at the CWC, as indicated above, was "an ancestry that takes you back to the continent of Africa." In its simplest form, this ancestral theory of African identity maintained that a person was African if she or he had living relatives of African descent or could claim a more remote ancestor who was born in Africa. A person who had some African ancestors will also be thought to have some African blood. If one did not know one's specific African ancestors, being Black was considered sufficient evidence of a primarily African ancestral origin. In this case, a person may be considered "African" by virtue of ancestry even if she or he did not self-identify as such.

However, it should be noted that from the perspective of the CWC's key "African born in America" leadership, "if a person of African descent persistently denies or disowns it [his or her African ancestry], a person can lose all connection to her African heritage. So, yes, you can be black in terms of skin color and not be African . . . Africanness is primarily ancestry and spirituality—skin color is not as important."[9] So, a biracial person, if she or he continually rejected his or her African ancestry, may "become something else—not African." Sara, who was a CWC African leader, described a counseling session with a very emotionally distressed "biracial" woman which illuminated these notions of embodied Africanness. Sara was a key participant in this study and the official representative of its values, mission, and programs. Born in Mississippi, she had lived in the Twin Cities for twenty-five years where she was a prominent community activist around health issues. The founder of an elders' network and rites of passage program for African American girls, she was the recipient of local, national, and international recognition for her innovative community programs.

I met with this young woman—about twenty-seven or twenty-eight—who didn't have a trace of Blackness in her. In the way she talked—the way she talked about her experiences is very different from other Black women. You know, Black women have this way of talking to other Black women. We put our hands on our hips, standing akimbo, look you straight in the eye, and tell you just what you need to know and don't want to hear. I knew instinctively—although she didn't say a word about it at first. But I knew that she was very disconnected from her Africanness . . . Then she revealed that her mother was German and her father was Black. And until that day she had not had an experience with another Black woman. Can you imagine going through your life as a Black woman and not having that experience? Sickness is just this disconnection between the psyche and spirit.[10]

"Blackness" here had to do with the elder's interpretation of how the woman presented herself—her style of both verbal and nonverbal communication, not skin color. "Blackness" was the embodied Africanness partially represented through skin color, behaviors, and ways of thinking that demonstrated at least a subconscious and, ideally, a conscious connection and identification with even a partial African ancestry. In a follow-up to this discussion, I asked the elder how she would approach her work with this participant. She explained:

a biracial person is someone of multiracial heritage who needs to reconcile within themselves the multiplicity of parentage. I would work with this person to become spiritually grounded in an African spirituality. I would help them use journaling—writing their own stories—to listen to their own thoughts . . . In 90 percent of the cases, these people become reconnected. But there are some cases when a person continues to say "I'm not [African]; I'm something else." The ancestors will not continue to own you if you continue to deny them.[11] I know there are some people who think that once a African, always a African. But the disconnection can become so great, where it's complete. You can just look at them and tell. This complete disconnection, this severing the tie is brutal, and sometimes it's too late.[12]

In such a case, persistent denial of the embodied drive towards Africanness would decouple Blackness from African identity. Such a person might be black in the sense of a skin color or some other phenotypical feature, but no longer be Black, that is, possess Blackness or Africanness in the CWC sense of cultural identity. While the CWC's "African born in America," leadership made this subtle distinction between acknowledged and accepted "Africanness" and "Blackness," other "African born in America" participants maintained that a person who is "Black" will always be "African" regardless of whether they accepted it, largely because Africanness was considered indelibly marked on the body through, as the participant quoted above put it, "the vibrations of skin and memory."

An African ancestry may or may not be immediately evident from a person's appearance. A biracial person may not necessarily be deemed to look African or black but would be considered "African" once a partial African ancestry was known, for example, a child with an African and a European parent. Another ethnographic example helped to clarify this point. In a meeting of the Health and Wellness Committee[13] to plan a special project to devise a community "report card" with indicators of African American health status, there was an exchange about whether the term "people of African descent" was appropriate. Ultimately, the CWC's key "African" leader decided that the term "people of African heritage" was preferable over "people of African descent." In her words, "the term 'people of African descent' might exclude people where the direct line of African ancestry has been broken. The word 'heritage' includes everybody with African roots." In this definition, African heritage, regardless of whether it is recognized, accepted, or self-defined by a biracial person, would take precedence in defining the identity of people of multiracial ancestry. One CWC participant of African heritage who worked in the public school system and happened to be married to a continental African, explained that "one of the issues for the public school system in working with multiracial children is that eventually—sometime usually when they are teenagers—the African inside of them comes out. They're searching for their African self but don't know how. As result, they sometimes act out in school, but the school system doesn't know how to work with parents to help them."[14]

According to this participant, the latent African inside the body will eventually come out—this African identity was stronger than the other identity of biracial children and will naturally and ultimately direct the identity of people of mixed ancestry.

However, not all "Black" participants who would be described by the CWC leadership as "of African heritage" agreed with this perspective. For example, Joanne, a health professional with a Ph.D. who described herself as "ethnically African American," was married to a "White" man, and had a biracial biological child and an adopted child whom she described as "looking black," had a very different perspective. Joanne, in her forties, was an executive at a large public health agency. Her approach to identity was also informed by her stay in Haiti and Benin as a Peace Corps volunteer in the 1980s. Joanne made a distinction between her "ethnic" identity and her "cultural" identity.

Ethnically I am Black or African American, but I'm more a part of middle-class American professional culture. Practically—I mean on a day-to-day basis—that's how I practice my culture. I would say that as someone married to a White person with a biracial and a Black child, I just represent a late twentieth-century African American and all the contradictory, mixed up things that involves.

I would not say that I'm African because I'm not. I lived in Africa for several years in Benin as part of the Peace Corps. Although that was a long time ago—over twenty years—I know that there are a lot of cultural differences. In fact, the people there thought of me as White although to most people here I definitely look Black. I also worked in Haiti in some villages and I would say that Haitians are closer to African than African Americans, although I could fit in better there because people often saw me as part of the Creole intelligentsia since I was considered light and am well-educated.

I don't believe that you're suddenly African because you wear African clothes, look black, or have lots of African art. It's more than that and there are real cultural differences. My children are African American but they are not, culturally speaking, African even though *some* of their ancestors are African. American society will see them as African American—with all the stigma that's attached to that category— whether they like it or not. What about my husband's ancestors? So, I can't say that they [the children] are exclusively African.[15]

Mavis, another participant who described her identity as "African American," and who would be described as "African" or "of African heritage" by the CWC leadership, made an implicit distinction between political and ethnic identity. Mavis, in her thirties, worked as a clerk at a hospital and had moved to the Twin Cities about ten years earlier from inner-city Milwaukee. She was also part of a CWC support group for people with diabetes.

For me, being African American means dealing with stress and a lot of illness and an economical situation where you don't have a lot of money. It is also means not being able to step out of your door without being bothered by people. I would say that my ethnic group is African American, but to me African American and black are the same thing. African American means that I am American because I was born here and I should have the same rights as any other American person. Really I'm American—a black American. Anyway, that's what the government says; you know the whole thing that if you have even one drop of African blood you're black. So, in a way, if a white person is born and raised in Africa, they're a "white African" just like I'm a black American—their ancestors are European, but they are African citizens. But you know for those white Africans, they are usually rich and make the black Africans suffer and then they [black Africans] end up needing to come over here. But yeah, I guess you would still call them [white Africans] "African" . . .

The African or black part means that my ancestors are from Africa. In fact, that's what I've been told by my mother and father—that their ancestors in the South [southern United States] were from Africa. But you know how we are. My father is a mixture of African and Indian, but he was always claiming that he was Irish or something else. But for black folks—somebody—somewhere down the line—came from Africa, even though people don't accept it . . .

Some people are really into the African stuff and because their ancestors are African, they say that "Africa is my home"—even though they might be from the south side of Chicago. For me, my ancestors are African, but Africa is not my home. I would be lost if I went there because I can't speak the languages. Some people are into the African stuff, but I'm realistic. Being African American means that you have this special understanding and identify with what your African ancestors had to deal with, but personally I'm from Milwaukee—I'm American and want my due here.[16]

This participant, while conscious of an African ancestry, would not describe herself as "African" because, for her, place of birth or political citizenship was the most significant component of identity. Therefore, even though she acknowledged that she had African ancestors, she defined herself as African (for ancestry) American (for place of origin) to underscore her rights as an American citizen. She did not see the "African" part of her identity as relevant in terms of her current lifestyle or cultural practices— only as a referent for ancestry and the North American racial classification of a "black" person.

For many CWC participants who described themselves as "Africans born in America," the term "African American" was explicitly rejected as an accurate descriptor of cultural identity. Nefertiti, the CWC's African dance instructor, represented this perspective well. "If you ask Black people about their identity, they will claim that they are anything else but African—Irish, Indian. They're so quick to be in line with everything else . . . But when you begin to understand what "American" really stands for—this whole false history about the land of the free and brave stuff—how can you say you are both African and American [as in the term African American]? . . . I prefer to say "people of African descent." This is a more holistic name. You can choose to take on a nationality but your culture stays with you."[17]

In the very early phases of this study, I asked the CWC's medical director, who is a licensed pediatrician and a Haitian woman of African heritage, to review an initial version of my research plan. Throughout the document, I used the term "African diaspora" as it is commonly used in scholarship to include individuals with historical origins, however defined, based in the African continent. The medical director, who self-identified as "African," explained to me, "We just prefer the term 'African.' There are so many ways to divide us: 'African American,' 'Afro-American,' etc. that we just say that people are 'African'—basically all these people are Africans."

I went on to explain how the term is used in anthropology and that my goal was to accurately represent CWC participants' understanding of their own identity, not impose my own. However, I would need to use terms like "Africa diaspora" to translate the CWC's worldview into terms nonparticipants could understand. She accepted my explanation, but throughout this research I was careful to use and document participants' self-descriptors. This approach, while occasionally the focus of gentle ridicule, helped me to establish and retain credibility as a native ethnographer while exercising the discipline's expectation that I present the emic perspective.

Elaine described herself as both "African" and "African American" depending upon the context:

. . . I would say that I'm African in terms of how I personally see myself. Being African refers to how I got here—my connection to the Middle Passage. It's also my skin color. I don't care how White people act and how considerate they are, skin color still matters.

So, yeah, skin color is a part of it, but not all of it. Because being African also has to do with how you live. So, my upbringing was different. When I was coming up, everybody in my neighborhood had something to say about what I was doing. It could have been the town drunk, but if he stopped my mother while he was sober and said, "Mrs. Smith, I saw Jane pulling up her dress and dancing on the curb," my mother would believe him and I would get in trouble for it. Being African means— but this is not true so much today—being raised in a village. And I think this is something we kept going from Africa, even though we may not be aware of where it comes from.

But there is also an internal piece to being African. It's got to do with spirituality—what you think and what you believe. It's the whole way I think about myself. I am extremely cognizant of who and what I am and where I come from—who my ancestors are and the whole Middle Passage.

Now although I think of myself as African, I don't always call myself "African." I sometimes use "African American." When we have to fill out government forms or applications and they give you some options for heritage or identity, you would usually not see "African." That's because some people take exception to not seeing "African American" because they want to make a distinction between those that came here involuntarily—"African people born in America" and "African people born in Africa." You know, also society often defines identity in terms of where you were born—your citizenship . . . but your ancestry can make you African even if you weren't born there.[18]

The CWC's "African born in America" leadership would explain the above participant's experience of being raised in a village as an extension of "African intuition." In the leadership's construct, Africanness was "intuitive," felt and experienced in the body, not only through the skin or the blood but also through the heart. As explained by an elder, a very active CWC participant who describes himself as an "African," born in the Caribbean, the shared components of African culture cannot be explained or reduced through "European" or (by extension) anthropological categories like race, history, or socialization, because they are "spiritual" and understood intuitively. In many contexts, several participants, particularly "Africans born in America," spoke of the "intelligence of the heart" to refer to a subconscious sense of what are considered core and constant African cultural principles. For example, one ongoing discussion in the African parenting support group focused on helping participants be assertive in various family, work, and community relationships without being offensive. The group facilitator, a CWC "African born in America," leader advised them to follow the "intelligence of the heart": "Africans have a kind of sensing to know and predict what is happening. You can strengthen it. It's an intelligence of the heart, and the CWC can help you develop it. We, as Africans, function almost exclusively at this level of knowing."[19] In another session, when discussing the same topic, the group facilitator explained that the intelligence of the heart was "being in touch with one's spirit as indicated by good intuition—know it when you feel it and how to interpret and apply it. Intelligence of the heart is speaking the truth—knowing when to say it; how to say it. Don't give up being African, whatever religion or philosophy you practice, don't give up being African. Do what you say you are going to do."[20] "Blackness" was a sort of bodily vessel for holding this intelligence of the heart and the African cultural memory that accompanied it.

At a workshop on understanding African culture presented to students— who were primarily European—through a partnership between the CWC and a well-known area medical school, a key CWC "African" elder encouraged them to "remember to focus on relationship building, using your intuition and reading nonverbal behavior when working with African Americans.[21] Africans work from this basis. Your instincts will be critical in the healing process because it's part of our cultural health practices."[22] From the perspective of CWC leaders, particularly participants who defined themselves as "Africans born in America," this intuition—this ancestrally informed and skin-embodied intelligence of the heart—was a distinctive way of knowing what made an individual of some African ancestry, however remote or "mixed," "African," regardless of place of birth, nationality, or current country of residence.

While many "Africans born in America" participants regularly referred to the skin as the locus of Africanness, Blackness, or a historical memory of an African past, for many "continental Africans," that is, African immigrants, Africanness was not primarily retained in the skin or heart, although the skin, and other phenotypical features, could be an external indicator of Africanness. Instead, they made more frequent reference to "the blood" as the defining component of who is African. In the words of a professional Somali woman, Haidia, who worked with the CWC and lived for many years as a teenager and adult in several Middle Eastern countries and the United States:

Your culture, your ethnicity is determined by blood—your blood origin. It's the natural way of things. Your origins have to do with who your ancestors are. It's not necessarily geographic because your ancestors stay the same no matter where you are living. But your ancestors tend to be from the place you were born. So, I am Somali first, because that's who my ancestors are, and African second because Somalia is in Africa. Whether I say I'm Somalian or I'm African depends on who's asking and how much they know about Africa. If I'm traveling in Europe and talking to someone from there who asks me "What's your culture?" or "Where are you from?" if it doesn't even seem that they even know where Somalia is, I might just say something general like, "I'm African." But if they seem to know something about Africa, I would probably tell that I'm Somali. If they are from Somalia, I would tell them my village. Since my children also have Somali ancestors, they too are Somali even though they live here in America.[23]

For several continental African CWC participants, a person of African blood or ancestry would need to consciously define himself or herself as African, consistently do certain things, and/or think in a certain way to "keep their culture" and identity. Haidia, cited above, continued:

HAIDIA   To keep Somali culture alive, you need to tell stories from the old country. Do things like take children for visits back home, speak the language, and maintain your social relationships so the children know who they are. But losing some of Somali culture is not necessarily a bad thing. It depends on the thing you're losing from the old and what you take from the new one [American culture].

JCC   What about the people you call African Americans? [I had heard her use this term in other contexts] What do you mean when you say that they are African American?

HAIDIA   [Pause] This is a tricky question. African Americans can be Africans because they do have some sort of African ancestry. However, some African Americans don't want anything to do with Africans or Africa. If they accept their African heritage, then they can be African. If they reject it, then they are not.

Akin, a Yorùbá immigrant from Nigeria who was a manager at a local nonprofit organization and part of the CWC's African elders' council, presented his perspective on African identity in the following discussion:

JCC   What about people not born in Africa who have African ancestors but also other ancestors, are they African?

AKIN   I would consider them African. I consider all African Americans African.

JCC   How is that? Why are they African, even though they may have not even visited Africa or have no idea what their original culture was?

AKIN   The part that they don't know does not mean the fact is not there. That is different between the reality and what we know. And the fact, to me, as far as I know, is that their family tree is from Africa. If they cannot trace—if they are somewhere here and therefore they cannot trace this part, it's a different issue . . . [referring to a sketch he made of a family tree to represent his notion of African American heritage]. And, therefore, you think you are an American because you were born in America, but I still consider that person African. So, the part that the person cannot locate—where in Africa and when and who—does not mean that he is not African.

       Another example is if you see Irish, they still claim to be Irish. I talked to somebody at the conference today who said, "I'm Scandinavian," and even though . . . his parents are born here in America, he still claimed that. I think it's only among the African Americans that this is not common. The Germans, they say, "We're from Germany," even though they were born here. Even you see people living essentially within proximities. That's an area is known to be German area, that's an area that is known in America to be Scandinavian areas, Irish areas. The city of Milwaukee, they said is a German city . . . So that's the way I look at things.

       As a matter of fact, I look at people from the Caribbean as African. Let me expand a little bit. The difference between nations, nationality, and the origin is different to me because it's just like an English person—it could be in Canada, it could be in Switzerland, it could be anywhere—that's their nationality. Africans in Cuba, their nationality is Cuban. Those that are in Brazil, their nationality is Brazil. But their origin is Africa. That's the way that I look at it.

JCC   So, the fact, for example, that most African Americans or what some people would call Black people that I know don't speak an African language, and we mentioned the fact that they may not know their original African culture, that's not relevant to the origin?

AKIN   That's not relevant to the origin because even within Africa we are beginning to see African people who cannot speak African language . . . who cannot speak Yorùbá because they went to nursery school, kindergarten, and from there they go to English speaking school. So, my kids don't speak Yorùbá now . . . There are some people in Nigeria who can speak French like anything, more than English. But that does not make them to be a French person. Language is something we can acquire or decide not to acquire . . .[24]

I first met Akin in a meeting with the CWC director about a new project and state contract that he had to provide culturally appropriate family planning counseling to women of African descent. He was exploring how to collaborate with the CWC in providing these services. Akin was also very active in Ẹgbẹ́ Ọmọ Odùduwà,[25] a Twin Cities-based mutual aid society for Yorùbá immigrants. Akin identified strongly as Yorùbá but also identified as African. In a less formal conversation than the interview session excerpted above, he said that he would describe himself in some contexts as a "Nigerian," but for him Nigeria was a political artifice created by the British that was no longer tenable. He supported Yorùbá efforts to secede from Nigeria and form an independent country because the "Yorùbá can make it on their own and will never get their due in Nigeria because it's dominated by the North."

Interestingly, as implied in the interview citations above, continental Africans, even those who like Akin, above, insisted that "African Americans are African," in everyday conversation made a classificatory distinction between "African American" and "Africans." However, the fact that a terminological distinction was made by continental Africans between "African" and "African American" did not mean that CWC African immigrant participants did not consider African Americans "Africans" in some sense. The semantic distinction between "African" and "African American" seemed to be more a statement about the specific place of origin rather than cultural identity. Interestingly, the term "African American" as used by both continental Africans and "Africans born in America" never referred to African immigrants who had American citizenship. Such individuals still referred to themselves as "African" or in reference to their country of origin or African ethnic origin, for example, "Somali," "Liberian," "Yorùbá" and so forth. Even if they had American citizenship, no CWC continental African participant described himself or herself as, for example, Somali-American, Yorùbá-American, or Liberian-American. CWC African immigrants seem to reserve the term "African American" to distinguish between people of African heritage—those who Akin also called "African descendants" or "African descents"—who were born here, particularly those whose ancestors arrived in North America through the seventeenth- to early nineteenth-century transatlantic slave trade, and those who were born in Africa and emigrated to the United States more recently.

As indicated by Haidia above, depending upon the degree of specificity required for a particular conversation, continental Africans may have also described themselves by their country of origin or ethnic group; she was both "African" and "Somali." Similarly for Akin, he strongly identified as "African" and "Yorùbá." The identity that was most prominently expressed or acted upon depended on the context. When speaking about Nigerian national politics, whether he was in Nigeria or at a Minneapolis meeting of Ẹgbẹ́ Ọmọ Odùduwà, Akin most strongly identified as Yorùbá. However, in most American social and political contexts, he most strongly identified as "African" in contradistinction to Europeans, Asians, or other non-African-derived American ethnic groupings. For CWC continental Africans, there was no apparent conceptual conflict between an "African" and "tribal" identity.[26] They identified as both, although how they described themselves varied according to the particular social or political context. Indeed, much of the CWC's work can be seen as providing African diasporan participants, both American- and African-born, a conceptual model for defining and positioning their translocal identities: for example, what it means and how to be African, Yorùbá, and American all at the same time.

African immigrant participants, who maintained relationships with family members living throughout the world, made a subtle distinction between "political" and "cultural" identity that was more prominent than among those CWC participants who defined themselves as "Africans born in America." For African immigrant CWC participants, the correspondence of blood origins and place of birth with ancestry was incidental; place was not the primary determinant of African cultural identity, but it was for political identity.

Both CWC participants who defined themselves as "Africans born in America" (African Americans) and African immigrants—who generally referred to themselves as "Africans"—saw African identity primarily as a matter of ancestry. However, for "Africans born in America," equal emphasis was given to physical indicators of "Africanness" based on notions of "Blackness" as sometimes externally indicated by skin color.[27] While African immigrant participants also had a sense of physical indicators of Africanness based in part on skin, primary emphasis was given to ancestry as determined by blood or biological relation or ancestry. However, as will be described below, physical indicators of "Africanness" were given more importance among those CWC Africans who have experienced racial discrimination in North American or European countries.

African immigrant CWC participants tended to have a stronger sense that people of African ancestry should make a conscious decision to define themselves as African to be considered such, although there was significant variation on this point. Those who had worked with the CWC's "African born in America" leadership the longest (for example Akin, quoted above) seemed to share the view that an African ancestral origin, even if unknown and unacknowledged, made an individual "African."

Those African immigrants who were newer to the CWC had the sense that self-identification as "African" was a necessary prerequisite for African identity. One could not be "African" unless one perceived and described oneself as such. Because of the strong emphasis placed on the combined notions of "Blackness" and ancestry, participants who described themselves as "Africans born in America" tended to believe that people of African heritage were still African even if they actively rejected or denied an African ancestry. Continental African participants, almost unanimously, maintained that people born and raised in Africa who did not have an African biological ancestry, regardless of level of acculturation—for example, White Kenyans or White South Africans—were not African in terms of cultural identity, either attributed or self-ascribed. However, because of the African immigrant distinction between political and cultural identity, people of European ancestry could be politically African in terms of their nationality. Most African American participants who described themselves as "Africans born in America" maintained that such individuals were not African by any definition—they were "Whites" or "Europeans" living in Africa. The participants of African heritage who did not define themselves as "African" and instead defined themselves as "African American" or "Black American" placed more emphasis on place of birth or citizenship in defining identity. For them, people not born and raised in Africa could not legitimately define themselves as "African," although their African ancestry was recognized by the inclusion of the terms "African," "Black," or "black" in their ethnic descriptors. For self-described "African Americans," people of European ancestry could be "African" if they held African citizenship or were born in an African country.

CWC "Africans born in America" tended to justify a common "African" identity across the diaspora in part because of a shared history of racism and discrimination. For example, Sandra, an "African born in America" school social worker, described this commonality in spiritual terms:

I feel more of a connection with Africans around the world than I do with Europeans. . . . It's just a natural, kind of spiritual connection. So, it's like if you're talking to a family member, you're more likely to share. But then other people from other cultures can also be very interested and make a good connection and you can be more intimate too. It just kind of depends. But, there is something special about and is spiritual with African people . . . It is a shared heritage. A shared sense of suffering. I think that wherever we are on the planet, we have had some degree of suffering that is historic and that continues based on the color of our skin.[28]

Race-based discrimination produced a kind of "Africanness" or "Blackness," which derived in part from a shared history of suffering. So, as a general rule, for both self-described CWC "Africans born in America" and "African Americans," skin color figured more prominently in defining how to accommodate African ancestry or heritage in one's identity theory than it did for CWC continental Africans.

However, it seemed that as CWC continental Africans acquired more direct experience with racial discrimination in North America (and other places, most notably Europe) they too were moving to incorporate race as part of their identity theories. Racial discrimination seemed to be providing a relatively recent historical and contemporary social experience that facilitated some level of common identification between CWC African immigrants and African Americans (both self-described "Africans born in America" and "African Americans"). This seemed to be particularly true for CWC African immigrant participants who were highly educated, or had distinct and marketable technical skills and/or training (for example, in computer programming or accounting), and arrived in the United States expecting reasonably unfettered upward mobility within their professions based on merit and fair competition. There was widespread frustration with what is seen as discrimination against African immigrants, particularly, but not exclusively, in housing and employment, because of both their "Black" racial and immigrant status.

For example, in a life history interview, Selassie, an Ethiopian immigrant and former CWC participant who had been in the Twin Cities for about eighteen years, recounted how encounters with African Americans and North American racism led to the formation of a grassroots nonprofit organization with the help of African American community leaders, some from the CWC, to advocate for East Africans living in the Twin Cities.

There is discrimination in Minneapolis. I don't have to take discrimination. I learned that from my ancestors and African Americans here. My grandfather [now deceased] told me about how they [Europeans] sold African people, but I know that I am a human being.

In my apartment complex, they would give us—especially mothers—problems every time we would try to use the community room. [This was in 1993.] They would call them niggers. There were repeated incidents with people telling them to "get the hell out of the country!" They would take their pictures by force—it was something like weird conservatives or the KKK. [Selassie's face was flushed and his eyes began to fill with tears.] It happened to me too. But you see, East Africans are shy people. They didn't want to confront the tenants or the management; so they don't tell the problems. Instead, they would come and tell me. I got the mothers together and we marched to the management offices at the apartment complex. We asked the management to investigate and to get photos . . . The management was unresponsive. They didn't listen whether you liked it or not . . .

Something in this country is turned way upside down! The White man here is very prejudiced. The management just kept saying, "Well, I don't know. Well, it's not my problem." That's when I formed PEACE ["PEACE" is an acronym for "People of East Africa's Common Effort"]. Before that I was looking for a way to get people together. By 1994, we really started to get on fine . . . This summer [1998], I want to have a camp to bring African immigrant and African American youth together to reconcile about the boyhood and sisterhood that was separated by force . . .

I've experienced a healing process by living among African Americans. I learned of many things that need to change . . . One of my first best friends here was Dennis, an American-born African [an African American] who died. He told me the hurts. He suddenly became homeless right before my eyes. He even lived with me for a while . . .

It's only if all Africans can get along that slavery and colonialism will stop. After all, are we really slaves or not? Are we still slaves? When you think about a slave, it's not just physical—it's [an] emotional and mental slavery. If you want to be free, you don't go to the people who made you unfree. *You* must untie the ropes.[29]

After a life history interview with Hara, a female Ethiopian immigrant amd CWC leader, I talked with her about her community work to promote positive relations between African immigrant and African American youth. Hara, a social worker, worked as a community liaison at a high school. I asked her, "You keep working at this issue—trying to bring African immigrant and African American youth together. With all the challenges you've described Ethiopian immigrant families facing, why do you keep working on this? Why are relations with African Americans worth so much of your time?"[30] She replied: "It's so important for Africans and African Americans to come together because of discrimination. [She extends her arms and holds out both of her hands with upturned palms her and fingers spread apart.] Many threads combined [She interlocks the fingers of her two hands into a prayerlike position] can slay a lion. We can build community if we work on these issues."[31]

Akin, the Yorùbá CWC leader quoted above, has felt particularly frustrated by employment discrimination.

AKIN   One of the big areas I have confronted discrimination is in the job environment . . . This condition that African Americans are facing is so basic and then even those of us who are just coming to America, we face that too . . . What I mean is that a majority of White people are not comfortable to work with you. When I worked with the state, out of about ten or twelve counselors in my office, I was the only Black person. Beside the team meeting that we have every Wednesday, nobody knows my house, I did not know anybody's house. You know, I was confused when I first came here because all the White people would smile at you. And, you know, back home, if somebody smiles at you that usually means they would not mind being your friend. Well, not here. People smile at you and don't want to take anything to do with you. What happens is that we don't relate to each other. The rest of them know each other's houses. They know each other's family. Except my kids come to my office after school, they don't know us . . .

I think we have more opportunities in Minnesota than in many other places. When I was in Detroit and I know you can't, unless you are outstanding in your field, you can't get a job because they want to balance their political position, which sometimes they do in Minnesota. They give you a job as a token, for cosmetic reasons. And if you are given that chance and you are able to prove yourself, then you are given additional opportunity. Otherwise they might just keeping you in the same place for the purpose of keeping their records . . .

JCC Did you always have the perspective—like when you were teaching back in Nigeria—that African Americans were also Africans?

AKIN No, because I don't know much about what they are going through here. I think I know a little about Blacks in America, just like I know there was Blacks in Cuba, there was Blacks in Brazil. I know Blacks are all about our countries, that what they are going through, I don't know how it was going to affect their thinking. And identity was not a factor. You see the composition of Nigeria and there are no White people, per se, except the ex-patriots that work in the embassies or companies. So, I don't deal with race in Nigeria. I deal with the tribes because we deal with tribalistic issues. So, I can't relate to race when I was in Nigeria. Until I got here, before I became so sensitive to issues of race, and it just took over me . . . Because race is a big factor in America, whether we agree or not. We see practically everything by race. Sometimes we don't express it, sometimes we do, both in governmental policy and social interactions. If I see you [referring to me as a Black person] in the bus stop and I see another White person, I might not talk to you but I probably with my eyes make eye contact with you and disregard the other White person. I believe the majority of us would do that. We might not say, "Hi," but at least we would communicate in one way or the other to relate to each other. To me, these are the sort of ways in which we practice our racism here . . . But that kind of eye contact I would have made here would not be a relevant thing there [in Nigeria]. I'm very sensitive to the issue of race in America.[32]

In life history interviews I found that well-educated African immigrants, particularly those who had been in the United States or other countries, especially in Europe, for ten years or more, were more sensitized to issues of racial discrimination than more recent arrivals and had a stronger sense of a common "African" identity based on experience of race-based discrimination. These encounters with racial discrimination have, in many cases, promoted a sense of Africanness based on race. There is also a tendency to emphasize race or "Blackness" as a component of defining who is "African." Thus, being seen and classified as "Black" has created a partial basis for common identification with African Americans among CWC African immigrant leaders, often leading to conscientious efforts to work with African Americans to promote better relations and a sense of shared "African" identity.

 The core question of this section is: Who is African in a global ecumene? The CWC's leadership attempted to construct a common ground for African identity across three key conceptual fault lines: place, race or ancestry, and cultural practice. These issues are also found in anthropological debates about the definition and locus of culture. The data clearly demonstrated that notions of "African" culture and identity were being created, in large part self-consciously, by the leadership. However, crosscutting the leadership's broader agenda, there was a dynamic discourse about who is "African."

For self-described "African American" participants, African identity was mostly a matter of residence and citizenship (place); therefore, even with a partial African ancestry, one cannot be "African" while living and/or having citizenship in America or some other non-African place. For those who defined themselves as "African American" or "Black American," biological ancestry was a part of, but not a determining factor of, identity. Place of birth and citizenship primarily determined identity. These participants tended to emphasize the cultural differences (most notably, language and other social customs like polygamy) that exist among people of African heritage and focused on race or a common history of racial discrimination in defining identity.

For many self-described "Africans born in America" and African immigrants, African identity was primarily a matter of both biological and, by extension, historical ancestry. For these participants, if one had even a partial African ancestry, one was "African" regardless of residence, citizenship, or cultural proficiency (for example, fluency in an indigenous African language). For African immigrants, those who had citizenship in an African country but not biological African ancestry (for example, Afrikaners) had a political but not cultural African identity. For "Africans born in America," it was theoretically impossible for a person of European ancestry to be "African" in any sense. Still, for other participants of African heritage, particularly the CWC leadership, African identity was primarily a matter of demonstrating "Blackness"—considered a unique, embodied cultural style purported to exist among "people of African heritage" regardless of citizenship or residence. Blackness may or may not be manifested in phenotypical features and was not necessarily represented through skin color. However, it was definitely expressed in, for example, what was thought to be verbal and nonverbal communication styles and a sort of intuition—a uniquely African truth-telling, an intelligence of the heart—that is an embodied ability to sense, understand, and express the underlying motivations for people's behavior. Some CWC African diasporan participants combined these three criteria of identity—place, ancestry, and Blackness—with varying degrees of emphasis to create a coherent identity theory that accommodated the decoupling of place and culture that typifies various diasporas.

All CWC participants, regardless of their definition of identity or preferred ethnocultural label (that is "African," "African American," "Black," and so on) shared the sense that Africanness was somehow placed, marked, or imprinted in the body—embodied either through the blood, heart, skin, or blackness, or physically expressed in the body through one's "race," most notably skin color. So, Africanized places and spaces became those where "African" people happened to live. Indeed, this was such a commonly shared view that in many instances, participants thought it strange that I, as an African American, would even ask questions with such seemingly obvious answers. The body seemed to be the predominant locus for defining and expressing Africanness at the CWC; it was the vehicle for carrying and transmitting culture. The CWC's leadership, in its notion of cultural wellness, was self-consciously building this notion that the body had a central role in retaining and expressing some sort of African identity, and elaborating it into a theory of Africanness and process for African identity building.

Ultimately, it was the body that sensed potentially conflicting identities (Yorùbá, Nigerian, American, African, Black, black, so on). Thus, the body must organize and integrate these multiple identities. Failure to engage the body in the construction of identity led to disease, both in the individual body and the African community. The sense was that the body was portable; it could carry, retain, and re-create culture across the various spaces and places where "people of African heritage" live.

The sense of embodiment, particularly as articulated by the "African" leadership, provided a rationale for a body-based identity that was not necessarily exclusively genetic or even racial in the mainstream North American framework. Africanness was sort of retained and replicated in the African body largely through everyday practices. Many people of African heritage were not conscious of the cultural basis of these practices because they have repressed knowledge of their origins. Part of the CWC's work in creating healthy "African" people was to make them conscious of this embodied heritage and teach them how to use it to guide their lives. Placing Africanness in the body in terms of this theory of embodiment enabled participants to transcend geographically bound definitions of identity.

The CWC's body-based notions of African identity also attempted to transform dominant ideas of race that construe the African or black body as inferior, animalistic, and violent. Dark or black skin color, conventionally a primary signifier of inferiority in North American racial hierarchies, was also partially re-created in the CWC's notion of embodiment. First, black skin color becomes a signifier, albeit not complete, of the Africanness unconsciously retained in the body. "Blackness" was not understood in terms of skin color but more in terms of cultural style, affect, and nonverbal behaviors. It was reproduced over generations and throughout the diaspora through purportedly unique bodily techniques motivated by embodied Africanness and honed by mundane everyday practices.

CWC "Africans born in America" rarely referred to themselves, or other people deemed to be "African," as "Black" in the sense of an all-encompassing identity. While people of African heritage were thought to possess or express "Blackness" as a sort of embodied cultural essence, black skin color did not define identity. Instead "Blackness" was considered a partial signifier—along with ancestry and "spirit" in three-part African theory—of Africanness that is retained in the body, that is, "embodied." At one level, Blackness was ideologically dismantled by appropriating it as a component of embodied Africanness.

However, while the CWC's theory of embodied Africanness in some ways transcended race, it also accommodated certain uniquely North American racialist notions. For example, the CWC's notion that any African ancestry—whether or not phenotypically manifested or genealogically verifiable—made one "African" was clearly reminiscent of North American notions of hypodescent, whereby "one drop" of African blood defines one as Black. At the same time, it also provided a basis for people of very diverse African-related origins to claim that they shared some commonality based on ancestry.

From an anthropological perspective, the CWC can be said to be constructing a pan-African ethnic identity to transcend the stigma and strictures of North American racial ideologies. The effort to circumvent dominant racialist notions of African diaspora through creation and promotion of "ethnic" identities is well documented in the literature (see Harrison 1995:58). So too are the efforts among other diasporan groups such as Filipino Americans, Chicanos, Puerto Ricans, Asian Americans living in the United States to create a sort of pan-ethnicity based more on sociopolitical interests than cultural commonalties (Mullings 1979; Espiritu 1992; Sanjek 1994; Takagi 1994). The CWC effort to create a sort of Twin Cities-based "African" identity is in some ways an attempt to create a pan-ethnicity.

However, the CWC leadership self-consciously eschews any notions of "ethnic" identity. Positing a body-based, but not racial, locus for "African" identity was seen an attempt to convert what might be defined as racial identity by dominant society into what the CWC might describe as cultural identity. On many occasions, a CWC "African" leader corrected me or other new participants when we referred to the CWC's various constituencies as "ethnic groups." In her words, "I have a problem with *ethnic*. It sounds political." In most CWC literature and among its leadership, the preferred term was "cultural groups" or, simply, "my people" or "your people." The CWC's insistence on using what were considered less "political" terms, like "cultural groups" instead of "ethnic groups," is another indication of its efforts to emphasize the alleged similarities among people of African heritage and underplay the very real but potentially divisive political and economic competition that existed in the broader Twin Cities socioeconomic context.

By examining the identity models of "Africans born in America," self-defined "African Americans," and "continental Africans," I have presented the first component of the CWC's identity model: how participants of various national origins define who is African. Regardless of national origin or ethnic self-identity, CWC African diasporan participants perceived "African" culture as being inside the body, that is, carried and expressed in either the blood, skin, or heart. The focus on the body as a place where identity resides is partially a result of the fact that the CWC focused on health. Shared encounters with dominant North American notions of race, as well as systems of racial discrimination and stratification have produced a tendency to define African identity in terms of the body and not in terms of geography. Thus notions of race were transformed to provide at least a partial basis for a transnational, nonterritorial sense of African community.

The CWC's discourse on African identity was framed by place of residence, ancestry, and cultural practice. However, race and its definition and role in relation to who and what was African was a constant and unavoidable undercurrent in CWC "African" identity formation dynamics. Just as anthropology continues its historic debate about the analytical relevance of race in the study of human variability, community-based nonprofits like the CWC which work with transnational populations find that they must somehow address issues of identity that affect their constituencies, including race. The CWC's leadership and some participants also consciously theorized about race and its meaning and applicability.

Gilroy (1993:40) argues that regional, national, and global disjunctures in contemporary cultural flows have made the practices and ideologies which comprise race more unstable and contradictory. Despite compelling academic arguments for the nonexistence of race (see Shanklin 1994; Sanjek 1996), others argue that "race's vitality and volatility have intensified. While having continuities with its past, race assumes new forms and is reconstructed and manipulated within a range of contemporary contexts" (Harrison 1995:49). Barker maintains that race now frequently fits into a framework of "racism without races" in which a bounded and ahistorical concept of culture is the ideological device for essentializing differences and reconfiguring race (1990:21). The resurgence of the 1960s "culture of poverty" thesis in the guise of notions such as "cultural capital deficits" is a contemporary variant of neoracist constructs (see Balibar and Wallerstein 1991).

Within this context, the CWC's ideas of who is African present an interesting case of how a diasporan group was attempting to construct notions of identity that transformed conventional and contemporary variants of race and Blackness as well as underlying notions of culture. The CWC's treatment of these notions was, in part, an indirect form of resistance to mainstream North American conceptions of race which equate black skin with inferiority.

There are loose ends in the CWC approach. They result from the leadership's conscious African-focused programming, a partially unconscious resistance to dominant notions of race and culture, and the diverse life circumstances and opinions of its "African" participant base. These loose ends revolve around the relative importance of race, ancestry, or cultural practices in defining African identity. These factors framed the parameters of debate about who was African, and there seemed to be some correlation between country of origin and the importance placed on one of these criteria in defining identity. The CWC leadership tried to transcend these issues by providing an alternative notion of embodiment for identifying African peoples. It is not my interest to enter into the intense anthropological debate about the contemporary role of race in understanding human variability. Instead, recognizing that race is a political and cultural construct, I examine how a community group manipulates various discourses on race and Blackness in an effort to construct an alternative to place-based notions of African identity.

Organizing Across Diasporan Crosscurrents

In March 1998, a Somali immigrant driver was brutally shot and killed as he responded to a fare in a largely low-income, African American section of North Minneapolis. The incident, widely reported in the press, under-scored the broader socioeconomic context in which the CWC was attempt-ing to promote a common "African" identity.[1]

The cabs stretched for blocks on Monday along the quiet residential street that borders the tiny Minnesota Islamic Cemetery in Roseville [a Twin Cities suburb].

Inside the chain link fence, nearly 80 men huddled together against the icy wind as they watched the body of fellow cabdriver, Said Igal, softly placed into the frigid earth. Like Igal, most of the men were Somali immigrants who came to Minnesota seeking opportunity and a haven from the violence of their war-torn homeland. Some called Igal cousin or friend as they stood gathered on the barren ground in the mid-afternoon sun. But many called Igal, 48, a husband and father whose life was cut short over the price of a fare.

"He came here to escape the bullets, and now his life is ended by gunfire," said Abdul Ghani, a 31–year-old friend of the Igal family. "It's so tragic." Police still don't know who shot Igal at 27th and Queen Avenues North in Minneapolis. An after-noon news conference [called by the cab company for which Igal worked] quickly turned into a news conference on cab driver safety . . .

Mayor Sharon Sayles Belton [the city's first female mayor, who was also African-American] and other city officials said that some of the responsibility for safety also falls on owners of cabs and cab companies . . .

Cabdrivers know that theirs is one of the most dangerous occupations in the country. But many of the Somali and Ethiopian men gathered Monday said they are torn by an even deeper issue—perceived racial obligation.

While nothing about a suspect, including race, is known, many cab drivers are concerned about serving pockets within the South [the CWC is located in this area] and North sides that they consider to be high crime areas. Some of the implications have racial overtones.

"We are black, and if you see a black woman with children in the cold, you pick her up and drop her off, no charge; or older black people—let them go free," said Faysal Mohammed Omar, a former ABC cabdriver who worked with Igal. "They came first, we came after, but we are still in the same situation."

Sonbol [owner of the taxi company for which Igal worked] and several drivers said Monday that they believe Igal's killing will hurt cab passengers in parts of south and north Minneapolis.

"This will affect certain neighborhoods, because a driver will feel they are in danger and they will not go there," Sonbol said. "We can't force them" to bid on calls for service.

Another Blue & White driver who identified himself as Girma said that he feels a bond and sense of racial responsibility to other blacks, and that many of his North Side fares are black. He will continue to serve the North Side, but the killing will make him wary.

"The bottom line is, even with a good person, after midnight, you're afraid to go to the North Side, and that messes it up for the good people because all you need is one bad person," Girma said. "Another black person has died, and it doesn't matter, African-American or Somali, we're all from Africa."[2]

This article highlighted several issues in emerging models for the organization of African diversity in the Twin Cities. First, there was some level of perceived commonalty between African immigrants and African Americans based on race or shared experiences of racial discrimination. Second, "blackness" was associated with a common African origin. Third, Somali and Ethiopian cabdrivers interviewed for this article understood and struggled with a core component of North America's racialized model for organizing diversity: the presumed and culturally constructed correlations between criminality and skin color (that is "race"). Even though a suspect had not been identified, the interviewees assumed that the guilty party was a Black, specifically African American, person.

This and other incidents reported in the press, such as the one below, indicated how American racial constructs were an unavoidable part of how diversity was being conceptualized and organized among African peoples living in the Twin Cities. The neighborhoods in which the CWC operated had among the highest concentrations of ethnic diversity, immigrants, and poverty in the Twin Cities.[3] Because of its deliberate effort to build a shared sense of "African" identity in the Twin Cities, these broader convergences of class and diversity were illuminated at the CWC and manifested with unexpected clarity as I conducted research. Several critical events, many reported in the major newspapers and smaller ones serving the African immigrant and African American communities, occurred and publicly highlighted these issues. These events were important for several reasons. They reflected the broader sociopolitical environment that influenced the CWC's work; they showed that several of the key actors had connections to the CWC; and they reported debates in the media that suggested how mainstream models for perceiving and organizing diversity inform CWC cultural processes (Schneider 1999).

Haweya Farah studies hard to make Sanford Middle School's honor roll each quarter because she dreams of becoming a doctor. A Somali immigrant, she is determined to make a difference in her community.

Yet, on some days, no matter how hard she tries, the 14-year-old can't focus on her work at the Minneapolis school. Instead, she finds herself fending off verbal confrontations with African-American students. She swats away verbal insults that sting her soul, then spits back more slicing words.

In the three years since her family moved to Minneapolis after fleeing Somalia and living in Kenyan refugee camps, she has joined a strong Somali community, one of the largest settlements in the United States. She has adapted Western dress, wearing bootcut jeans, platform shoes, a gold stud in her nose. And like other Twin Cities teens, she enjoys going to the movies and shopping at the Mall of America. The biggest problem Haweya and other students like her have found in fitting in is bonding with African-American youths, people whose skin tones reflect the same rainbow of brown as Somalis.

A recent argument with a young African-American man hurt her. "He told me to go back to Africa," she said. "Where does he think he's from? If they came to Africa, we wouldn't be treating them this way. We would welcome them home."

At Sanford Middle School, where about one-third of the 636 students are Somalis and another third are African-American, the two groups constantly find themselves in conflict.

Somalis thought the blacks they found here would be allies. African-Americans thought Somalis wouldn't act as if they think they are better.

"They don't want to get to know us from the inside," Haweya said. "They only know us from the outside. We are all black . . ."

Sanford Assistant Principal Ohadiwe M'Geni, an African-American, tries to help students understand that they have more commonalties than differences.

He addressed students during an assembly earlier this school year: "You Somali kids need to understand you are black. You African-American kids need to understand you are African."

From that gathering, M'Geni and Irvin Mitchell developed the African-American-Somali Group to help students better understand one another.

Consequently, the number of hall and cafeteria brawls has diminished. Some of the students have become friends.

"We shouldn't be against our color," he said. "If we're going to be against anyone, we should be against the people who brought us here. If it wasn't for them, we would all still be in Africa" [14–year-old African-American student].

"They tell us you don't have a house. You have no shoes. You only have this when you came to America," she said. "I wish they knew more about our country."

Haweya wishes she had some African-American friends. "We're all supposed to be proud of who we are."[4]

As was the case with the cabdrivers, the students in this article had adopted dominant notions of the partially racial basis for organizing diversity. "Black" people were part of a common category with some level of presumed affinity. At the same time, this model for conceptualizing African diversity was influenced by the reality of cultural differences between African American and African immigrant students. Somali immigrants and African American students were thought to be parts of separate groups— one defined in primarily racial terms and the other in ethnic terms. Mediators, such as the school principal and a teacher, devised a forum to highlight possible culturally based commonalties between the two groups (for example, African American celebrations like Kwanzaa based, in part, on East African cultural principles). Both groups seemed to have adopted certain mainstream, stereotypic notions of each other. African students were somehow less "civilized" and African American students were somehow of lower social status. Finally, the school mentioned in this article had a high concentration of lower-income students, suggesting that some of the apparent conflict may have been indirectly induced by partially perceived class competition among African American and African immigrant families who may have had incomes at the lower rungs of the economic order. The reported cabdriver murder and school conflict incidents demonstrated increased public debate about appropriate models for conceptualizing and managing the region's increasing diversity, especially with the increased migration of non-European nationalities and "racial" groups.

A letter to the editor written in response to the above school report highlighted some of these issues.

The Minneapolis public schools have experienced an interesting variation of an old problem. Ethnic tensions and outright violence have arisen as an influx of immigrant black students from Somalia have encountered, not the vanishing minority of white students left in the school system, but rather native-born African Americans.

There is no cause for alarm, however. The highest wisdom of the school district's administrators has been brought to bear on the problem.

The assistant principal at one of the affected schools, an African-American himself, convened an assembly of his school's students to address the problem. As reported in the *Star Tribune*, he instructed them: "You Somali kids need to understand that you are black. You African-American kids need to understand that you are African."

One cannot help but ask on what basis the assistant principal believes these students are to treat their fellow students and teachers who are neither African nor black with respect. Indeed, students appear to have drawn obvious inferences from the assistant principal's remarks. One such African-American student is quoted as observing: "We shouldn't be against our color. If we are going to be against anyone we should be against the people who brought us here." Is it not clear that there is something radically wrong here?

What is wrong, of course, is the inane multiculturalism that divides students into groups on the basis of race and ethnicity. It is this multiculturalism that pervades the Minneapolis public schools and underlies the assistant principal's instructions to his students.

New York Times reporter Richard Bernstein has studied the curriculum produced by multiculturalism in Minneapolis. According to Bernstein, the most notable feature of the curriculum is "the veritable cult of difference . . . the power of the pressure on pupils to think of themselves as members of small groups whose character and identities stemmed from that association." This multiculturalism is profoundly misguided . . .

The teaching of the Declaration [of Independence] that all men are created equal and are endowed by their Creator with certain inalienable rights forms the only true basis on which respect among racial and ethnic groups can be predicated or demanded. If the Minneapolis public schools have abandoned this teaching in favor of a misguided multiculturalism, we should not be surprised as the schools come to resemble Yugoslavia rather than America.[5]

During this period, the Minneapolis public school system was in a fierce community debate about whether to include multiculturalism in its curriculum. The above letter to the editor expressed some of the fundamental issues in this debate. Opponents of multiculturalism, who might be called "monoculturalists" or assimilationists, saw many public institutions as overemphasizing and thereby creating cultural difference that made political order and democracy difficult. The school's assistant principal, who was considered a multiculturalist from the letter writer's perspective, saw himself as respecting preexisting differences and reorganizing them into more inclusive levels of cultural identity and social cooperation. Public discourse on the organization of diversity was often posed in terms of multiculturalism versus assimilation as the only two options for perceiving diversity and for organizing diversity through various agents, for example, schools, politicians, corporations, and nonprofit organizations. Both these models assumed what many anthropologists would consider conventional, reified theories of culture associated with socially predefined, immutable ethnic or racial groups.

Public discourse about how to organize diversity was complicated by parallel debates within African immigrant communities. For example, soon after Igal's tragic murder, and after the reported incidents at Sanford Middle School, African American community groups organized a community forum with representatives of the Somali community in North Minneapolis at Lucille's Kitchen, a popular soul food restaurant. The meeting had been planned before the shooting and the high school tensions as part of an ongoing series of community forums held at the restaurant on issues of importance to Twin Cities African Americans. The forums were funded by several area foundations and cosponsored by the city's only Black-owned radio station and a black newspaper.[6]

Perhaps the only time the majority of Twin Cities residents hear about the presence of the Somali community in Minnesota is when tragedy strikes: white hoodlums attack young Somalis in Rochester; Black and Somali students exchange hostilities; or the recent murder of cabdriver Said Igal . . .

But on this day members of the Somalian community came, not to dwell on the negative situations which plague their homeland and some of their compatriots here in the United States, but to introduce themselves to the community and build a bridge to their African-American neighbors.

Ayeh said first his people had to find a way to unite themselves and overcome mistrust and disunity which exists between Somalis from different tribes, which are essentially large extended families. Ill feelings between tribes, said Ayeh, presented community organizers with a challenge. "It became very difficult in the beginning to bring all of the [Somali] people who are in a meeting so that they could really talk about forming a community."

Eventually, said Ayeh, one representative from each tribe, regardless of the size of the tribe, would have a seat on the governing body. In addition to equal representation, the chair position rotates on a yearly basis, so no one person has a monopoly on the leadership. The CSCM's third chairman, Ayeh said this system has helped over tribal barriers.

"Before [the confederation] two people would meet in the street and not greet each other because there was mistrust," said Ayeh. "Now they can come together in tea shops and coffee shops and gatherings and they can talk without any problems. They develop friendships. The community doesn't have any difference in Minneapolis . . ." According to Fahia, [also a representative of the Somali confederation] most Somalis live in predominantly Black neighborhoods and relations are generally positive with a few exceptions." Of course, there are tensions," he said, due in part to "cross-cultural misunderstanding" and "different religious observances." Sometimes those "cross-cultural misunderstandings" have led to cross-cultural fisticuffs. But according to Fahia, those incidents are "blown out of proportion" by the media.

To overcome these differences, Fahia offered some advice to help African Americans better understand his people. "African Americans should know that Somalis, like many other Africans who come to the United States, have never been enslaved; they come with a clean slate. They have never felt different or lower than other people, they have never been discriminated against."

Sometimes, said Fahia, that "may cause a Somali to not realize they are being discriminated against. An African American could understand that a White person is discriminating against an African, but the African may not even feel it."[7]

This passage provided several insights into how diversity was being constructed among some Somalis. Common language and geographical origins rather than political conflicts or clan affiliation were becoming the basis for creating a shared Somali identity in America. In addition to adapting the idea of ethnicity as a conceptual basis for managing diversity, the passage suggested that Somalis were also creating new ideas of community in terms of social networks, as represented, for example, in the nonprofit board. At least in the largely African American context where the community forum took place, there was an emerging sense of Somalis and African Americans being part of a "Black" diaspora based, in part, on mainstream notions of race defined by phenotype and common African ancestral origins.

Turning to the role of the CWC in the negotiating of diverse perceptions, it should also be noted that CWC was a philanthropically and publicly funded nonprofit organization. These cultural dynamics illustrated here may be driven in part by the funding requirements of state and private philanthropic notions of diversity. To receive funding, nonprofits, such as the Somali organization represented in the above newspaper article, were encouraged to define their diversity in terms acceptable to these institutions. Implicit concepts of inclusiveness and participatory democracy in the philanthropic sector motivated many African immigrant mutual aid associations that wanted to become formal nonprofit groups to include members of diverse indigenous groups from their country of origin. There was a reluctance to provide support for exclusive services to particular African ethnic groups, for example, an Oromo program. However, funding for "Ethiopian" nonprofits would be considered. As the African market for culturally appropriate services grew, interethnic nonprofits were forming.

One example was a nonprofit organization originally begun to provide support to Ethiopians which over time defined its constituency as all people of African origins, as well as others. The ability to create institutions that accommodated more inclusive levels of diversity was financially rewarded in grants from the philanthropic and government sectors.

The state, by collecting data through public health agencies, the Census Bureau, and others, was another agent in promoting mainstream notions of diversity based on race and ethnicity. Survey forms used to collect data provided a particular range of categories which encoded certain ways of conceptualizing diversity. The most ethnically specific category available for African diasporan respondents was generally "African/African American" or "black," although there seemed to be general movement away from the latter racial designation. Some forms gaining currency among the public health departments referred to national origins, for example, Somali, Ethiopian, Liberian, and so on, the equivalent of American ethnic groups. Rarely did forms refer to indigenous African ethnocultural or linguistic categories, for example, Oromo or Yorùbá. Therefore, the American tendency to define ethnic groupings in terms of country or national origin may have tended to underplay indigenous African diversity and encourage the formation of more encompassing ethnocultural units.

Nonprofit groups, as well as schools and other public entities, were clearly a locus for conflict among these emerging groupings, such as Somali versus African American. However, these institutions were also becoming key forums for collaboration among individual agents of African American and African immigrant origins who were leading efforts to create new models for dealing with diversity. Thus, partnerships between Black leaders and their Somali counterparts, as reported in the Black media in the passage above, forced public discussion of diversity issues. These interactions also tended to promote the conflation of ideas of race and ethnicity in the emerging concept of an African or Black diaspora in the Twin Cities.

The nonprofit sector and its various leaders were becoming important agents whereby mainstream notions of race and ethnicity were reformulated. Many African immigrants and African American leaders felt that in order to influence the political process, African immigrants must organize across ethnic and national lines and ally with African Americans on issues of common concern to achieve mutually beneficial rewards and an influential political voice. The political reality was that while the numbers of African immigrants, and migration of African Americans from other states attracted by Minnesota's strong economy, grew significantly over the 1990s, the number of African immigrants and African Americans was still quite small as a proportion of the overall population. However, concentrations were much higher in the central cities and, to a lesser extent, in first ring suburbs. Formal, collaborative political action was still only in its infancy, but the collaboration among mutual aid and nonprofit organizations could be seen as a training ground for future action in several ways.

This collaboration provided a forum for African immigrants new to the Twin Cities political system, to learn the nuances of American political organizing. Being able to manipulate mainstream ideas of diversity, for example, race, was clearly a critical skill gained in these efforts. Establishing social relations and networks at more encompassing scales of African diasporan diversity could provide the basis for a constituency that could influence the political process. Thus, African diaspora nonprofit sector activities provided the training ground and infrastructure for potential organized political action.[8]

As alluded to by the Somali leader cited above, there was a recognition of the political potential of nonprofit sector collaboration. There was also a sense that mainstream media were more inclined to report incidents of conflict and competition between African immigrants and African Americans, while underplaying their efforts to bridge their communities and work cooperatively. This was often expressed as an effort of the power structure—"the system"—to inhibit organizing and ethnic identification that might lead to an expanded and influential diasporan political base.

Contests and negotiations over these constructs were being played out in various institutions and reported in the mainstream and black ethnic media. This discourse both described and partially shaped the direction of the creation of new concepts and mechanisms for managing African diversity. Pivotal agents, individual community leaders of African American and African immigrant backgrounds working in nonprofit and public institutions, were taking the lead in shaping ideas of diversity and building social networks to convert these new constructs into new social institutions. Collaboration seemed to be a largely African immigrant and African American middle-class phenomenon, both in terms of agency and leadership. At the same time, particularly in areas with increasing concentrations of poverty among native-born African Americans and African refugees, there was fierce competition and conflict. Yet leaders of both communities were cooperating, at least to some extent, to define common interests, which, as the community grew, could be used for political action.

The Twin Cities are a prominent center for multinational corporations, so the area has an established infrastructure to facilitate transnational ties. Piggybacking on the region's global economic networks, African American leaders, many of whom have experience and connections in the corporate or philanthropic sectors, seemed to have developed, particularly during the 1990s, a particular interest in promoting business and development collaborations with African immigrants to work in various African countries.

Reflecting national trends, available data indicate that there was simultaneous growth in African American concentrated poverty as well as an increase in the middle-class.[9] For example according to 1995 U.S. Census Bureau data from Minnesota, the state also had the nation's highest percentage of college-educated African Americans. They were also twice as likely as their White counterparts to have a college degree.[10]

Middle-class African Americans and African immigrant leaders were taking a leading role as agents in taking the social networks created in the nonprofit sector and using them to promote economic interchange between the two continents.[11] Indeed, although this cannot be definitively validated, cultural exchanges and business collaborations between Twin Cities African Americans and African immigrants seemed to have been growing during the 1990s, a period which coincides with the remarkable growth in the state's African immigrant population. For example, a recent newspaper article about a conference to promote Minnesota's business ties with Africa noted: "Minnesota has dozens of ties to Africa in business, culture, technology, education, government and religion. After this week, some of those connections are expected to grow stronger."[12] The major sponsors of the conference referenced in the article were Twin Cities-based multinationals, for example, 3M and Cargill, who have investments in various African countries. Crosscutting these corporate ties were various partnerships promoted by prominent African Americans, most notably several Hennepin County judges and other business leaders. For example, as cited in the article,

The only American in an international group of public defenders visiting Kenya and Ethiopia in May and June, Hennepin County public defender [an African American known to wear Nigerian-style agbadas and dashikis to the court room] spoke to lawyers, judges and professors from 20 African nations. He suggested how to develop public-defense and legal aid systems in Kenya, where 90 percent of people charged with capital crimes other than murder represent themselves. As a result, Kenya's parliament is expected to adopt a legal system that incorporates a handful of Minnesota-style programs.[13]

A critical event and its aftermath illuminated how increased transnational economic activity between the Twin Cities and Africa might have influenced the translocal organization of diversity. In March 1998, the Ghana Association of Minnesota (which had about five hundred members according to its president), the chair of the Midwest Black Publishers' Coalition who was also owner of the Twin Cities Insight News Group (a major Black-owned community newspaper company in the Twin Cities), and the Council on Black Minnesotans (a state-supported political advocacy group which had been attempting to expand participation to African immigrants) cosponsored a visit by a high level delegation from Ghana to explore trade relations between Ghana and Minnesota, particularly between Ghanaians and African Americans. The event was held one morning at Lucille's Kitchen, a modest but popular Minneapolis soul food restaurant where one can buy everything from sweet potato pie to deep fried alligator. A cross section of the Twin Cities African American community showed up for the event, including a recently retired dean at a major area university, several nonprofit and corporate leaders, a prominent Hennepin County judge, as well as community people with no particular organizational affiliation. The community meeting, entitled "The Re-Emergence of African Civilization," featured a panel discussion with members of the African delegation, the chair of the publishers' association, and the local Ghanaian immigrant mutual aid association.

Ghana's deputy minister of trade, Dan Abodakpi, opened the discussion by stressing Ghana's interest in "networking with its brothers and sisters in the diaspora." Abodakpi recounted the history of African American relations with Ghana, including invoking the names of W. E. B. Du Bois and George Padmore. He said that "Ghana needs the wealth of its brethren in the U.S. to work jointly to rebuild African civilization." The president of the Black Publishers' Association stressed: "There are not only economic benefits to working with our brothers in Ghana. There are social benefits. For example, we all know that our court system doesn't work. We need to think about how we can explore and adapt Ghana's rich culture, like customary courts, to promote justice in our community."

Ghana's tourism minister, Mike Gizzo, did a presentation on two events being organized by Ghana: PANAFEST, a pan-African cultural festival, and African Emancipation Day. He opened his presentation by saying that the delegation was

invited to talk about how to link up to save our mother. After all, what does it gain you to have all the riches in the world and your mother is walking around naked? You have a home and you have to come help us build our home. Thirty-four of the forty-three slave dungeons in West Africa are in Ghana. Ghana served as a point of exit and departure for our people. Now it is serving as a point of return. We can reunite the African family—together we can join our resources. These events are a cultural forum dedicated to enhancing development—improvement in our quality of life. We have a commonality of interests—we are not asking you to be benevolent. It is your birthright to the continent. There is an Emancipation Day that celebrates the abolition of chattel slavery. But it's celebrated mostly in the Caribbean. Now we will have it for the first time in Africa. We will rebury at Elmina the interred bodies of runaway slaves from New York and Jamaica. Ghanaians want to be involved in restitution and atonement because some of our factors were involved. It is said that 300 million people were removed. But you can come back! The 21st century will be the century of the African!!

The pronouncements drew animated applause and affirmation from the audience of mostly African Americans and some Ghanaian immigrants.

These pan-African declarations, however, were more than mere rhetorical devices. The speakers built their perceptions of shared diasporan identity and related social networks into new paths of transnational economic exchange.

Three months later, *Insight News*, a Twin Cities newspaper owned by Al MacFarlane, reported that Kojo Yankah, Ghana's minister of the central region, and MacFarlane, also president of the Midwest Black Publishers' Coalition, signed a memorandum of understanding stipulating that the coalition would be the sole marketing and promotion agency in North America for PANAFEST '99. The later PANAFEST '99 was a transnational cultural festival that was held in Cape Cost and Elmina with the theme, "Uniting the African Family: The Agenda for a New Millennium."[14]

Ghana's Emancipation Day took place with much fanfare in the local black Twin Cities press. One article, "Ghana Welcomes Black Publishers' PANAFEST '99 Business Initiative: Marketing the Re-emergence of African Civilization," provided helpful insights into ways local African and African American leaders promoted translocal ties and resource flows through the African diasporan segment of the global economy.

Discussions August 4 in Accra, Ghana, at the Osu Castle with Ghana's vice president, His Excellency John Atta Mills, concluded a week-long awareness tour and two days of negotiations between the executive board of Midwest Black Publishers' Coalition, Inc. and Pan-African Historical Theater Festival (PANAFEST) Secretariat . . .

McFarlane [said] . . . "PANAFEST '99 will be unique and significant because it will widen the floodgate, allowing and encouraging thousands more people of African descent to make the pilgrimage to the sacred sites that evoke solemn remembrance of the atrocities of slavery—the African holocaust" . . .

"Most importantly, we see ourselves promoting the notion that Africans in America and every descendant of Africa, should visit the slave castles that dot the African coastline, should see firsthand the genesis of the cruelty of European imperialism and tribal warfare conspired to visit on our people, and say to ourselves and to history 'Never Again, Never Again . . .'"

It is no accident that European Americans have fueled the growth and prosperity of European nations even after the ravishing devastation of two world wars. They have relationships with their families and friends and culture that shape American foreign and fiscal policy towards Europe. The same is true for growing Asian and Spanish-speaking populations here, he said.

"Your return to Africa cannot be merely symbolic: it cannot be merely to ancestral memorials or to the shrines of your original spiritual homes," he said. Mills said though the commemorative sites are full of the energetic presence of the spirit of ancestors, the sites are all in near ruins. He said though at times there is conflict or mistrust between African Americans and Africans, we must recognize that our relationship is still "disturbed by the shadow of the one who intervened between us. There are times when our ties are weakened by ignorance, self-protection instincts, and cultural reflexes borrowed from others.

. . . Let us defy those who seek to marginalize us: let us defy anyone who seeks to keep us under tutelage in any shape or form. Let us build the future as free and proud people."[15]

As these articles and events indicated, the media had a particularly powerful role in shaping identity and creating vehicles for transnational exchanges of images and resources. Resurrecting and marketing Ghana's history as an important site for the creation and promotion of "Panafricanism," along with the reinterment of African slaves from the Americas, and atonement for African involvement in the slave trade, also promoted a model for organizing culturally diverse groups across the African diaspora to emphasize shared historical experiences as opposed to cultural differences. Representatives of the Midwest Black Publishers' Coalition not only saw themselves as marketing PANAFEST and Emancipation Day but also as educating African Americans about Africa and establishing networks for trade. Coalition representatives promoting a transnational sense of "African" identity were creating an expanded market for Ghanaian tourism, which could be translated into an emerging transnational Ghana-Twin Cities track in the global economy. The marketing partnership between the Midwest Black Publishers' Coalition and various high levels of Ghanaian government were, of course, facilitated by the leader of the Twin Cities Ghanaian mutual aid association, a long-time middle-class Ghanaian immigrant to the Twin Cities who helped organize the trade delegation that first visited the area in March 1998.[16]

What these examples show is that efforts to promote a shared sense of identity were occurring in a context where a critical mass of Africans and African Americans, particularly those of the middle-class, were collaborating not only for its own sake and to address social problems, but also to promote translocal marketplaces for mutual economic gain and development.

While there were clear economic competitions and intergroup conflicts, there were also high-profile efforts to mobilize pan-ethnic identities to enhance political power and economic capacity. Leaders in the African immigrant community attempted to help constituents negotiate complex North American conceptions of race, while building alliances with native-born African Americans. All of these organizing efforts occurred in a context where there was public discourse about the appropriate model for conceptualizing diversity, as seen, for instance, in the debate over multiculturalism in the schools.

These broader dynamics in the management of diversity provides a useful context for understanding how these issues were manifested in the CWC's approach. The CWC can be seen as one of several nonprofit agents that was reconstituting translocal cultural, economic, and ideological flows through the Twin Cities diaspora. The CWC attempted to organize people of different backgrounds and assembled a network of agents to reformulate the African diasporan ethnicities in creative ways. While ensconced in these translocal flows, it was not fully determined by them.

The CWC's "African born in America" leaders saw the Center as a bridge connecting the groups that comprised the African diaspora and as providing a politically neutral organizing space that transcended ethnic, class, political, or religious affiliations or specific historical experiences.

A part of the CWC's organizing mission was to establish an authority pattern in which African Americans were seen as the most appropriate intermediaries as they had lived as "African" in the United States long enough to learn and share lessons learned about efforts to assimilate. Most active CWC African immigrant participants also saw CWC African Americans who self-consciously defined themselves as "African" as having this unique leadership role. As explained by one Yorùbá participant:

It is very difficult for anyone to claim to be an authority in all aspects of Yorùbá culture. It is very complex. Just Ògún itself is huge, if you want to study it. On its own, you can spend all of your life studying it [Ògún] and not go by everything . . . Sara and Rashad [pseudonyms for two CWC "African born in America" leaders] were telling me at one of their meetings that Yorùbá is not just a culture, it's also a religion . . .

I realized right away that these are the words or the statement that have never been made to me before, and most of us [Yorùbá] have never even thought about that . . . And after that, I've used that with many people because once they said it, I can see the cultural aspect of Yorùbá, I can see the religious aspect of Yorùbá that all these practices go together . . .

When I talked to Rashad, I think his knowledge of Africa is more than I've seen of anybody, including Africans. He takes you from the roots; it's just something I always liked listening to. Things that I always liked to hear. Every time I have the chance to talk to him, I feel stronger than I was before I sit down to talk with him.[17]

This passage was an example of the acknowledged leadership role granted to "Africans born in America." From this position the leaders were able to propose and teach new constructs and strategies for perceiving diversity. The new concepts were adopted by African immigrant and other African American leaders who, in turn, used them with their constituents.[18] This had the effect of spreading new constructs for organizing diversity across networks in the nonprofit sector.

The following exchange between two Ethiopian immigrant women in their thirties, the first of Amharic and Tigrean heritage and the second of Oromo heritage, both very active in the CWC, and a senior Somali woman, for whom this was her first interaction with the CWC, highlighted the perspective of some African immigrants about the CWC, and its African American leadership, as being a key institution in connecting people of various African backgrounds. It also indicated women's important leadership role in cultural reproduction:

AMINA (through an interpreter)   I know about the different social services for Somalis. But when you go there, it seems that, really, they only serve certain clans or tribes. And I don't like that. It makes me feel uncomfortable.

ZELA   Well, it's not like that here. The CWC serves everybody. It's the only place where it does not matter where you come from. This is an organization to deal with the needs of all Africans—whether immigrant, refugee, or born here. Anyway, the issues are basically the same.

AMINA   (through an interpreter)   I like that. I have never been any place here [in the Twin Cities] where you get so many different Africans—Kenyans, Ethiopians, and Somalis [Looks around the room and nods at women who seem to represent each of the national/ethnic groups she mentions.] You know, we must remember that we are here on the backs of African Americans. These people came here from Africa first, and they didn't want to. It's their suffering that made it possible for us to have somewhere to go—to come here to America and live.

SHEBA   Here we work together to overcome our differences. It's the only place where women can come together and put aside tribe and nationhood. The other organizations, they are run by men. Women are better at working together on these things.[19]

The perceived authority and, in some ways, greater authenticity and cultural consciousness attributed to self-described "Africans born in America" to organize diasporan diversity was indicated in another conversation. The day after a meeting of CWC teachers of various ethnic backgrounds, a key CWC "African born in America" elder who facilitated the meeting commented on the participation of African Americans: "I am proud of my people. I see knowledge of our traditions, history, and practices coming together. African Americans are in a better position to promote traditions that are purer. For continental Africans, sometimes the traditions can go sour but they have become part of the myth and they just keep going anyway. So, like how the Yorùbá sacrifice chickens to *orisha* [I nod my head]. It's not necessary and it's really traumatizing to children."[20]

Birth and socialization in Africa did not necessarily grant a person the level of cultural expertise and commitment considered necessary for effective cultural reconstruction and organizing. An African-born person could be so completely disconnected from what the CWC's leadership might consider "African traditions" that she or he could lose his or her Africanness. The words of a Hausa immigrant from Nigeria and CWC participant, married to an African American, explained this perspective:

. . . There are some African Americans who embrace Africa 100 percent and who want to help Africa, who want to go back and rebuild and reeducate the people and tell the stories of how the White man has destroyed us. And there are some continental Africans who would swear they would never want to go back to Africa. Do you understand? So who is better at being an African—the African American or the continental African? It's just what is in the heart. What are we doing for our own salvation? What are we doing for the reeducation or reclaiming of us as a people? That's the underlying question.[21]

For the CWC African leaders, consciousness of African heritage and self-conscious efforts to support the interests of African people were the primary determinants of authenticity—not place. This approach to knowledge and heritage provided the rationale for who was an appropriate authority figure. Demonstrated skill in recalling, re-creating, applying, and thereby sustaining some sense of "African" culture—not place of birth or citizenship—provided "Africans born in America" a passport to leadership.

Many CWC African immigrants concurred, because the leadership was seen as having expertise in balancing or combining aspects of African culture and dominant "European" culture in America. Leaders could extract and apply to health, politics, family, or community relations the essential elements of "African" culture seen as more impervious to historical change, linguistic or cultural difference, and political tensions. Leaders could teach people how to "keep your culture." One African immigrant participant explained her approach to keeping the culture: ". . . What I have been able to do to myself and to my family is the system of incorporation of the best. It's not assimilation, it's incorporation. And it's not integrating either. It's *incorporating* the very best. There are some of the cultural aspects that are unbroken that remain for us or for me as an African woman. Those remain strong, and those will be the ones that I will carry stronger than some of the ones that I may incorporate along the way."[22]

The CWC leadership was seen to have the skills to promote a kind of selective incorporation that built on what was valued in various traditions to which people were exposed—not assimilation into a broader "European culture" in America. Indeed, assimilation was defined and interpreted as a major cause of illness, disease, and social problems. Instead, the CWC promoted a model of incorporation in which participants reconciled their re-created and rediscovered cultural traditions with those of the dominant society.

However, not all African immigrants embraced this division of labor for organizing African diversity. The most active African immigrant participants tended to be emerging or established leaders in their communities of origin, for example, Liberian, Ethiopian, and Yorùbá, and had the broadest vision of "African" identity. African immigrants who were less active did not necessarily believe that African Americans who defined themselves as "Africans" had either any particular leadership role or were legitimately or authentically "African." For example, one Somali participant at a CWC conference, who is knowledgeable of but not actively involved in the CWC, complained that "these African Americans who are really into Africa think that they're somehow more *African* than the real

Africans [people born and raised in Africa and/or born to parents who are natives of Africa] themselves."[23] This is one reason he was reluctant to become actively involved. This perspective was probably more widespread in the Twin Cities' African immigrant community but was not widely represented at the CWC. The African immigrants who were most attracted to and active in the CWC tended to espouse and assertively promote some variation of a pan-Africanist perspective. The CWC's African American leadership also gravitated towards collaborating with African immigrants who shared its vision of "African" identity. One CWC African American leader said: "I want to work with continental Africans who are about building community. You can't just come here and rent space and not collaborate with other Africans at the CWC. In its work the CWC is modeling a vision of African community where different people of African heritage are working together and supporting one another. So, to have you here, and Rameses working with the children, Nefertiti teaching dance, and Haidia working with the Somali parents is a way of showing how a healthy African community would work."[24]

The CWC was both a conceptualizer and an organizer. It created new ideas about African diversity and drew on translocal flows to build new social networks and organize capital to support them. As an organizer of diversity, one of the CWC's primary activities was to "build community" through effective social networks of mutual support among African peoples in the Twin Cities. This involved facilitating social relationships between individuals and institutions. Cosponsorship and incubation of start-up African immigrant social services and advocacy projects were ways that this community-building work was undertaken. The intention was that the projects would spin off as independent programs or organizations as they developed their administrative capacity and acquired independent funding, office space, and staff.

One such organization, which was envisioned by its Ethiopian founder as a cultural organization for East Africans of various nationalities and ethnicities living in the Twin Cities, became independent and was working on efforts to engage African Americans in development efforts, particularly those related to health care and other social services, among immigrants in the Twin Cities and East African countries.[25] The organization actually started as a way to organize African women who were being racially harassed in an apartment building.[26] This leader continued to provide support for these women, and eventually became interested in creating a formal nonprofit program to provide ongoing family services support. The organization was featured in a poignant front page article in Minneapolis's major daily newspaper, highlighting this former CWC participant and the personal impact of the AIDS crisis on the approximately 35,000 East Africans living in the Twin Cities:

Selassie has been crying.

He's crying for his youngest brother, who died seven months ago, and crying for another brother who is on his deathbed. And for months, Selassie, 36, of Minneapolis, has been crying each time he gets another call or letter from his native west-central Ethiopia telling him that someone else he knows has died of complications of AIDS.

Selassie, founder and executive director of an area social and social service group for East Africans, and leaders of other Twin Cities-based African organizations are coming together to find ways to get people to talk about the issue, their grief and suggestions for helping those back home.

One idea is to take a group of black Americans to Africa next year to help with AIDS prevention education. Africans don't take seriously the advice of white relief workers who distribute condoms . . .

The Twin Cities is home to about 35,000 residents from that region: Ethiopians, Eritreans, Sudanese, Somalis, Kenyans, Ugandans and natives of other East African nations. Many of them remain anxious about the poverty, lack of medicine, poor hygiene and other problems in their war torn countries. They worry about relatives enduring life in refugee camps while awaiting admittance to the United States and other countries, and about whether loved ones have been killed during the latest battles.

Now they have added AIDS to their list of worries . . .

So, Robi and Maire [both Sudanese immigrant directors of two other Twin Cities-based social services agencies specializing in Sudanese community] are organizing a group of black Americans to go to East Africa early next year for an AIDS education mission. They say that it is essential for blacks to travel to Africa to help the effort to reduce the spread of the AIDS virus. They can be key in breaking cultural obstacles to practicing unprotected sex, Maire said . . .

"At home we are taught to respect and be courteous to all visitors," Maire said. "But if they are white telling them how to live, they do not listen . . ."

Meanwhile, Selassie wants to end his suffering and the pain of others living in the Twin Cities. "We can sound our voices together," he said. "If you are one, nobody can hear you. If you are many, you can be heard."[27]

Using the Twin Cities as a base, many of the activities of grassroots, formal nonprofit and mutual aid societies referred to in these passages were designed to improve relations across various diasporan groups and were not local, but transnational. The African immigrant groups seeking to collaborate with Twin Cities African American nonprofits sought to work on issues of common concern. Although many were primarily in the planning stages, they also tried to work on projects benefitting Africans living in various countries in the continent—most notably Sudan, Ethiopia, Ghana, Somalia, Liberia, and Sierra Leone. It was not relevant whether African Americans had the specific cultural or language expertise to work effectively on "transnational" health advocacy efforts, as proposed by the Ethiopian and Sudanese leaders in the article on AIDS cited above. What was most important was that the African American and African immigrant participants *believed* there was some basis of common identification and knowledge, as well as, in some instances, mutual socioeconomic and political interest, to justify formation of such efforts.

The CWC was a mentoring and training ground for African immigrant leaders. Through community building and incubating start-up nonprofits, one of the CWC's linking functions was to form new social networks that would crosscut the cultural counterflows of a transnational African diaspora.

The Twin Cities have become an intercultural crossroads for diasporan peoples from across the world. In the region's broader sociopolitical and economic contexts the CWC was taking on a role, along with a number of other institutions, in organizing and managing the diversity of the Twin Cities' African diaspora. Analyzing the CWC's cultural dynamics was complicated by the fact that it linked subcultures and institutions to create alternative ways of perceiving diversity at multiple levels: within and among the various ethnic subcultures that comprised its constituency (that is, the African, Asian, Chicano and Latino diasporas, American Indians, and Europeans); across the various neighborhoods that constituted the Powderhorn planning district; into mainstream medical-related institutions (for example, hospitals, medical schools, insurance companies, health care foundations) and grassroots mutual aid and nonprofit organizations; with individual agents; and in the Twin Cities region and other metropolitan areas where the African diaspora lives.[28] Conventional models of culture and ethnicity do not neatly accommodate the staggering diversity and jagged transnational edges of the CWC's cultural processes.[29]

A recent stream of cultural analysis provides alternatives to geographically bound notions of culture and ethnicity that can be used to understand cultural production in the Twin Cities African diaspora.

Anthropology's difficulty in theorizing the African diaspora, and intercontinental cultural phenomena more generally, is indicative of a fundamental problem. Scholars are confounded by the breakdown of boundaries that demarcated "a culture" and resulted in blurred distinctions between the local and global and the compression of time and space. A culture is no longer necessarily coterminous with a "people," a nation, or a village, or a neighborhood—the various spaces and places that many anthropologists (and others) thought contained single cultures and shared systems of meaning. With world migration and the influence of various communications and media technologies, cultures are increasingly placeless (see Harvey 1989; Kearney 1995:547). Many collective systems of meaning (what has been conventionally called "culture") can meet in one place; these systems are not necessarily shared or cohesive but are in flux as influenced by power relations and historical dynamics. The greater emphasis on the study of meaning in the context of shifting power relations has also undermined the assumption that collective systems of meaning are somehow customary or self-perpetuating (Hobsbawm and Ranger 1983).

Identity formation studies in Africanist and African diaspora scholarship have conventionally focused on models of nation and ethnicity. Recent contemporary critiques have demonstrated how each of these models assume the universality of essentially conventional Western notions of culture as bounded, integrated, homogenous, and continuous in time and space (Fardon 1987; Handler 1988; Barth 1989; Appadurai 1990). Depres (1984) questions the universality of the Western idea that "nationhood" necessitates "ethnic" homogeneity. Worsley (1984:187) suggests that societies of different political organization have different approaches to organizing different "cultural communities." He also suggests that societies have varying levels of tolerance for cultural difference, due largely to political philosophy. Barth (1984:84–85) makes similar observations when he notes that the sociopolitical organization of the Sohari of Oman and certain key cultural concepts such as honor produce different conditions for the definition and organization of cultural diversity (see also Fardon 1987; Foster 1991). Concepts of nations as not only politically but culturally and economically independent also do not address transnational dynamics in identity formation (Bhabha 1990). Ethnicity, pluralism, and nation—and to some extent even the underlying concept of culture itself—are increasingly losing their credibility as universal models for understanding complexity comparatively. Instead they are being seen as alternative ways of organizing and managing diversity.

The breakdown of the conceptual underpinnings of conventional approaches to culture has led to a proliferation of alternative terms: "public," "transnational," "translocal," "global," "global ecumenes, fields, and flows," "creolized," and "postmodern," to name just a few.[30] Definitional debates about these terms aside, all may be seen as attempts to understand how cultural and politicoeconomic factors intersect in the production of increasing, overlapping, sometimes contending, and more encompassing systems of collective meaning, especially in the contemporary global economy. These attempts to build "global culture theory" (Kearney 1995) are heavily influenced by Wallerstein's world systems theory (1974, 1984), but they are more concerned with tracking the development of new systems of meaning in the context of the contemporary global flow where geographically bound distinctions of center/periphery or local/global are less clear cut. They also emphasize the declining significance of the nation as a forum for creating identity, the continuing significance of cultural difference, and identity formation.

Another concern is with the legitimacy of "culture" itself as the foundation for anthropological analysis. One stream of this debate maintains that the term is so laden with baggage from conventional theory that it cannot be productively redefined to fit within the structure and operation of contemporary collective systems of meaning. This line of thought also proposes that the term has been politically appropriated for various purposes—from the creation of the "primitive/civilized" dichotomies used to support colonialism to various social debates in America, such as multiculturalism and the reemerging "culture of poverty" thesis (Abu-Lughod 1991; Wikan 1992; Ingold 1993).

However, discarding the notion of "culture" will not somehow remove the social and politically contingent nature inherent in the study of collective ideational systems. Any alternative conceptual framework will necessarily be bound by the sociopolitical context in which it is created. The comparative ethnographic study of collective ideational systems in the context of political economy, social systems, and history continues to be a valuable and almost defining niche for anthropology.

Appadurai (1986, 1990, 1996) maintains that contemporary translocal processes of cultural formation make outmoded the notion of "culture" as shared meaning within a distinct geographical area. He proposes an essentially adjectival use of the term to describe the process whereby groups mobilize difference to construct identity (1996:27–47). He suggests a model of "scapes"—comprised of key fields of transnational exchange in the global economy—to characterize these cultural dynamics.[31] Some of these are, for example, "financescapes" for the disposition of global capital; "ideoscapes" for key concepts, images, and associated words such as "freedom," "democracy," and "rights"; and "ethnoscapes" for intensified global migration. These "scapes" intersect in unpredictable ways, coalescing into "diasporic public cultural spheres" where individual agents manipulate and negotiate these contending meanings and resources to direct the local construction of identity as informed by transnational processes. A fundamental challenge of contemporary cultural (re)production is to create "localities," the conventional focus of ethnography, in the face of these crosscutting and destabilizing arenas of human interaction.

Hannerz's (1992, 1996) recent approach to the organization of cultural diversity is also helpful in analyzing the CWC case. Building on earlier usages of the term in anthropology (see Kroeber 1945:9; Kopytoff:1988, 10; Foster 1991), he proposes that we break up the conventional boundaries that were thought to contain culture and instead consider collective systems of meaning as part of a broader "global ecumene" of translocal cultural flows in which there are different and overlapping "habitats of meaning" (see also Bauman 1992:190–91). Here culture is seen as meanings and meaningful forms which we shape and acquire in social life. In Hannerz's distributive, processual approach to culture, the extent to which culture—that is, a "habitat of meaning"—is integrated, shared, distributed, or is tidily coterminous with a distinct geographic area will vary across societies and historical periods. Hannerz's analysis focuses on the pivotal role of "world cities" as conduits for global flows of meaning. He proposes a model of "double creolization" whereby world cities exchange cultural flows, recombining them in new ways with immigrants adding new habitats of meaning to the process. Hannerz also emphasizes the important role of a diverse array of agents—for example, social institutions, corporations, the state, and individual actors—in the creation and management of these variously distributed habitats of meaning.

In the Twin Cities, which as the highest concentrations of Somalis, Hmong, and urban American Indians in the country and growing immigrant populations from other countries, a vigorous public discourse and contest has emerged about appropriate models for organizing diversity. To use Hannerz's term (1996), the Twin Cities may be seen as an emerging world city—a conduit where all the cultural flows brought by these diverse groups converge with the local political economy to create crosscutting scapes that frame translocal cultural production. The Twin Cities are experiencing "double creolization" whereby the area exchanges culture with metropolitan regions throughout the world, with immigrants adding new streams of culture at both ends of the flow.

The Twin Cities African diaspora has become a transnational field, a black public sphere, applying Appadurai's view (1996:169), composed of intersecting scapes of ethnoracial, financial, ideational, and media flows. These scapes are translocal points of contact where the global and local meet, creating unpredictable permutations of cultural meaning without tidy social or political boundaries. African diasporan nonprofit organizations like the CWC, in collaboration with individual leaders from the government, corporations, and philanthropic entities, are key agents in conceptualizing and managing these flows to create more encompassing levels of common cultural identity. These new identities result from the interaction of imported models for conceptualizing diversity with deconstructed and reassembled mainstream notions of race, ethnicity, assimilation, and multiculturalism.

Implicit in both assimilational and multiculturalism perspectives is an assumption of monoculturalism, which, increasingly, many anthropologists and others suggest is a conceptual framework that may be specific to Western societies (Moore 1987). In monocultural approaches, defining self by one cultural identity is the norm. Those with multiple cultural origins are aberrant and require assimilation into a dominant, putatively more homogeneous identity group established as the norm. The CWC accommodates multicultural origins but proposed that "African" approaches to health and wellness form a common cultural thread beneath which various ethnic, sociopolitical, and other differences can and should exist. Within this "African" cultural framework, multiple "indigenous" cultural variations are accommodated, but they are seen as manifestations of a shared African theme. The CWC approach allows for contextual identity. Although a person might claim to be Oromo, Ethiopian, Christian, or Muslim in a particular social setting, if he or she has some partial African ancestry, the person is still considered "African." The CWC sees its model for conceptualizing diversity as teaching people a way to "stay African while living in America."

African diasporan nonprofits like the CWC have taken on a lead role in managing diversity across these global scapes of cultural flow. They act as intermediaries among various African diasporan peoples to construct alternative models of identity. They also link these various constituencies to institutions that provide capital (government, philanthropic, corporate), media access, and exposure to American cultural constructs to devise social institutions that provide vehicles for mutual aid and potential political action in these new transcontinental communities. They establish a mechanism to convert these translocal social networks into transnational economic ties between the Twin Cities and various African metropolitan areas, where immigrants often maintain active connections. Because of the increasing concentration of poverty among racial minority groups in the Twin Cities, there is competition and conflict. This is manifested, for example, in major public institutions like schools where racial minorities come together. However, a countervailing trend seems to be the deliberate effort of members of the African diasporan middle class to establish commonalties and economic cooperation to address common social issues. These groups form a potential basis for increasing the scale of political influence in the Twin Cities beyond the various ethnoracial groups that comprise it.

These ethnoscapes of exchange are more accurately described as ethnoracial scapes, as various African groups conflate mainstream notions of race and ethnicity to create multiple levels for perceiving identity at progressively more expansive and contextual levels of inclusiveness, for example, from clan or tribe to a Twin Cities Somali "community," to a transnational Ghanaian or Somali ethnicity group, to a "Black" or "African" diaspora with transatlantic social and economic networks.

The African Body Resistant

The CWC's folk notions of history, identity, and the body were integrated into its guiding policy statement, called "a people's theory of health and wellness." This "people's theory" was seen as providing the CWC's rationale for its particular approach to "cultural wellness"—the building of consciousness of heritage and its application of specific cultural healing practices that purported to promote wellness and prevent illness not only for individual people of African heritage, their families, and communities, but for the ethnically diverse constituencies represented by individuals and families of the Phillips and Powderhorn neighborhoods.

The people's theory was created by the precursor organization to the CWC, Community Health Initiative,[1] and noted that

The CWC was born from the ideas of citizens and health practitioners in the community who had been meeting in CHATs (Citizen Health Action Teams) as part of Community Health Initiative. It was a two-year initiative [1995–1996] funded by a major area health care foundation, the Allina Foundation, to engage citizens to work together to improve the health of the community. Forty-one ideas were generated at those meetings, including a Farmers Market, now in its third year, and the CWC, where many of the other ideas are still being carried out. One of the major conclusions from the work of Community Health Initiative was the importance of culture and community upon health. Again and again, we documented that people need a strong network of relationships in order to be healthy. When these community and cultural connections are broken, people's personal health and the health of the entire community decline. When people are engaged in their own healing, have kinship networks, participate in community life, are connected to their culture and heritage, know their neighbors, are closely connected with and take responsibility for generations other than their own, and have a spirituality that connects them to something beyond themselves, then personal health and community health flourish.[2]

The CWC sought to nurture links to others, to the past, and to spiritual growth. Community people, working in Community Health Initiative and now the CWC, had created a bridge between the conventional health system and cultural and alternative health practices. The CWC saw itself as cultivating an organic community care-giving system where people could be in touch with the resources they need to heal themselves and their community.

In the people's theory of health, a downward process of illness and disease, community violence, and decay was produced by a combination of factors: individualism, loss of community and culture; loss of a sense of belonging and worth; isolation and disconnection from community, and depression and lethargy—all seen as the results of a technologically driven, individualistic, capitalistic Western society. As succinctly stated by the CWC's director in a community forum about funding community-based health programs and announcing a major public study on minority health: "The people said that individualism, the loss of community, and the loss of culture can make you sick."[3] The CWC's work was to stem the tide of ill health, disease, and community decay by promoting an "upward process of health and wellness within a safe, flourishing community. A philosophy of community embraces a positive sense of belonging and worth, interaction and connection (i.e. strong families, elder, and neighborhood networks); optimism, energy, and power."[4] The CWC board, which included medical doctors, high-level public health officials, and community healers and activists of various ethnic backgrounds, had developed a policy statement articulating its Principles of Community/Cultural Health Practices. It stated:

Cultural health practices exist within a knowledge system founded on a set of underlying assumptions. In this system, life is not limited to the aliveness of the physical body. The person is understood as a reflection and an extension of his/her place within the universe, the environment, the community and the family.

The person is the place where powerful forces of relationships intersect. These relationships include interactions with family, elders, children, community, as well as with work, nature and the invisible elements. Cultural health practices are based on a relationship way of thinking where disease which expresses itself at the physical level has parallel manifestations in the emotional, mental and spiritual.

Healing at any level would then also have parallel manifestations at the other levels. More than the causation of disease, cultural health practices focus on "the message" inherent in a particular disorder for other aspects of a person's life and vice versa. The aim of cultural health practices is the restoration of harmony; the process is anchored in relationships. Many tools and techniques—herbs, manipulating the environment, symbols, stories, rituals, chanting, bodywork and manipulation—are used to support the fundamental process of restoring harmony.[5]

The CWC also described these cultural health practices as the "medicine of reconciliation." The goals of the medicine of reconciliation were to help participants to "reconcile, be in harmony with other cultures and other traditions; reconcile with our past; reclaim the knowledge from which we have been disconnected; regain balance: male/female, heart/mind, being/acting; relearn the ancient wisdom of our people."[6] The same program flyer goes on to say that: "Stress-related habits and illnesses have their roots in these issues. True health and well-being needs the medicine of reconciliation."[7] CWC physicians and staff, along with various cultural elders and healers, worked with people within the context of their culture to improve their health through lifestyle changes, cultural health practices, and education.[8]

"Cultural immersion training" was one of several CWC strategies used to practice or heal through the medicine of reconciliation. This training enabled a person to "connect yourself to a community that can give you support and a sense of belonging. Replace a sense of isolation with a sense of community. Study your heritage and culture to strengthen your identity and purpose."[9] The CWC logo was composed of three circles, each encasing a symbol representing a component of a healthy community and related CWC services:

> a healthy individual *body* (promoted by CWC "Core Member Activities")
>
> a healthy *mind* (the CWC's "Invisible College" to teach community members and health professionals cultural health practices through, for example, journaling, storytelling, family tracing)
>
> a healthy community/individual *spirit* (CWC "Health Institute" services to promote connections among various community members and to connect conventional medicine with alternative or indigenous practices through, for example, birthing teams, healing circles, elders councils).[10]

The three circles intersected; the intersecting sections were shaded like a Venn diagram representing a community and individual where the body, mind, and spirit were in harmony.

Participants saw these core program principles as an alternative to the mainstream medical system's approach to health. These attributes were also interpreted as fundamentally African by most "African" and many "European" CWC participants. Thus, CWC resistance to mainstream medical models provided the conceptual apparatus to reconstruct notions of African identity through the surrogate discourse of health and wellness.

The CWC theory of African identity was based on a notion of embodiment in which Africanness was thought to be literally retained, albeit it in varying degrees of a consciousness, through a kind of built-in intuition inside the bodies of all people of some African heritage. It was guided by the African ancestors. Even in its unconscious state, African intuition caused the body to move and express itself in particular ways that were considered common to people of African heritage. Failure to develop an ability to consciously hear the ancestors and be guided by their wisdom produced illness. The CWC's notions of embodied Africanness as indelible were an attempt to construct an alternative framework for African diasporan identity that, while accommodating the social reality and some key North American notions of race, especially hypodescent, sought to transcend and resist the stigmatizing connotations of Blackness.

Generally speaking, these were not the terms in which the CWC's work was officially expressed. The CWC's people's theory and notions of the medicine of reconciliation and cultural health and wellness replaced folk notions of identity, race, and culture with more mainstream frames of reference. These core program principles provided a legitimized trope for the CWC's African and broader community-building agenda.

Cultural wellness at the CWC was a sort of cultural critique. Western notions of the body disconnected it from the mind (rationality) and spirit (intuited heritage and culture in the CWC framework), and these produced sickness and social disharmony. Tensions in European-African relations, discussed so explicitly in many interviews as well as various CWC events, were displaced into a more general critique of Western capitalism and attendant individualism. The critique of Western culture dealt with "disharmonies" created by capitalism: for example, mind/body; men/women; individual/society; Black/White. CWC attempted to reconcile disharmonies by promoting its conception of cultural health.

This was not the stereotypical message about oppressed, inner-city minorities whose negative lifestyle choices had caused a concentration of illness and poverty. Instead, the people's theory proposed that an inherent, unnatural disharmony of Western culture caused illness. Western culture and capitalism were equated with fragmentation, sickness, and decline.

Reconnection to one's heritage and its "ancient wisdom," as it was called by the CWC, enabled a person to reclaim traditions to prevent illness. So, it was the heritage of people of color that provided the key to health. Without explicitly critiquing European-African relations, the CWC theory reversed power relations so that "Africans" were the standard to which others should aspire. "European" participants were then in the position of attempting to assimilate so-called indigenous (or African[11]) cultural principles in order to achieve well-being.

This interpretation of the people's theory and the CWC's other program discourse (such as the medicine of reconciliation) was further supported by the CWC's official mission statement: "to unleash the power of people to heal themselves." Implicit was the notion that Western society somehow untaught the generations-old holistic cultural practices that kept African individuals, families, and communities healthy. Western medicine disengaged individuals from their social networks and heritages and instead created an often unnecessary reliance on the expertise and artificial medicines of the doctor. Very reminiscent of Foucault's (1980) notion of "docile bodies," the CWC's perspective was that mainstream Western medicine's reliance on medication, physical symptom-focused treatment, and the assembly line-like time restrictions of managed health care were increasingly creating people who, unlike their ancestors, did not know how to use their cultural practices and social networks to treat underlying cause of illness.

The mission statement implied a more subtle meaning. The *power* that the mission referred to was the inherent power—sometimes called "ancestral energy"—that every person, especially people of color and Africans, were literally thought to have inside their bodies. Although often lying in a dormant state, if cultivated and unleashed, this embodied power reconnected people with ancestral healing practices. This kind of power contributed to curing sickness and promoting holistic health and wellness.

This power focused on the individual, but it also indicated a kind of social healing and reconciliation. Cultivating the healing energy or power inside the body was understood and taught by the CWC's leadership as providing a sort of mental template that enabled a person to make life decisions—not just physical health decisions—informed by ancient wisdom.[12] This lessened dependence on mainstream institutions, not only medical institutions, but also mainstream cultural constructs and institutions.

There was also an implication that this power was unleashed in a social context. Embodied power was both individualized and collective, and CWC classes and support groups were deliberately designed to be microcosms of healthy social networks. A key CWC African leader described the groups as forums to "give people an experience of culture and teach them to build community."

Cultural healing countered the notion that the Black body was a stigmatized racial symbol of violence, primitivity, unbridled sexuality, poverty, and intellectual inferiority, as conventionally proposed in North American racial constructs. Instead it became a site of "ancestral energy," wisdom, and power that had been sustained, at least in a dormant state—in anthropological terms, "embodied"—throughout the displacements of the diaspora. Building on current trends in the nonprofit philanthropic sector to emphasize and encourage community participation in program design, community-based solutions, empowerment, and the social assets of financially poor communities, the people's theory provided a mainstream construct in which the CWC's notions of the empowered African body could operate without being interpreted as radical or antiestablishment.[13] Furthermore, the people's theory located the body as the vehicle for transporting and sustaining core cultural practices through social relations and connections that transcended locality, were transnational, and expanded Minnesota's affective social networks throughout the globe.[14]

Most of the CWC participants accepted, at some level, its program mission and principles, but in significantly different ways. The proposition that "the people," particularly inner-city people of color or Africans, were the cultural standard-bearers of health and wellness was a potentially contentious notion that was played out in many ways during CWC program encounters.

The discourse about what was "really African" in the CWC's philosophy, mission, and programs involved its two most prominent and active groups: "Africans" and "Europeans." It was not always contentious but was a potential source of tension and conflict of which leaders were always aware. This discourse was a useful lens on the complex dynamics of resistance that underlay the CWC's effort to create alternative notions of culture, wellness, and race so as to construct a translocal African identity.

African people, according to interviews with CWC African participants, shaped the development of the CWC's program philosophy, mission, and strategies in its formative stages. The CWC founder's story of how the people's theory and the broader mission developed clarified this perspective:

When we were starting Community Health Initiative, I read a lot about Cuban, Haitian, Japanese traditions and the WHO [World Health Organization] literature on how African countries and villages care for themselves and the role of culture. The so-called third world has figured out some ways to survive. At the same time, I was heavily involved in strengthening African culture through my own volunteer work in the community. In developing Community Health Initiative and the CWC, I wanted to remain true to my [African] philosophy—this work fueled the development of the CWC. In fact, a lot of the early work in the CHATs, [Community Health Action Teams] particularly the community meetings that led to the people's theory and philosophy of community, were facilitated by Rashad [pseudonym for a Twin Cities "African" elder and active CWC participant] . . .[15]

So, despite the self-acknowledged fact that this leader and CWC co-founder conducted research on various cultural health practices, some of which were arguably not African (for example, the reference to research on Japanese traditions), to devise the CWC's mission and programming, essentially the approach was considered African. This was in part due to the fact that many of the originators and significant numbers of active participants were of African heritage, and they saw themselves as transforming other cultural practices into something African.

The overall CWC purpose and mission were understood as providing a general framework for promoting the health and wellness of the broader community, not just what was defined as its African components. Indeed, its African leaders maintained that various "European" CWC leaders recognized the leadership role of people of African heritage in its work. During an interesting and sometimes emotionally charged exchange at a community forum on racism, Pauline, a CWC European leader and social worker, stated:

Why does my body feel this way? All these different cosmologies running through my body—the liberal tradition, ancient European traditions, and then, the Adam and Eve story which is essentially about hatred of women. [The woman was crying. Her face was red and her body was noticeably trembling.] I am not so much worried about my sons getting killed on the street but I am worried about their spirits being killed. Like liberal white women who have stolen drumming; we know that your [comments directed at one of the "African born in America" speakers] culture has something we need—we want to learn.[16]

While Pauline sought African knowledge, on other occasions European participants acknowledged that the African role in setting and implementing the CWC mission was a source of interracial tension. Several "African" participants seemed to be conflicted about what was sometimes described as the appropriation of the CWC's African people's theory and approach to cultural wellness by its European participants. For example, Akbar, an African born in the Caribbean participant and leader, expressed uneasiness about how "some Europeans are genuine in their search for their heritage. But at the same time, they can take what is yours, incorporate it, call this ancient knowledge 'New Age' and then your people don't get any credit for it."[17]

This ambivalent sentiment about the role of Europeans was also expressed in the CWC's "African" leadership's concern about "African" participants' reluctance to participate in the CWC's interracial activities and programs. For example, Korman, one of the Capoeira teachers and an "African born in America" who was a devotee of a Yorùbá *orisha*,[18] explained: "The CWC is a place where we can come practice in an African way—you can just be African—be with other Africans without having to explain, justify it as African, or explain what we're doing."[19] Nefertiti, the dance teacher, described the tone of an ongoing seminar held to teach all CWC instructors its official cultural wellness philosophy and practices:

... I've noticed that something about the tone of the conversation changes as [when] black people [are] in these classes. We have our own collective words that we use, but in these classes we're talking about it from a different perspective. We're really talking about getting a consensus on the language we use—the energy we use—in the classes as instructors. It's not about the interracial harmony—the melting pot theory thing. A lot of Europeans are benefitting from what the CWC has to offer. People of color are not finding ways to access it enough ... Sometimes I'm not sure of how to interact [with "Europeans"]. The CWC is teaching me how to deal with people of non-African descent—how to do that without giving up yourself.[20]

On the other hand, several "European" participants commented that the CWC seemed to cater to its African more than its European constituency. Sara mentioned that a "deliberate effort needs to be made to make Europeans feel welcome because they are not yet in touch with their own heritage or comfortable with indigenous cultures." The CWC leadership, both European and African, made sure that the diverse cultures represented in the broader community felt welcome. For example, the exercise room once had an African theme. It was changed to have a rotating art exhibit featuring works of neighborhood artists of various cultural heritages. However, it was frequently expressed, largely because of the predominantly African-inspired interior design and dedicated participation of a regular group of "Africans," that the CWC's primary constituency and focus were African. In keeping with this general perception of the dominance of an African spatial and design aesthetic, the multiple European and Asian artifacts in the office were frequently, nonetheless, identified as African.

The CWC often explained its notions of cultural wellness and medicine of reconciliation as "spiritual," that is, they transcended or integrated the dualisms thought to characterize European ways of knowing. The European and African leaders saw the "spiritual" perspective as African, and the organization as an apolitical tool for reconciling the various oppositions inherent in European ways of knowing, for example, African/European, spiritual/material, Blackness/Whiteness, sacred/secular, and so forth.

The different Black movements faltered because they were looking for White people to give freedom. After long study and analysis, I decided that White people can't free me, and didn't care about whether they gave us citizenship. If White people can't give their own people rights, how can they give me rights? My people have to deal with different issues. Black people have to ask themselves a series of questions and only Black people can provide the answers. "Why have my people been conquered for so long—enslaved for twenty-one generations? How do we get back our equilibrium, harmony, and power?" I don't know the answers, but I know that I won't let it happen to my children or anyone in the next generation that I have anything to do with.

This realization brought me to a spiritual understanding of these issues—a "cosmological" understanding. Cosmology is universal. It is grounded in creation and belongs to my people too. I don't have to ask anyone's permission to build my cosmology . . . A cosmological approach does not ground liberation in material or political world. It's a spiritual liberation. It's not defined or constrained by dominant culture or power structure.[21]

Here there was an implicit juxtaposition of the "spiritual" and the "political," with the political being part of the material world and the spiritual being a more cosmological approach to solving earthly problems. Similarly, the CWC's "African born in America" leadership had a particular aversion to the use of classifications such as "lower class" or "middle class" or "ethnic group." In several meetings I was asked not to use these terms as they were "too political." The CWC leadership also often distinguished itself from other similar community-based projects, particularly those created by government, as being cultural as opposed to political. The thinking was that political approaches to "community building," or what the CWC would call reconciliation, were doomed to fail because, as implied by the above quote, they were working within a framework constrained by material divisions. The CWC saw its cosmological (spiritual or cultural) approach to reconciliation and healing as transcending the inherent conflicts of politics.

Contained within this cosmology was a particular philosophy and epistemology of identity and community. It proposed that each "culture"—in current anthropological terms, "ethnic group"—had a heritage and cosmology, from which they had been disconnected, particularly people living in diaspora communities in dominantly Western (that is, North American or European) societies. Each person must find a way to reconnect to this heritage and make explicit their people's cosmology as it provided a guide to cultural and societal wellness. With everyone working within a cosmological framework, constructive racial reconciliation was possible as it enabled groups to recognize each other as coequals defined in terms of cultural, not material, worth or political advantage.

The cosmological perspective was not most accurately described as apolitical. It transcended the political and material world, while, at the same time, providing an independent philosophical basis for African liberation. While the spiritual was perceived as somehow transcendent of the material or secular in the CWC African way of knowing, it was not disconnected. European ways of knowing were seen by CWC leaders as keeping these dualisms in destructive opposition. From a CWC African cosmological perspective, these dualisms were, in fact, inherent in nature or the universe itself and were the basis of creation. The CWC saw itself as helping people accept and balance, or "reconcile," these natural tensions in the promotion of individual and social health and wellness. From the CWC African leadership's perspective, before "racial" reconciliation can occur, "your people must understand how they relate to creation; and my people must understand how they relate to creation." Teaching African people what the CWC defined as their way of knowing and cosmology was seen as a prerequisite for cultural wellness and a first step in promoting reconciliation across the various divisions among the Africans and with Europeans as well.

Despite the leadership's extensive theorizing to construct a kind of apolitical conceptual framework and practices for organizing, participants were aware of the political context in which they operated. Their apolitical, cosmological view qualified as "African" because it was considered the polar opposite of what was described as the European worldview: the African sought balance; the European fragmented and based analysis on dualism. In the CWC's approach, the body, and the universal human need for physical wellness—what it called cultural wellness—became the mediator of cultural difference and political conflict. It was where the cosmology of a particular people was practically experienced, even if not cultivated, and viscerally understood. Thus, reconnection of the mind (consciousness) to the body and spirit was the key to cultural wellness and social harmony, and African cosmology provided a means of achieving such a reconciliation at two levels: philosophically through the integration of mind, body, and spirit, and inter-ethnically by creating shared levels of identity among, for example, Somali, Amharic, Oromo, Yorùbá, African American constituents as well as among the other ethnocultural groups that comprised the broader community. This power to proactively bridge the disconnections suggested to have been caused by Western culture was understood to represent a sort of transcendent spirituality, as opposed to materially based political liberation.

The CWC's mission and program principles repositioned the stereo-typed and stigmatized African body and thereby attempted to transform bodily perceptions into positive and valued representations that made the body the main locus for situating African identity. The discourse expressed in the CWC's official people's theory, and other program principles as well as public meetings, translated its underlying folk theories of identity into terms more understandable and acceptable to the power system—specifi-cally, funders, public officials, and wealthy donors who provided financial and other support for its work.[22]

Although not overtly political, the CWC, like any institution, was en-sconced in a set of structured power relationships that pervaded every as-pect of life (Foucault 1980). Ferguson (1994) and others (see Rahnema 1992; Escobar 1995) argue that public or private funders of nonprofits—or nongovernmental organizations (NGOs), in international development parlance—have a tendency to co-opt and transform alternative ideas and institutions such as the CWC. NGOs, the so-called independent sector, they suggest, rather than transform the power structure often ultimately sup-port the status quo. Ferguson's (1994) seminal study of international de-velopment in Lesotho demonstrates how the structural interdependencies of nonprofits and the development industry can depoliticize power rela-tions by treating local conditions as "problems" requiring "technical" as op-posed to political solutions.

The equivalent U.S. nonprofit sector, one could argue, is health care and the community development industries of which the CWC and its funders are a part. I do not claim that the CWC, which was still in its early forma-tive stages during this study, had become part of the antipolitics machine of the Twin Cities community development industry. However, its discourse and practices demonstrated some of the same oppositional dynamics. These dynamics express both the inherent tensions and contradictions of resisting dominant forms of race, culture, and identity, while depending on the financial support of representatives of many of the institutions that may sometimes perpetuate these notions, either consciously or unconsciously. The CWC's discourse and practices of resistance bring into sharp relief the broader political context which informs the African community as it at-tempts to find common ground.

Many ethnographers of American culture as well as analysts of American

ethnography (see Ortner 1997b) note a general American aversion to recognizing the role of class factors in determining their social status and, instead, associate themselves with a broadly defined middle class. Another
tendency, pointed out by (1997b), is to represent class through other categories of social difference: gender, ethnicity, or race, and, I would add, certain concepts of culture as in the culture of poverty thesis. Ortner argues
that until recently, with very few exceptions (for example, Hannerz 1969;
Stack 1975), anthropologists of North America tended to avoid class analysis and instead focused on "ethnicized" subcultures isolated from broader
power relations (1997b:164,166–67).

This tendency to avoid recognition of class factors and displace them
into cultural terms is evident in the CWC's discourse about power, identity,
and the body. While the CWC's constituents, both members of the diverse
group that the leadership defined as "African" and other constituent
groups, represented the full spectrum of the city's class differences, discussion about class was notably absent from the CWC's program materials. Instead, the CWC had two parallel discourses about race and identity: the
discourse in its official program materials, which used concepts familiar
to its powerful funders and upper-class participants, such as "community
building," "cultural health and wellness," "medicine of reconciliation," and
healing of the individual body. In what might be called its more culturally
specific programs and classes, as well as in special topic events such as the
community dialogue on racism, the CWC's discourse bordered on more explicit political critique and analysis. But even its analysis of racism was
couched in what it called "cultural" terms, such as "cosmology," and self-
conscious discouragement of explicit political discourse, as indicated by
the insistence that its approach was "spiritual," not "political," and by a general aversion to politicized terms such as "ethnic group." The effort to create alternative cultural constructs, that is, new collective ideational systems,
was also seen in its effort to promote a "cosmological" approach to racial
reconciliation as opposed to political solutions. This process was also the
backdrop of the CWC's effort to engage its entire range of ethnic constituencies in its project of "unleashing the power of citizens to heal themselves," its medicine of reconciliation: strengthening African ethnic
identity while constructing broader levels of community identification.

Although this complex topic was beyond the scope of this study, it should
be noted that the CWC was a nonprofit organization, largely dependent on
funds for programs and operations from wealthy mainstream individual
donors, philanthropic institutions, and, to a lesser extent, government con-
tracts. This predicament presented interesting challenges as it attempted
to resist, at least indirectly, dominant ideologies of poverty, race, and culture. It was an ongoing challenge for the CWC to raise funds for even its official articulations of its mission.

The CWC leadership was aware of the inherent tensions involved in this process and consciously attempted to devise marketing and fundraising strategies that enabled it to retain the integrity of its mission and underlying philosophies and theories. For example, the CWC offered a range of health-related training and support-group services to nonprofits (particularly medical school students), public health agencies, and some corporations. Several large local health maintenance organizations (HMOs) reimbursed patients for "alternative" or "complementary" health services, particularly acupuncture and chiropractic, as these were seen as potentially preventive and cost-saving health measures. The area's major medical school had even developed a graduate minor in complementary medicine. The CWC leadership investigated the possibility of becoming HMO-certified to receive health insurance payments for services rendered to covered patients who were CWC clients. However, it concluded that the various HMO requirements would severely constrain its ability to provide services based on its values and mission, and it did not pursue that strategy.

Participants were encouraged to become members and were charged fees for some services and classes. The leadership preferred that individual members financially support its activities through membership and donations, as these strategies promoted community ownership. In reality, however, many CWC constituents did not have the financial ability to pay. Therefore, the leadership in many cases did not collect fees, or attempted to have another entity, for example, a hospital or public health agency, sponsor individual participation in certain programs. At some level, it can be argued that the CWC accommodated some aspects of the culture of capitalism in its partial commodification of culture for the purposes of program marketing and fundraising to mainstream funders. At the same time, CWC services were not driven by a profit motive or bought and sold on the open market.

On the one hand, the CWC's cosmological approach might be described as part of the antipolitics (Ferguson 1994) which several authors claim typifies the relations of nonprofit community revitalization groups and their funders. From this perspective, the CWC's apparent displacement of power inequities and class conflict in terms of "the body," "cultural wellness," "cosmology," or "spirituality" could be seen as obfuscating political organizing and protest among its constituents, many of whom live in areas with the cities' highest concentrations of poverty. Applying this approach, the CWC can be seen as helping to perpetuate the very power structure that enabled the widening disparities of wealth and illness rates between people of color and White people. Furthermore, the CWC, while suggesting different underlying notions of race, culture, and the body, also, to some degree, perpetuated the largely reified and stereotypic depictions of "Africans" as more inherently "spiritual" and "Europeans" as somehow more rational and materialistic. However, as is often the case in studying the dynamics of cultural or political resistance, the situation was much more complex.

The CWC's claim of apoliticism was one means whereby it kept such diverse African immigrant participants, many of whom were at war in their countries of origin (for example, Ethiopians and Liberians of various ethnicities or the various Somali clans), engaged in collaborative work. As indicated by the popular media accounts, many of the conflicts between African immigrants and African Americans were between those of modest financial means, many of whom were competing for a limited number of low-skilled, living wage jobs. In this context, deemphasizing class and political divisions among various African diasporan groups enabled the CWC's leadership to emphasize the historical and cultural commonalities that their model of translocal African identity suggested. Attention was diverted from intragroup class and political tensions, and instead, potential political organizing energies were focused on mainstream institutions and structures. Given the relatively small numbers of African Americans and African immigrants in the Twin Cities region, creating a common ground, although not politically motivated, could facilitate formation of political consciousness.

The focus on the body as both a tool and conduit of transformed identity reoriented political analysis and critique—displacing it, in a sense—from overt conflicts over territory, power, or economic resources to one focused on a universally shared concern: the power to determine individual health and wellness. The CWC's extension of the notion of personal wellness to include reconnection with heritage and community well-being enabled a kind of emergent, indirect political resistance to dominant notions of race, the body, and culture which underlie mainstream medical and public health approaches. The focus on the body as a reservoir and conduit of historically preserved energy could be interpreted as a kind of power that, if cultivated, not only promoted health and wellness but offered an empowering strategy for living, and potentially, deliberate political action.

Furthermore, the perception of CWC leadership of the entire people's theory and cultural wellness approach as fundamentally an "African" construct was another form of indirect political resistance. Although it was not without tension, the belief that the entire mission and approach was African could transform dominant power relations in an important way. It suggested that "Africans born in America" and elsewhere, were the cultural standard-bearers to be emulated by other groups. Thus, notions of inherent European cultural and institutional superiority were dismantled, although there was some ambivalence about the alleged appropriation of African culture, as well as discomfort, particularly by some CWC Europeans, regarding the perceived dominance of Africans in CWC programming.

The CWC approach could be seen as both incorporating and transforming key cultural constructs to create a philosophical and practical basis for local and translocal African connections. The CWC's discourse mitigated against the kinds of political and class-motivated ruptures that could prevent the broader level of pan-African cultural consciousness it was trying to promote. At the same time, its discourse provided a framework for political analysis and transformation of race relations, in which "people of African heritage" were repositioned, not as stigmatized, oppressed people, but as the key to cultural health and wellness for society at large.

Part III
Creating "Africa":
A State of Mind/Body/Spirit

I am an African woman wherever I am.

—Sara, CWC African leader born in the United States

Healing the Mind:
Embodying an African Epistemology

There was an ever present discourse on the distinctions between "African and European ways of knowing" at the CWC. After all, as noted by a key CWC African born in America participant, "The CWC taught me that the two systems of thought—African and European—are in conflict." In constructing an African way of knowing, the CWC attempted to explicate the fundamental distinctions between these conflicted systems of thought and reconcile them. Its epistemology juxtaposed perceived European individuality with a purported African way of knowing that emphasized community or intergenerational responsibility informed by ancestral intuition. For example, the class titled Old Ways of Parenting for Young African American Parents taught young parents of African heritage "how to participate in and receive extended family assistance with discipline and cultural teachings." In one session, a parent was seeking advice on choosing from a confusing array of lifestyle choices which she felt conflicted with her responsibilities as a single parent. In addition to advising her to develop and follow African intuition—"the intelligence of the heart"—Sara cautioned her:

In the European way of knowing, you are just open to everything. This is freedom, and rationality is supposed to help you choose what is the good thing. The CWC teaches a different way of knowing—a way of choosing—that will keep you African. You need to ask yourself, "What will keep me African?" not "What will keep me an individual?" As parents, you need a grounding in it—you need to have a vocabulary to talk about it—so that you can teach it to your children. The children need a philosophical ground to help them relate to others and their people. We used to teach this to our children, but we are not teaching it anymore.

If you are open to everything, then everything will come. That's the problem with this generation; it has too many choices and society reinforces the openness. You need to choose what is right and what is wrong. As an elder, I will tell you very clearly what is right and what is wrong. If you choose the wrong way, then you will have to suffer the consequences.

We don't want to get stuck in all these different experiences. The question you need to ask is "What will keep you African?"—despite all the different choices, the lifestyles and cultures, that are open to this generation. The question is not the European question: What will keep me an individual? From an African perspective, it is not your actualization as an individual [that counts]. You must be concerned about our actualization as a people; you must be concerned about our future. The old African way of thinking is generational. Our [African] civilization is based on generational thinking—not based on the individual. We were not only conquered physically, we were conquered in other ways. Our spirituality, ways of thinking, customs, beliefs, and sexuality were also conquered. So, we must intentionally learn and teach the ways of our people.

First, the African way of knowing (the "old African way of thinking") that guided the ancestors was stifled and distorted as a result of European conquest. It was a holistic way of thought that included customs, spirituality, and so on. It continued to exist inside the body and people like CWC teachers helped Africans to tap into, learn, and teach the old ways and apply them to new times.

Interestingly, the teacher also used geographic metaphors to describe the African way of knowing/being.[1] These geographic references were used in several CWC contexts to explain how the African way of knowing/being could orient people's sense of self. The "grounding" of people in this epistemology could be seen as a substitute for territorial markers of identity, thus, facilitating the body and not the land as the foundation of diasporan community.

Because of increasing diversity, a dizzying array of lifestyle choices were available. The African way of knowing continued to reside in the body as informed by ancestral energy; therefore, it could help people make life decisions that helped maintain and strengthen the person in the context of family and community. In contradistinction to the African way of knowing driven by a historically informed intergenerational responsibility, the European way of knowing was based on a notion of unbridled individual freedom divorced from accountability to community or history.

This passage demonstrates how participants were taught to think about embodiment. Behaving in what was defined as "European ways" would lead to practical negative consequences in one's life. Being open to other lifestyles also meant literally opening up the body to "wrong" ways of knowing that impaired development of innate Africanness and led to physical illness and negative social consequences for other African generations, most immediately one's own children. Although the class did not explicitly focus on the body, participants were taught to believe that their physical bodies were affected by their mastery of CWC African ways of knowing. It was teaching a way of actively connecting life philosophy to real-life behavior that encouraged embodiment of CWC beliefs.

The second component of the CWC's "African way of knowing," implicit in its notion of African intuition, was the idea of spirituality. In the CWC framework, Africans had a more spiritual worldview than Europeans. This notion was articulated in many CWC contexts, both those that were predominantly African or European as well as ethnically diverse situations.

One particularly insightful opportunity to understand the CWC's conception of African ways of knowing was a series of community dialogues on racism held in spring 1998. During internal planning meetings in preparation for the forums, as well as in the forums themselves, CWC staff and community members articulated their understandings of African ways of knowing. Participating were several key CWC African and European leaders. Susan, a jack-of-all-trades, had worked most recently in the construction business. She was also a CWC cultural healer who lived with her partner in the Powderhorn neighborhood, where she was also an activist on lesbian and gay rights issues. Bonnie had worked with Sara, a key CWC leader, at the CWC's precursor, the Community Health Initiative. Along with Susan, she facilitated the diabetes wellness group and many of the classes on European health and wellness issues. She also assisted with CWC administration. Baktre, who was originally from the Caribbean, was a social worker and relatively recent addition to the CWC staff. Among her CWC roles was to consult with African people on spirituality issues.

SUSAN, EUROPEAN STAFF PERSON 1   The Western model is based on the rational—it separates to analyze. The indigenous model [African, the CWC's] helps figure out interrelationships. It is a more integrative approach.

BONNIE, EUROPEAN STAFF PERSON   The Western model also separates in order to conquer. The holistic [African/indigenous] model is opposed to the rational model because the European model is dualistic. It sets up oppositions like win/lose, top/bottom, us/them. But dualistic thinking is not the only way of thinking. The holistic way of knowing focuses on the place of connection and unity. This holistic/unified way of thinking makes the whole notion of race ridiculous; there's no place for it.

> This whole Western culture of rationality has a hatred for anything that is seen as nonrational. Any culture or gender, like women, that is seen as nonrational is devalued. It puts Western rationality at the top, so the Western is seen as civilized, then you get this whole hierarchy of rationality.

SUSAN   So, like when people look at a piece of African art and say that it's nonrational, so it's primitive.

> It's like reason is supposed to make some human beings above others—other cultures. It's a tradition that puts everything in a hierarchy. The [Western] tradition uses observation/analysis/categorizing—comparing and contrasting all categories . . . It makes the European seem superior over those cultures which seem irrational. The dominant culture has an oppositional approach. It thinks we

have to define ourselves in opposition to other people. In the CWC's cosmology, we define ourselves as an aspect of a whole.

BONNIE   Europeans have to reconcile what happened in their culture. We [European leaders at the CWC] are trying to heal the effects to get along with any other culture. We must recognize it for what it is and deal with it.

BAKTRE, AFRICAN BORN IN THE CARIBBEAN STAFF PERSON   Indigenous peoples have a spirituality—a way of knowing that Europeans tried to destroy. There are no limits in European worldview—you can destroy anything.

EUROPEAN STAFF PERSON   Destroying indigenous cultures destroys the knowledge that was protecting the planet.[2]

During a community session on racism, a dialogue between two European participants and an African participant further illuminated the distinction made between rationality (European) and spirituality (African): "Race is a political construct that doesn't really exist. To maintain material privilege, Europeans had to trade off the spiritual—a spiritual price—that's the deal that got struck for European material privilege. That's why Europeans have no culture."[3]

What was particularly instructive in this dialogue, as well as in numerous other CWC contexts, was the equation of spirituality with culture and the identification of the secular or material realm as somehow not cultural. Spirituality was seen of the basis of culture—"the way a people knows a thing"—that transcended material or secular concerns. Because the European way of knowing, in the CWC model, was based on secularism and materialism, it was not cultural.

From the CWC European perspective, it was almost as if the CWC African was defined as the Other because Africans were thought to "have culture" ("spirit" or "soul"), in contrast to Europeans who had at worst lost their culture and instead had materialism, or at best had ancient culture and traditions that were more deeply repressed in the body's historical memory. CWC Europeans saw people of African heritage as generally less disconnected—from each other, the earth, ancestors (history), and the body. CWC African epistemology was considered a means whereby culturally disconnected Europeans could recapture their heritage and, thereby, promote cultural health and wellness.[4]

While the CWC deconstructed what it saw as the essential differences between African spirituality and European materialism, it did not reject the material as subordinate. The leadership maintained that the African worldview was "cosmological" in that instead of emphasizing the points of tension and separation in the cosmos, it sought to integrate the conflicting forces of creation—for example, rationality with spirituality, children with elders, and mind with body—that were in opposition in European ways of knowing. As indicated by one of the CWC's prominent elders, "it's [cosmology] the way that your people define themselves as a part of creation—a part of the universe." This cosmological approach, in which the sacred and secular as well as other dualisms were in harmony, was considered a core component of the African way of knowing as taught by both CWC European and African leaders.

During a community forum on racism, Bonnie, a CWC European leader, explained this perspective using an example from her own personal experience:

Somebody says that cosmology provides the language to describe this teaching. It is a gift of African people. I feel like all my life I have been saved by African people. I lived in a very segregated, isolated, homogeneous community in New Jersey. I remember once, for some reason, my family wanted to go to the opening of the new Kennedy Airport in New York. I got lost at the airport. This African American man walked up to me and helped me find my parents This became an important metaphor for my life. I had my first job as a clerk filing. It was a monotonous, mechanical kind of job and I hated it. I worked with mostly white people and no one really talked to each other. Then later I did the same job, but it was in a primarily African American office, and it was so much fun. People were laughing and joking. The atmosphere was warm and inviting. I began to ask, "What are my people missing? Where is my soul? What have we done to ourselves that we are so spiritless?"[5]

What was critical here was not only the purported contrast between African spirituality and European secularity, but also the ways in which the CWC European leader recounted experiencing these differences: through the social atmosphere of the workplace, and the rhythm of work. She juxtaposed her "monotonous," "mechanical," "spiritless" work with European workers with the more social and soulful, and therefore, spiritual work rhythms with African Americans. This implicit contrast—between the more spiritual African way of knowing, based on social relationships manifested in the body's rhythms, and the European way of knowing, based on atomistic individualism and technological or material relationships—was a core theme in the CWC's epistemological discourses.

This CWC cosmological approach was understood as "spiritual," that is, transcending or integrating the dualisms thought to characterize European ways of knowing. Because it was spiritual, the CWC leadership saw it as an apolitical tool for reconciling the various oppositions or dualisms its leadership defined as inherent in European ways of knowing, for example, African/European, Blackness/Whiteness, sacred/secular.[6] The cosmological perspective, and the African way of knowing that flowed from it, were seen as ways to transcend the political and material world while at the same time providing an independent philosophical basis for African liberation.

While the spiritual was perceived as somehow transcendent of the material or secular in the CWC African way of knowing, it was not disconnected. CWC participants were keenly aware of the sociopolitical context in which they worked. For example, in one interview session with the medical director, I mentioned that despite efforts to promote and create an independent African way of knowing/being, CWC teachers constantly referred to its distinctions from European ways of knowing. For example, Dr. Abana, an African born in Haiti who was the CWC medical director, explained: "Yes, it's true. On the one hand there is this African cultural essence that we are all trying to reconnect to. But it's like doing it in a fishbowl. There is always the European there in the background. We are all involved in this intricate dance—moving back and forth to sort out who we are in this kind of European fishbowl."[7]

The cosmological approach expressed in the African way of knowing was often described by both CWC African and European leaders as a sort of "chalice" that seeks to hold various dualisms—including African and European—in creative tension.[8] From a CWC African perspective, these dualisms were inherent in the universe itself and the basis of creation. The African way of knowing/being was understood to provide a nonpolitical means of reconciling these natural tensions in the promotion of individual and social health and wellness.

The CWC African leadership also saw the African way of knowing as integrating the sacred and secular—intuitive and rational knowledge—on two levels: in terms of self-perceptions of identity, and in everyday life. The following passage from my field notes describes a conversation from a session on women, spirituality, and leadership presenting the CWC perspective on reconciling the secular and the sacred.

As I walked in, Sara was discussing how we could all better integrate our "sacred" and "secular" knowledge in our everyday life—"the two lands," as she called them. Another way she posed the question was "How can we remain present on this earth while we operate from spiritual knowledge and guidance?" She said that she did not want to be seen as "flaky." She went on to explain that by "flaky" she meant that she did not want to seem inaccessible or dishonest as many spiritual leaders can appear. She wants to be straight with people and "be of this earth," not operating "up there" in a place where she seems inaccessible. "I do not want to be put on a pedestal like many spiritual leaders—that is bullshit!"

She went on to say, "We are all teachers and students, and to teach, you must also be present in the moment—experience the world as the people you are teaching do. If you can't do that, you cannot teach . . . I am an African woman wherever I am. That does not and cannot change. I am consistent—I'm not flaky." [As an example of how the spiritual and sacred were integrated in everyday life, she walked over to an African mask on the wall and said] that the art was "earthy," that is, of the present—it was "functional"—but at the same time it tells a spiritual message, "it links the two lands."[9]

In many contexts, the CWC leadership emphasized the importance of everyday ritual in connecting these "two lands"—the spiritual and the secular. For example, in another session on women and leadership, Sara explained that ritual was a critical method for being "guided by spiritual knowledge while living in the present . . . Rituals like brushing your teeth—your morning routine—mundane things that you do over and over again that seem to give your life a sense of order. You know that you have ritualized your morning routine when you have guests over and they disrupt your routine. Fill those mundane routines with deliberate thoughts about the sacred as a way of linking the spiritual and secular in leadership on a daily basis . . . Sometimes the mundane task of a ritual can have a deeper spiritual purpose."

The teacher was urging students to create ritual moments that would enable them to take on spiritually informed bodily practices. These moments provided opportunities to blend thought and action in everyday practice. They can be seen as a deliberate strategy for embodying African ways of knowing/being. Being spiritual *and* "grounded" in the present were considered to be effective strategies for balancing the two lands—the secular and sacred—misconstrued as polar opposites in the European worldview.

The "two lands" was a wide-ranging metaphor that referred to balancing various divisions that were thought to impede cultural wellness. The CWC leader quoted above emphasized that, although she could provide leadership at a spiritual level, she was also "grounded," that is, she was an African women regardless of her location or social context. The metaphors of "land" and, again, "grounding" were symbolic landmarks for orienting the identity of people of African heritage who the CWC would define as displaced from their original homeland. The emphasis on ritual as a tool for grounding ways of knowing/being in the body was an effort to produce a sense of embodied African community. The "two lands"—conflicting Africa and America (and related epistemologies)—were harmonized and collapsed into the body. Knowing was still another nonterritorial means for situating identity within the African body. The "land" was converted from territory to an embodied metaphor in order to reposition culture and identity throughout the displacements of the African diaspora.

Napier's (2003:17–20) analysis of how embodiment happens is also useful in understanding the connections between CWC discourse, ritual and identity formation. According to him, although the current fashion in the field is to eschew the study of ritual for the mundane world of everyday living, ritualizing powerful metaphors, for example, in the CWC case, "the land" and "grounding," inscribes an embodied senuousness into seemingly secular activities. Partly through ritual the CWC discourse on cultural healing and the associated elaborate symbolic language were transformed into an embodied feeling of cultural wellness and African identity. Following Napier (2003:17), "ritual, then, is not an 'unreal' mode of living, but is a very special kind of social activity that most modern secularists are at a loss to understand." In the CWC's words, "it links the two lands"—the spiritual and the secular—and is integral to the healing process.

The CWC notion of the mind/body unity was not only a principle of its emerging epistemology. It was also constitutive of the CWC's distinction between African and European people. The mind and body were two realms of being that the CWC taught were severed by the European way of knowing. As noted by Susan, a European leader, "It is a way of thinking [the European way of knowing focused on rationality] that comes from a lack of a cosmology—something about us that divides the person into parts—and makes the mind superior over the rest of our body." In a session on women and leadership, Sara emphasized that "society—through therapy, college, formal leadership courses—teaches people to objectify themselves, to live outside their bodies, to analyze themselves from a distance. Well, with this dissociating from our bodies, insanity can descend upon us!! [laughter from group] . . . We need to remove this artificial separation between the 'mind' and the 'body.' We think with the entire body."[10]

In further illustration of the CWC's notion of mind/body unity as constitutive of the distinction between African and European epistemologies, these remarks were prepared by a European leader for a group of medical students on the influence of culture on European medicine: "Ancient traditions are more affirming of the mind/body connection . . . Since Descartes, the Western world has taken reason outside of the body. 'I think, therefore I am' made reason—the mind—above everything else. It started a focus on controlling the body—controlling nature. We even use the language of war when talking about the health of the body—like 'conquering disease.' Indigenous cultures know how to live with the body and the environment. To be well, we have to learn to live in—to be in—our bodies."[11]

CWC notions of the body and mind were somewhat culturally specific. Strictly speaking, "the body" did not only refer to the physical body and "the mind" did not exclusively refer to thought or cognition. The body was inclusive of the mind, and the mind was informed by the body. Cognition, rationality, thinking, consciousness, or the psyche were literally inside the body and composed the person along with his or her ancestral energies or heritage. The CWC's African worldview focused on the points of integration between what is popularly understood as the "mind" and the "body."

The body—this juncture where mind, spirit, and physicality met—was an energy field with impulses, a sort of built-in intuition, which guided us. Sensitivity to these impulses helped people make dietary and other lifestyle choices that were healthy. As explained by an African leader born in the

Caribbean, ". . . for Africans, health is not isolated in the body. It's a sort of vibrational field in the community that can make you sick or well."[12]

After explaining my understanding of "the body" at a session on women and leadership, a European leader cautioned me not to misinterpret the CWC's notion of the body as physical in opposition to the mind or the spiritual. According to her, the CWC saw the body as more of an active vessel for an "aura," a desired point of integration between physical, spiritual, and rational being.

Another means for defining and expressing African ways of knowing was to compare and contrast African and European healing traditions and approaches. The CWC had several forums that brought together what they called "conventional health practitioners" or "medical doctors" with "indigenous" or "traditional" healers. These sessions involved CWC staff, volunteers, and participants with some of most influential members of the Twin Cities medical and public health community, including prominent university professors, medical doctors, and county commissioners, some of whom also received services from CWC-affiliated "cultural health practitioners."

One such arena was a committee that advised the CWC on devising policies and practices to influence mainstream medical education and government funding of unconventional medicine-related organizations like the CWC. A monthly training session called the Medicine of Reconciliation convened doctors and alternative healers of various ethnic backgrounds to help develop the CWC's healing policies and practices. This training also attempted to construct a network of CWC practitioners called a Circle of Healing, that would enable practitioners to support and advise each other and provide an integrated array of services for CWC clients that promoted holistic health and wellness. The CWC also had a contract with a major university to teach medical students the "cultural health practices" of the diverse ethnic groups that comprised its constituencies. Medical students also frequently participated in a range of other CWC support groups and classes, often acting as observers and sometimes as volunteers.

Many of the discussions at the health policy committee meetings focused on how the CWC should approach its educational work within the medical community. For example, according to the CWC's African leaders, who facilitated many of these sessions, one of the key barriers to their teaching "cultural health practices" to the conventional medical community was that they had fundamentally different approaches to culture. An exchange between the CWC's African medical director with medical school residents and a CWC European "natural healer" showed these distinctions.

DR. JONAS,[13] CWC EUROPEAN LEADER AND PUBLIC HEALTH AGENCY EXECUTIVE
    (directed to students)   How does the CWC experience influence your thinking about our role in medical education?

MEDICAL STUDENT   CWC experience is very powerful. I'm very wary of institutionalizing it. It's like the university's required sexual education classes. First it was a good idea, but now students fight it because they are forced to do it. When you require people to talk about culture, it changes it. The CWC has so much power because it's outside of the fray of the infighting in medical education. [Teaching culture in a classroom] can be a marginalizing exercise. Just like our ethics classes—you have to deal with it; you have to confront and get into it.

DR. ABANA, CWC MEDICAL DIRECTOR   It's not like what people call cultural competence. It's more like cultural immersion . . . You can't just give a lecture, because things happen once you get involved and you need follow-up. So, exposure may be the wrong word; students need *immersion.* Students need to be here at the CWC and experience it. We also need to emphasize that conventional *medicine* is also part of Western culture and works in that cultural context. We need to ask questions like, "What makes it so hard for medicine to deal with other cultures?" . . . It's because of the way that medicine is practiced that the schools isolate culture into one day in the classroom. Medicine is part of culture itself; it does not stand outside of it. The medical community hasn't accepted this yet.

MEDICAL STUDENT   But this is difficult for doctors. You know, it's hard for us to accept that we can't completely heal someone. This attitude automatically discounts other approaches—like in alternative medicine—and the kind of work the CWC is doing.

DR. ABANA   We need to have people [medical students] come to the CWC to work with people [clients or patients] at a deeper level—we have to immerse them in it. In that way, we can teach them to promote wellness, instead of fixing sickness.

SUSAN, CWC EUROPEAN LEADER   We need to promote a fundamental change in the system's concept of healing when we work with students. We need to promote our idea of a Circle of Healing where a physician might take you so far, then an elder takes you to another point, then an alternative healer to another.

In an Executive Health Briefing, a series designed for physicians and public health officials, a conversation between a prominent professor at a local university and a doctor, who was also a CWC client, further suggested the purported distinctions between the Western and indigenous (African) ways of knowing: "[The CWC] is a place where talking abut spirituality can happen. You can't talk about it in the mainstream Western world, and it limits our effectiveness as healers. Residents are never trained in this stuff because the Western model just doesn't deal with it. As a faculty member, you don't talk about it. But culture is a factor. Sometimes a bright, competent, compassionate doctor comes up against some cultural blocks and it could have stunted their career if it weren't for the advice of the CWC . . ."

These discussions, and many others like them during the course of fieldwork, highlighted core distinctions used to express the differences between Western (European) and African (indigenous) ways of knowing, and Africanness itself. First, the two approaches proposed essentially different approaches to culture. Again we saw the suggested equivalence of spirituality with culture and the African or indigenous way of knowing. In contrast, the Western or European way of knowing was considered devoid of culture or spirituality. From the CWC African perspective, culture, defined as a way of knowing the world, was integrated into every other aspect of life so that one learned culture through experiencing it. With the Western approach, as expressed by the conventional medical education system's tendency to teach culture in a classroom context, culture was segmented out of experience, dissected, and seen as utilitarian. Students were taught how to use it almost as technology—to learn "cultural competence" in working with the Other—but not how to experience it in their own lives.

The Western approach to healing also saw itself as somehow transcending culture. Culture was something that the Other possessed, an irrational set of beliefs that impeded scientifically based healing that could be mastered and manipulated by the scientific, omniscient physician. The CWC saw its approach as equally applying to physician and patient, European and non-European. As noted by the CWC's African medical director in another context, "Many people in my own community are relearning what their culture is. Actually, we are on a more equal ground, and the CWC can promote parallel learning."[14] The cultural immersion process that was emerging sounded almost anthropological in that it required that the physician also self-consciously study his or her own culture and understand what the CWC's medical director called "the culture of conventional medicine."

Applying the CWC approach, one medical doctor participant who worked with the CWC when he began his medical residency spent a year in both Ghana and Eastern Europe to study indigenous Ashanti cultural health practices and "discover his Scandinavian and Jewish roots." According to him, "If you as the doctor are disconnected from your own culture, you won't be able to heal people. You need to not only learn about *them* but take the journey to study your own culture. That's how you become a competent medical professional who can bridge culture and health."

The CWC's process for constructing, or, in their parlance, reactivating, an African way of knowing and sensing involved creation of a new epistemology to reverse the essential, unnatural, and unhealthy fragmentation of mind/body/spirit believed to define the "European worldview." The

African way of knowing/being was considered integral to the cultural healing and wellness process. It provided the philosophical basis—a mental template—for cultivating the bodily practices thought to be at the base of African community.

The CWC could be seen as an all-encompassing cultural immersion process whereby participants engaged in an effort to learn cultural healing principles through a kind of intense study comparing their own heritage with those of others—in the European case, Africans, and in the African case, Europeans. The reflective process, combined with storytelling, journaling, and bodywork classes, enabled instructors and participants to translate teachings into new bodily practices that promoted cultural wellness. In this way, what was considered essentially African ways of knowing/being were embodied into the healing practices of medical students of diverse backgrounds.

The CWC's African and European leadership mutually constituted each other in an effort to define alternative ways of knowing and being based on notions of cultural wellness. African was defined, in part, in contradistinction to what was European. European was defined, in part, in contradistinction to what was African or "indigenous." CWC African leaders' articulation of the African worldview also formed a standard upon which CWC European participants attempted to re-create and reconnect with ancient European cultural traditions and health practices. This interlocked process was based on reconciling a series of dualisms (see Table 1) which, from the CWC African perspective, were thought to be inherent in nature.

In its idealized, African way of knowing, these dualisms were a series of creative tensions that defined the universe. The cosmos sought to hold these tensions in harmonious balance because they were the basis of creation. In the European way of knowing, these dualisms were diametrically opposed and set in a hierarchical relationship with the secular or the scientific "conquering" or being superior to the spiritual. Disconnecting the poles of these dualisms, rather than reconciling them as was done in the European way of knowing, made people sick. The more holistic African way of knowing was thought to balance the dualisms of nature and present a path to cultural wellness. The African way of knowing was the basis of what the CWC called its medicine of reconciliation—its core healing practice—for bridging the dualisms that separated people from their heritage and from each other in a diverse community like Powderhorn, or American society in general.

At the CWC, "African" could be seen in two ways: as the cultural or ethnic identity of some participants, and as a specific way of knowing, being, and experiencing the world that was also being constructed, taught, and modeled by European participants attempting to "get in touch" or "reconcile" with their heritage, culture, and related healing traditions. This perspective would most assuredly be a cause for heated discussion and

TABLE 1. WAYS OF KNOWING, BEING, AND SENSING:
A CWC MODEL OF AFRICANNESS

"African Ways of Knowing"	*"European Ways of Knowing"*
African/European	European vs. (over) African
Blackness/Whiteness	Whiteness vs. (over) Blackness: : White vs. (over) or (is the opposite of) the Other
Male/Female	Male vs. (over) Female
Mind/Body	Mind vs. (over) Body
Nature (Environment)/Technology	Technology vs. (over) Nature (Environment)
Sacred/Secular (The "Two Lands")	Secular vs. (over) Sacred
Spiritual/Material	Material vs. (over) Spiritual
Rationality/Intuition	Rationality vs. (over) Irrationality : : Science vs. (over) Religion
Freedom/Discipline	Freedom vs. (over) Discipline
Individual/Community (Society)	Individual vs. (over) Community (Society)
Holistic	Fragmented
Natural	Artificial
Cultural	"Not Cultural"

controversy among some CWC African participants. However, given the CWC's diverse participant base and the leadership's promulgation of the essentially African underpinnings of its mission and philosophy, in some way European participants could be said to become more African in their ways of knowing, particularly as related to cultural wellness and healing.

The CWC efforts to redefine African identity did not occur in a sociopolitical vacuum. They occurred within what one African born in America leader called a "European fishbowl"—the dominant political structure and social structure of the Twin Cities. The data here indicate other ways in which the CWC's work was a form of indirect resistance against the established power structure. Both the content and process of constructing and embodying African ways of knowing/being suggested a reversal of power relations between Black and White Americans. In a reversal of the power relations involved in identity formation, as explicated in Said's seminal study (1978), Europeans, and mainstream North American culture, became the Other in contradistinction to an African cultural norm. The CWC's work suggested a broader level of indirect social critique that transcended race relations.

Some aspects of the CWC's African epistemology are similar to those proposed in the works of Afrocentric scholars such as Molefi Asante (1987, 1990). Asante's Afrocentricity proposes an alternative epistemology based on African philosophy to counter what is considered the implicit Eurocentrism of much mainstream scholarship. It also provides a set of interpretative principles that scholars and others can apply to historical research, sociocultural analysis, and social action. In contradistinction to Eurocentric and modernist philosophy (beginning with Kant and Hegel), Afrocentric philosophy defines itself as derived from ancient Egypt (Kemetic philosophy). This approach emphasizes certain core notions, for example, the ideas of harmony, community values, and spirituality derived from the ancient Egyptian goddess Ma'at. These notions are very similar to the timeless, essentialized distinctions between African and European thought created at the CWC. Asante's Afrocentricity suggests that these principles are somehow perpetuated by African peoples, largely unchanged, throughout history and the diaspora.[15] Despite these broad similarities, culturally specific CWC data also suggest important differences from Afrocentricity as espoused by Asante.

The CWC leadership, especially Africans born in America, were very well versed in Asante's theories and the broader Afrocentric literature. Interestingly, they adamantly maintained that their work was not an expression of Afrocentricity, even though outsiders might have seen similarities. In fact, even with my many hours of fieldwork, the term "Afrocentric" did not even come up until I raised the question almost at the end of the fieldwork period for this study. There were several possible reasons for this apparent contradiction.

The African born in America leadership generally felt that Afrocentricity was too abstract a philosophy to enable a practical community wellness and community building agenda. Unlike Afrocentricity, in the leadership's view, the CWC offered a theory and contemporary practices that practically linked the "two lands"—the past and present. Africanness was not just retained as an article of faith. Instead, the CWC saw itself as providing concrete and current evidence of a dormant African identity that could be revitalized through its wellness programs.

Furthermore, for some leaders, the commercialization of African culture had somewhat discredited Afrocentricity as a legitimate effort to reclaim, re-create, and promote an authentic African identity (see Stoller 2002). The CWC made conscientious efforts in its funding practices to avoid commodification of African cultural experience. The grassroots involvement of everyday people in building African community was seen as a more genuine healing process than the efforts of Afrocentric academics.

The CWC African diasporan participants' diversity also made it difficult to strictly classify it as Afrocentric in the specific sense of Asante's theories. While some CWC African Americans and the Africans born in America (or the Caribbean) may arguably be seen as holding Afrocentric-type views, generally the "continental Africans" did not. Their affinity with African Americans was based more on shared social or political interests. However, it did seem that the longer they remained in the United States, the more open they were to what would be better described (for reasons noted below) as embodied, as opposed to Afrocentric, identity theories. The so-called European participants were certainly not Afrocentrists, even though many adapted what they saw as African or indigenous cultural practices for their cultural wellness efforts.

Furthermore, the CWC leadership would reject the claims of some "Afrocentric" social analysis that asserts a black racial superiority.[16] At the CWC, "African" was not only a identity but a holistic approach to life that could be learned and practiced as a cultural wellness strategy by all persons. In its own way, the CWC attempted to promote an identity model and underlying epistemology that uncovered and celebrated diversity but also created unity around its core "African" principles, particularly the notion of wellness. It also sought to position this African wellness model as the basis for promoting community across the various interest groups.

The CWC is not credibly defined as Afrocentric in the strict sense of the term, although some members of its very diverse participant base espouse part of this ideology's principles. The extent to which the CWC espouses Afrocentric principles is not what is most ethnographically interesting about this nonprofit organization. Because its work occurs in a pluralistic sociopolitical system, there would naturally be a number of differences and similarities with other identity theories, including conventional notions of race, culture, and African history. What is most compelling about the CWC case, and other translocal nonprofits, is the opportunity to witness culture in the making and to better understand postmodern community formation.

As social science makes its earliest efforts to analyze Afrocentricity (Lefkowitz 1997), there is a tendency to presume that every African or African American effort to theorize and/or define identity vis-à-vis Africa is an act of Afrocentricity. Furthermore, in much scholarly discourse "Afrocentric" has become a very general descriptor for the interest among African diasporan peoples to learn about the African components of their cultural history, in addition to its European or American ones (Walker 2001). Thus, from this limited perspective, the CWC's work would be seen as Afrocentric, but so would any general effort to educate Americans, particularly Black Americans, about African components of their cultural heritage.

A more detailed analysis of African diasporan identity formation and historiography presents a more complex picture. Afrocentricity is just one of several often competing models in a longstanding African diasporan effort to define a transnational identity. Afrocentricity is more productively seen as just one stream of an alternative construct in a dynamic and variegated complex of African diasporan culture theory and historiography (see Du Bois 1939, 1990; Padmore 1956; Levine 1977; Drake 1982; Appiah 1992; Gilroy 1993; Walters 1993; Harrison and Harrison 1998; Moses 2002). Despite what may be our personal dislike for some versions of these theories, anthropologists can more objectively and productively understand transnational cultural collectivities by viewing them as examples of universal practices of culture production and community formation (Said 1978; Anderson 1983; Hobsbawn and Ranger 1983; Chatterjee 1986; Mudimbe 1988, 1994; Gupta and Ferguson 1997b).

CWC African epistemology, particularly the notion of mind/body/spirit unity was also a response to abstracted, ideational notions of culture that are arguably part of mainstream North American culture and much social science discourse as well (cf. Abu-Lughod 1991). CWC discourse suggested that this rupture between mind/body/spirit was caused by the fragmentation that accompanied capitalist culture. CWC Africanness and cultural healing was experienced as suturing the fissures caused by so-called European systems of thought. While CWC participants and leaders did not construe the CWC's theories of African mind/body/spirit unity as an explicit critique of social science theory, the parallels of its approach with anthropology's various embodiment theories were striking and instructive. The epistemology provided the philosophical basis for a body-based (that is, embodied) notion of culture in which the connections between cognition and bodily practice were theorized, often in the context of power relations. In the CWC approach, thought was at once cognition and action. The CWC created programs that taught participants how to self-consciously instill its epistemological principles into bodily techniques, for example, by ritualizing the mundane routines of everyday life. In this way the "two lands"—ideation and practice—were inextricably linked into a seamless cultural experience as suggested by various embodiment theorists (e.g., Csordas 1990, Napier 2003).

Interestingly, although the CWC leadership was unfamiliar with the work of Stoller, their "African" epistemology echoes components of his efforts to promote sensuous scholarship (Stoller 1989 and 1997). Using his long experience with the Songhay of Niger, his work demonstrates how Western scholarship has created a false dichotomy between mind and body that constrains ethnography's capacity to fully apprehend and express social life. The work of embodiment theorists (for example, Bourdieu 1977, 1984 and Csordas 1990) attempts to redress the conventional bifurcation between thought and action. However, according to Stoller, much of embodiment theory reflects a "Eurocentric" conception of the body and analyzes it in primarily intellectualist and textual terms. Like the CWC's cultural wellness program and the approach attempted in this study, Stoller (1997) argues for a fully sensual ethnography that expresses the whole body's experience of cultural life, including its smells, tastes, textures, and other sensations. Such an approach expands anthropology's knowledge base beyond its conventional focus on vision and speech (also see D. Howes 1991) and bridges the culturally specific mind/body divide inherent in much of Western philosophy and social science.

The CWC example highlights the epistemological biases inherent in mainstream approaches to healing. In addition, a simultaneous accommodation and reformulation of dominant constructs of race, culture, mind/body, and society was also evident in the CWC's African epistemology. This was similar to other examples of indirect forms of political resistance to capitalist culture and colonial-type power relations, now so well documented in the ethnographic literature (Hebdige 1979; Taussig 1980). Despite resistance to aspects of mainstream North American capitalist culture in a manner very reminiscent of Willis's classic study of culture and class dynamics among English working-class youth (1977), the CWC also replicated the elements of the dominant ideology. The CWC's African epistemology resisted dominant notions such as individualism, but at the same time displaced explicit class critique and politics in its notions of a spiritual or cosmological approach to social action.[17] Furthermore, although unintended, the epistemology's ideal constructs of "African" and "European" ways of knowing could perpetuate certain stereotypic notions of Africans and Europeans contained in racist constructs of Black people as more intuitive and less rational compared to their White counterparts. However, for CWC participants, this inherent potential to further reify racist notions of African and European culture would be seen as mitigated by the concurrent positioning of African epistemology as a universal blueprint and an alternative, nonterritorial basis for healthy transnational community.

Healing the Body:
Reactivating the African Habitus

The CWC's African way of knowing implied not only a particular cognitive understanding of the world but also a particular sensorial way of seeing, experiencing, and interpreting it. As explained by one CWC African elder, "It's a very different worldview—the African and the European. For the African, all phenomena are alive; they are invested with spirit. For the European, phenomena are objects; they're dead, inanimate. These different approaches produce very different ways of negotiating; very different ways of consciousness."

The CWC leadership devised a multisensorial spatial aesthetic to stimulate Africans' innate historical and cultural memory. The very deliberate way the office was organized, adorned, and used was thought to create an African space—a sensory and symbolic experience—that subtly and gradually awakened dormant Africanness. In many conversations, both formal and informal, CWC African leaders spoke of the uniqueness of "the African worldview." A common question during discussions, especially when someone paused to ponder or determine how to verbalize a statement, was "What do you *see?*" Seeing, or the "view" in "worldview," a synonym for "way of knowing" in CWC parlance, was not a literal visually based aesthetic but a more expansive kind of whole-body sensory understanding, integrating the aural, oral, visual, and kinesic into what was considered an African way of sensing the world. The best translation for the common CWC question, "What do you see?" was "What do you sense or understand?" or "What does your embodied, ancestrally informed intuition tell you is true?" Integrating the senses was seen as a tool and a complement to the CWC's effort to harmonize the dualisms proposed to have been embodied by people of African heritage as a product of European assimilation. Africanness was embodied when participants could actively use all their senses—not just visual and aural ones—to interpret and act upon the world. The CWC deliberately designed its own material world to facilitate this particular African way of seeing and experiencing the world. Through the manipulation of the physical environment, the offices were a surrogate for an actual African territory. According to Sara, a CWC African born in America leader, "this space belongs to African ancestors—it's guided by us. Our [the CWC's] philosophy is fundamentally African. The African can hold the other philosophies underneath it, but they can't hold us. The philosophy—the spirit—is African at its core. It's African medicine. Indigenous cultures feel comfortable here—the space will hold them. This brings a special kind of dignity because usually it's the African who's trying to fit in. Here people sense that they can be capable—it's visible everywhere."

Participants' experience of the CWC as a sort of African oasis was, in part, a result of the contrasting environment of the surrounding neighborhood.[1] One common theme raised in their migration stories and the informal or formal interviews with them was the comforting and nurturing feel of the CWC space. Many referred to the space as creating a sense of home in Minneapolis, or of having a place where time slowed down. I often sat in the reception area with people who would stop by to "hang out"—to sit on the sofas and chat with staff and whoever happened to drop by the office. For example, one day a young single mother had just finished her first counseling session with a CWC African leader. Instead of leaving, she walked around the space for about an hour with her toddler daughter, who squealed in delight as she romped through the office. She commented "My daughter really likes the open space here. She can just move around and I don't have to worry. There's a real peaceful feeling here 'cause of the art, pictures, the color and the dim lights. It's not like a lot of agencies where you just feel like a number so they can get that next grant. It has a real homey feel." Africans and Europeans generally had this reaction to the space; however, it was not unanimous.

Joanne, who described herself as "ethnically African American but as a culturally middle class, professional American," noted that the space was "nice but it's a little too much. Look at all this [pointing to what was actually an altar in commemoration of European women killed during the medieval witch burnings]. I don't know. But it's like they're saying that somehow if you put up a bunch of African art, that makes you African. But it's still nice and I like the feeling of being here—it's just a little overwhelming sometimes." What was interesting about this reaction was not only the participant's ambivalence about the space's symbolic messages, but her related assumption that all of the decor was "African." In fact, many of the artifacts were African, but others were European and Asian and some, were Latino and Native American. CWC African leaders argued that her misinterpretation of the artifacts' origins was a result of the general African spatial aesthetic upon which the CWC decor was based. Their power absorbed or held other aesthetics within them.

Akbar, an African born in the Caribbean leader, explained why he thought that African participants' generally described the space as calming, homey, or supportive, providing an important insight into the CWC's construction and expression of an embodied African epistemology and phenomenology. He said:

As people come together in the space [the CWC], they may not have the capacity to articulate feelings that are there; you have to listen carefully. Coming into the space is very unique.

There is a contextual field about how a space and the art present itself. [He pointed to a mask that was on a large white wall in their home with no other decoration. The piece looked like a large Baule mask in earth tones—mostly beige and brown with some rust accents. In the context of his description, I could see how someone might feel that the piece dominated the empty wall space surrounding it—as if it pulled the surrounding wall into it. It demanded attention as you walked into the room, taking over the room, and creating space—the mask and the surrounding wall—all its own].

The CWC confers some degree of ownership—of pride. It is part of the dynamic of feeling comfort. Psychological ownership is implicit in the process. Attached to the psychological ownership is a sense of pride that people feel. It is an affirmation of the African heritage that is in one's self.

It's different from art displayed in a public [that is, White-controlled] museum. [It is still an African spatial aesthetic] even though, for example, the art displayed is not being used in a ceremony or ritual as would be the case in "traditional" African contexts.

The context is different when the art is displayed in a place like the CWC or your home—[it] conveys a sense of ownership, pride, affirmation of African heritage; the symbolic messages of the mask activate the ancestral memory.

[With] African symbols there is also a [kind of] recall. [We have] been told that [our symbols] are pagan, animist, primitive. But the contextual field is different. It creates its own presence—it evokes its own presence. It is very present and alive. It shows that our culture is very present and alive. With White people there is a feeling of negation; we are silenced or dismissed. If it's African, wherever it comes from on the wall [of the CWC], it's better than having no presence at all.

The mask is a symbol that is very powerful in a context [Minneapolis] that is [almost] totally white. If you are in a museum context—a museum that is owned by White people where we have no authority—the space disconnects you from it [the symbol and its power to evoke ancestral memory and pride]. A change in ownership of the space changes the [meaning of] the context.

Your memory ["your" refers to any African in the CWC] is being activated as you talk with the many Africans who come through the CWC. You [as an African] find some attraction; some common ground. You might not be able to explain it, but there is a sense that you find fulfillment, satisfaction; something in you is nurtured. In America, there are very few places that the African can go and feel nurtured in terms of symbols—our cloth, art.[2]

Many participants seemed to have a subliminal feel for the integration of experiences that the CWC offices represented. Through its multifunctional use of rooms and mix of various cultural artifacts—for example, a computer desk with African print cloth—the space itself broke down the overspecialization and fragmentation of experience promoted by "the Western worldview" as represented in various dualities: African versus European (and others), or home versus work. The CWC's physical space was described as reminiscent of "home"—some long lost or forgotten African place of comfort, acceptance, and safety. As described by one leader, the CWC "creates a space that promotes African unity." It was a deliberate attempt to activate what leaders believed "embodied Africanness" to be. The CWC's space helped to internalize and deterritorialize Africanness by providing a surrogate sensorial experience and locality for expressing and feeling one's identity.

The CWC had a contract with a major public health agency to hold a support group for people with diabetes. The CWC leaders understood diabetes, and disease in general, as not simply the physical manifestation of symptoms, such as high blood sugar, but as a disconnection between cultural heritage and contemporary lifestyle, particularly as manifested at the level of dietary habits and exercise. Assimilation to Western culture in the United States caused people to become separated from the cultural knowledge that kept them healthy in their countries of origins. One of the most critical cultural distortions was the presentation of the body as a purely physical entity severed from the mind and spirit. The body in fact held ancient cultural knowledge and, if reactivated and cultivated, this knowledge directed people to lifestyle choices that promoted health and wellness.

As a result of assimilation or adoption of Western ways, people no longer "listen to their bodies." This deafness caused people to engage in a wide range of unhealthy dietary and lifestyle choices because they did not hear the knowledge of the ancestors. Instead they listened to the messages sent by their minds, now disconnected from the body and informed by mass media and socialization, to embody standard American approaches to diet, exercise, and life. Increasingly, and as a result, the mind was artificially segmented from the real needs of the body. Therefore, reflecting this more general mind/body cleavage, the mind's messages about which foods to eat or lifestyles in which to engage were perpetually distorted and unhealthy. Failure to listen to the body was both the result and cause of overassimilation to European ways of knowing. Such disunity impeded and severed people's consciousness and understanding of their heritage. The CWC's work with diabetic participants attempted to reconcile them with their heritage as a critical component of integrative cultural healing.

The CWC received referrals from several area physicians, clinics, and hospitals to provide group counseling and support to people with diabetes. About twelve regularly attending participants, including mostly Africans and Europeans, as well as an American Indian, a Guatemalan immigrant, and a Filipino immigrant comprised this group variously known as the Wellness and Diabetes Group or the Diabetes Support Group. The African participants included African Americans with (from the CWC African leadership perspective) varying levels of interest, understanding, and consciousness of their African heritage, and two CWC Africans born in the Caribbean. The group met twice a month for about two hours during lunchtime.

When first developed, the diabetes group was facilitated by the CWC's medical director, with the assistance of two other CWC European staff persons, one of whom was a natural healer and another who described herself as a specialist in ancient European (particularly Celtic) cultural and healing traditions. Increasingly the leadership became concerned that having a physician facilitate the group fostered participants' dependence on the mainstream health care system; it did not empower them to take control of their own health and wellness.[3] Therefore, over the course of the field work, the two Europeans, also called "cultural healers" in the CWC's terms, became the primary facilitators of the group. Cultural healers were those who were not formally trained health care professionals but who mastered the indigenous health practices of a particular society and could demonstrate successful application of them to heal illness. These individuals were also considered experts in "building community," meaning they helped people with physical ailments construct social relationships and identities that supported the healing and wellness process.

Because the physical ailments associated with diabetes were potentially debilitating, the diabetes group provided an important means for understanding the role of the body in the CWC's mandate to heal through self-recognition. The group had expanded through physician referrals and met more regularly with better attendance compared to when I began formal research. In addition to participant observation, I collected life histories and conducted interviews with some diabetes group participants of African heritage to understand their beliefs about African identity and how they did or did not conform to the CWC's model of cultural health and wellness. Between group meetings, I also volunteered to make calls to remind participants of meeting dates and times. What emerged from participation in and study with this group was an intricate picture of CWC theories of illness and wellness and how these processes supported the notions of embodied Africanness.

For the CWC, disease was not simply a physical ailment. It represented what one CWC leader called the "dis-ease"—the various disconnections between the participant and his or her heritage, spirituality, or lifestyle. Thus, dis-eases such as diabetes had what the diabetes group facilitators called a "character," "personality," or "psychology" that expressed the degree of disjunction between the various forces of creation that needed to be integrated in an individual's life to achieve health and wellness.

A key technique used to teach this perspective was to explore various ways that diabetes group participants related to food. A core topic of conversation was the cause and control of food cravings—an apparent, insatiable desire for a particular food, especially those with a high sugar or fat content not conducive to keeping the low blood sugar levels critical to diabetic health. In one session, the CWC physician and medical director did a presentation on the physiology of cravings, focusing on how some foods promoted the release of endorphins producing a feeling of pleasure. The problem with such cravings, she explained, was that they were often not filling; they only produced a desire for more of the same food. Interestingly, in a follow-up session, one participant, whose opinion was affirmed by several others in attendance, stated that the session was informative but "with all those big words like 'molecules' [you] didn't address the reality faced by many diabetics. What makes you want the food and how do you satisfy the craving, and what causes the diabetes in the first place?" For the next six sessions or so, the diabetes group focused on the issues of the causes of diabetes and related food cravings.

At a subsequent session, the Guatemalan participant noted that he did not have diabetes until he came to the United States and "started driving everywhere instead of walking." Several other meeting participants nodded in agreement indicating that their diabetes also coincided with a decrease in physical activity that accompanied a major lifestyle change like moving away from a rural United States environment and/or emigrating from another country. As participants recounted their own personal experiences and theories for how they contracted diabetes, a facilitator, focusing on the issue of food cravings, interjected:

SUSAN, CWC EUROPEAN CO-FACILITATOR   Diabetes is more than high blood sugar. It's a metaphor for a way of life that has become too easy. Diabetes is about taking the easy way out. What would happen, for example, if instead of going to the store and buying the pie, then eating it; you made the pie?

JOSH, AMERICAN INDIAN PARTICIPANT   Well, when that kind of thing happens, I'll make it [that is, make the pie], take a little bit to satisfy the taste and that's it. You can make it a part of your life and take a little bit instead of obsessing over it.

DR. ABANA, CWC MEDICAL DIRECTOR   Some foods, instead of leaving you satisfied, like chocolate, release chemicals in your body that tell you that you want more. What we have to do is eat foods that engage the whole body—the foods that goes back to when we use[d] to work hard—our *ancestral foods*. Ancestral foods trigger a signal in the body that "Hey, this food is good; it sticks to your ribs." We all have this built-in stop mechanism so that we don't overeat ancestral foods. But when we just get off on cravings for things like white sugar or white flour—these foods with all the nutrition taken out—the body says "where is the stuff?" Then you end up needing to eat more to satisfy the body.

SUSAN   Yeah, our food is overly processed, just like our culture is overly processed. We need to eat more *real* foods instead of all of these overly processed foods. Some real, ancestral foods would be like grits or whole wheat—they engage the whole body.

JOSH   Yeah, like corn meal or acorn meal in my culture.

SUSAN   I wonder what the effects of instant foods are on a culture. It has not only a nutritional effect, a physical, but a spiritual. What happens to a culture that wants everything in an instant? [I asked for more elaboration on the spiritual effects.] The attitude of having everything in an instant standardizes this notion in a culture. [It's the] spiritual effect of being disconnected from the earth—how food is produced. We're no longer as close to the earth.

BONNIE, CWC EUROPEAN CO-FACILITATOR   There is something special about making food with your hands. It's like the energy from your body is passed into the food. Have you seen the movie, *Like Water for Chocolate* [several people nod affirmatively], where a woman's emotional energy would pass through to the food she was making. So if she were sad; the people who ate her food would be sad. If she were happy; the people who ate her food would be happy. If she were in love or feeling romantic; the people who ate her food would feel sexy.

DR. ABANA   In mainstream medicine, in a clinical setting, there is not really a mechanism to help you absorb this kind of information. They teach a whole different culture of diabetes. They focus on getting you to take the medicine because you're sick; not doing what you can do to make you well. The CWC can take on this role and help us give leadership to our own health.

SUSAN   Diabetes has a personality based on this whole notion of doing things the easy way—instead of doing the hard thing—like eating the processed food instead of the real food. If you really look at it, you'll see that the character of the disease has parallels in our own lives. If we would stop this practice of doing things the easy way, we would see that it would break up some of the patterns in our lives that caused us to get diabetes. Changing the way you live might make the cells look and act differently.

In another session, I delved more deeply into some of the core concepts of the CWC's theory of dis-ease and diabetes. A facilitator was discussing the distinction made between real food and processed food, and I asked a question about soul food, a concept that had been raised but not fully discussed by an African American participant in a previous session.

JCC   I have a question about soul food. In my extended family, where many of the older and some of the younger people are diabetics, there are certain foods—that my family and many friends call "soul food"—that people like to eat, especially on special occasions. They like the smell of it; it has been passed down through the generations; it reminds them of their childhood. Food like chitterlings, sweet potato pie, and collard greens. Well, now when we get together I try to make soul food with healthier ingredients—like smoked turkey—no pork at all—and people don't generally want it. Like a sweet potato pie with whole wheat crust and honey instead of sugar. What do you do when people want what you call "ancestral food" but it is actually not good for them?

SUSAN, CWC EUOPEAN CO-FACILTAOR   Well, maybe it's not ancestral food—maybe it's food from America.

HATHOR, CWC AFRICAN PARTICIPANT   Yeah, it's really survival food.

JOSH, AMERICAN INDIAN PARTICIPANT   But for me "soul food" is any food that feeds your soul—it makes you feel good. In my culture, it's corn. So, I really enjoyed the corn bread [corn bread was served for lunch]. You can eat soul food once in a while but not everyday because it becomes poison . . . Like maple syrup. When my people ate it, we would just take a little bit for rituals. We didn't just pour it over pancakes. The Europeans started that and it's not good for you, even though it's a kind of soul food for my people.

So, "ancestral food" or "real food," the kind of food that should be the basis of a healthy diet and lifestyle, was that food which was thought to derive from some aboriginal state of culture, before infiltration by European or Western ways of knowing and related foodways. It was connected to the earth (minimally processed), eaten in moderation, and had energies that promoted a harmonious relationship with the environment. In other words, the real, ancestral food bridged the disjunctures (for example, technology over nature) created by Western habits. Soul food, depending on how it was acquired, prepared, and eaten, may or may not have been ancestral food. If the "soul food" that derived from foodways practiced by one's ancestors was eaten in moderation and was extracted and prepared in a manner that was respectful of the environment, it could also be ancestral food, like maple syrup. Instead of representing the foodways of ancestors, a soul food may instead have been a practical adaptation of purer and more healthful antecedents, developed out of necessity for survival by disenfranchised and displaced people. Unlike an ancestral food, traditional African American soul food represented the accretion of distorted cultural principles due to the constraints imposed by European political domination, for example, subsisting on food scraps from American slave owners. These contorted practices were discouraged in an effort to support health and wellness; they did not represent the wisdom of the African ancestors.

These critical concepts were continuously reinforced during my research. Food substances ingested by an ancestor-filled body was a metaphor for culture and an indicator of one's "spiritual state," that is, the degree of integration between mind/body/spirit and connection with ancestral practices. Food was a visceral connection between the individual and his or her culture and history. Distorted relationships with one's culture and history were revealed in one's foodways and poor levels of health and wellness. Encoded into the core distinctions between overly processed, Western foods and natural, non-Western (indigenous or African), "ancestral foods" was the fundamental epistemological distinction between the "European" and the "African" that the CWC's leadership was attempting to teach. Simply teaching these notions in a traditional classroom context would not induce the embodied experience of Africanness that the leaders sought to promote. Preparing and eating food was a complete sensory experience, especially when combined with supportive discourse that taught and reinforced CWC ways of knowing and wellness. Therefore, the diabetes group and other bodywork classes provided ideal forums to stimulate the kind of self-conscious, whole-body-focused experience of Africanness that the CWC attempted to facilitate. It also promoted the notion that the body was the mediator of cultural and historical experience.

One of the critical ways that this unconscious embodiment of Western knowledge occurred was through the acquisition, preparation, and consumption of food. Food contained energy, and its energy reflected the extent to which the various forces of creation inherent in the cosmos were in balance. Processed food was food with its nutritional substance removed. It was food with its culture removed. It promoted a kind of instantaneous preparation, as in the concept of fast food, that disengaged the body from the total experience of nourishment. Preparing and eating real food engaged the body in the consumption process and reinforced the body's absorption and understanding of the connections between people and nature. Ancestral food enabled a kind of embodied holistic African, or indigenous, way of knowing to occur, as opposed to the fragmented way of knowing promoted by Western teachings.

Ingesting food acquired, prepared, and eaten in a context where the forces of creation were in disharmony promoted illness. A diet comprised of mostly overly processed, instantaneously prepared, nutritionally empty, supermarket-bought food, often eaten in a rush and alone, made people sick, not only physiologically but also spiritually or socioculturally. The CWC saw the conventional medical system as addressing the physiological symptoms of disease, while it healed underlying sociocultural causes of disease. To be well, people had to reactivate the passively embodied cultural knowledge to acquire, prepare, and eat ancestral foods—"real" food that historically had kept African people and others healthy.

From the CWC's perspective, diabetes was caused in part by the adoption of American foodways focused on convenience and long shelf life. These foods, while they could be prepared quickly, had little nutritional substance, just as the CWC leadership saw American or European culture as lacking substance. Ingesting such food items hastened the body's absorption of American culture more generally and the resulting disconnection from one's own origins and susceptibility to dis-eases like diabetes. Reliance on American foods and technology, combined with the stress of assimilation, promoted elevated blood sugar levels and produced the high incidence of diabetes found among Twin Cities people of color, including immigrants.[4]

Adoption of American foodways promoted a kind of overassimilation in the body, facilitating its absorption of the false Western dichotomies that made people sick: mind over body, rationality over intuition, and technology over nature. Embodiment of Western ways of knowing was largely unconscious, as was the simultaneous process of suppressing ancestral ways of knowing. The CWC saw itself as making conscious these subliminally embodied Western ideas and making explicit the heretofore repressed ancestral (that is, spiritual or cultural) ways of knowing that resided naturally inside the body. The keys to cultural health and wellness were to expose the negative bodily effects of Western knowing and to recall indigenous or ancestral knowledge.

While the data support this interpretation, it should be noted that the CWC leaders rarely explicitly presented their theory of diabetes in terms of its approach to Western or African ways as presented here. The diabetes group meetings themselves operated very much like the CWC's typical support group in which the facilitators asked a series of open-ended questions to draw out personal stories and examples to explicate the issue being discussed, such as food cravings. There was so much storytelling and social interaction around food that it seemed that people rarely took time to write journal notes. Increasingly, one of my functions was to act as note keeper so that the leadership could document what they called the "indigenous knowledge" being created in this Invisible College support group.

Diabetes group meetings, in addition to teaching new ways of understanding diabetes and disease in general, coached participants to exhibit new habits, particularly around food and exercise. The meetings, in large part, revolved around food—teaching participants how to acquire and prepare real or ancestral foods. They were held during lunchtime and a "cultural" meal was always prepared.[5] Meals used minimally processed food ingredients, and recipes for the dishes that were served were provided to participants. In fact, by the end of my research, there were plans to assemble several of the recipes into a cookbook that could be used by diabetes group members, and perhaps sold to help support the CWC. Meals were relatively simple and included dishes such as red beans and rice, salad and pasta, soup, or burritos—always with whole grain bread and filtered water.

There was a sense of anticipation of a good meal when participants began to arrive. The smells of whatever was being prepared permeated the hallway. As participants arrived, they frequently attempted to guess what would be served. While they spoke informally, food was usually being arranged buffet style on a table with a lime yellow-green African tie-dyed tablecloth.

After eating, the meeting began with a discussion of the meal—the ingredients, their health benefits, where to buy or how to grow them, and the general recipe including the preparation time. Increasingly over the course of the meetings, facilitators and the cook would prepare "real" food with short preparation time to "show that you can eat well even if you don't have a lot of time"—a sort of ancestral fast food. Ingredients were usually vegetarian and organic and were purchased from one of the many food cooperatives in the Twin Cities region.

As the course progressed, this sequence of activities at each meeting took on an almost ritual quality, beginning with entry into the CWC's offices and participants' frequent efforts to guess what was cooking and ending with a homework assignment to explore or practice some component of cultural health and wellness for diabetics.

Several sessions focused specifically on the role of food rituals. Typically, a facilitator would start with an example of a food ritual she had either witnessed or practiced. She then asked a participant to discuss a food ritual with which she or he was familiar, thereby starting a dialogue on these practices by soliciting personal examples from most of the participants. Focusing on commonalties in the participants' commentary and on how the food rituals made them feel, the facilitator ended with a general statement about the function of food rituals and sometimes gave participants a home assignment to think about the food rituals they performed as a child. The following field notes passage highlights several of the key attributes of food rituals as a CWC cultural healing and embodiment technique.

BONNIE, CWC EUROPEAN CO-FACILITATOR   I had a Jewish friend who had a ritual for almost every activity in her life. A ritual—usually a moment of silence or prayer—before eating, for walking through a doorway—each of these rituals as marking different parts of the day—helps you slow down and be more contemplative. [At this point there was great silence in the room.]

SUSAN, CWC EUROPEAN CO-FACILITATOR   I know a kind of ritual for food. When I lived off campus in college, me and some of my friends established a "vegetarian house" where everyone took turns making dinner. We thought it would be a way of getting everyone together at least once a day. But everyone was so busy that they just gulped down their food, and there was hardly any socializing. To address it, people in the house came up with the idea of having minute of silence before eating the meal. They also decided to use chopsticks. This slowed down the meal substantially—initially. It seemed that people took more time to eat and talk and they began to feel better. But, of course, once they got the hang of using chopsticks—after about a week or two—they were back to their usual speed. But I never forgot this example, and today try to have a moment of silence before every meal with my family.

AKBAR, CWC AFRICAN BORN IN THE CARIBBEAN   Back home in the Caribbean they had certain food rituals and bush medicines to keep people healthy. Fresh fruit was always around and they ate a lot of it. Also, they would take fresh fruit to the river and share it with the river— you know, in the tradition of Shango [nods at me knowing that I lived in Nigeria and studied Yorùbá religion for a time]. The idea was that the earth gave you food and you should share it . . . We grew up as Seventh Day Adventists, so we were not allowed to cook on the Sabbath. So everyone cooked on Friday in preparation for the Sabbath. I remember that fresh baked bread was an important part of the ritual. My mother, every Friday, would give me a piece of dough and say "OK, now you go and bake your own bread." I had no idea what an affect this practice had on me. When my mother died several years ago, someone at the funeral mentioned her bread. I had the image of her giving me my dough to bake every Friday, and I began to cry. The image is still very powerful.

This notion of food ritual, like other rituals, providing an opportunity to slow time down and be more contemplative was integral to the CWC cultural healing process. Slower, ritual time, especially when it was self-conscious, enabled the participants to link the spiritual, ancestral world with everyday practice. Such reflective moments allowed ancestral wisdom to be heard; people could "listen to their bodies." It facilitated embodiment of African ways of knowing.

Within the general category of food, herbs—actually plants and vegetables in general (particularly organic varieties grown with no artificial pesticides)—were construed as a particularly powerful ancestral food. Herbs not only reconnected one with the ancestors, they were especially connected to the earth, retaining potent energies and medicinal properties. Part of the cultural recall process that was encouraged by diabetes group facilitators focused on remembering herbally based home remedies from childhood that could be encouraged as a routine part of participants' current diets and lifestyles. For example, in one session, while facilitators asked participants to recall food rituals from childhood, some began to detail their use of herbs in cooking and health care rituals. The following exchange demonstrated the role of herbs in the CWC's cultural healing process:

AKBAR, CWC AFRICAN BORN IN THE CARIBBEAN　We used bush medicines. Everyday I took a tonic made from boiled herbs from a tree that was used to "thin blood." My mother gave it to me regularly because it was supposed to clean the blood.

JOSH, AMERICAN INDIAN PARTICIPANT　Plants are alive; they are living things. There was this preacher I was working with. He was Native American but didn't believe in the old ways. Well, he has high blood pressure and I was talking to him and suggested that he use bergamot. He did and his blood pressure went down.

SUSAN, CWC EUROPEAN CO-FACILITATOR　Many of the medicines we use are from plants but just take certain elements. But since the plants are alive, scientists separate out and think it will still work. That's why we get side effects. With herbs we are taking the [whole] living thing and taking all its properties.

JOSH　I've had diabetes between five and ten years, but I can't remember exactly when I officially got it . . . I was a lumberjack and ate lumberjack food—steak and potatoes—lots of carbohydrates that I burned off when working. But when I stopped being a lumberjack, I just kept on eating the foods. I was diagnosed with diabetes but was in denial about it. I was also an alcoholic. I just kept eating what I wanted and eventually got a toe amputated. Now I'm doing much better. I'm going back to my people's old way of eating—eating mostly veggies with meat only as a seasoning. Drinking herbal teas and harvesting my own herbs—no store-bought tea because you don't know where it's been or whose energy is in it. I think of my herbs in the spiritual way. I have great regard for the plant and its energy—it's alive.

UNIVERSITY MEDICAL STUDENT　Have you heard of the science of the signatures?

SUSAN　Yeah, it says that every plant has a distinct signature. For example, the roots of Solomon root [an herb also known as Solomon's seal, used to alleviate arthritis symptoms] has gnarled roots and bends over to the side [as she bends over] resembling someone with arthritis. That's one way people knew what to eat.

After this session, one European natural healer and the diabetes group facilitator brought in an herb and shared it with the class. In particular, Solomon's seal, available in a liniment ointment and recommended for relief of muscle and joint aches, became very popular, as many of the participants had foot pain related partially to diabetes-induced circulation problems. They were given a sample in the class and directed to a neighborhood food cooperative where they could inexpensively buy a liniment derived from the herb. Also, various herbal teas were typically available in the CWC's kitchen. Presentation and explanation of the use of some herbal remedy was usually presented at the end of each diabetes group meeting. Herbs, used in cooking or for exclusively medicinal purposes, were the ultimate ancestral food as they had a particular closeness to the earth. The energy of herbs not only soothed pain but helped to make conscious embodied cultural heritage and helped people with "dis-ease" like diabetes to listen to the voices of their ancestors within the body.

In the CWC's "dis-ease" theory, Western assimilated people did not hear their bodies; they did not know how to listen. This could be particularly devastating for the diabetic as the body had an instinctive knowledge of what was good for it based on the innate wisdom of the ancestors. However, the reception might be blocked by several factors—adoption of European foodways or other kinds of epistemological dualisms, resulting in unhealthy lifestyle choices and, ultimately, illness.

The diabetes group not only taught this notion but attempted to provide practical exercises and techniques for participants to "get in touch with their bodies." An example of these practices to reestablish a conscious mind/body connection were demonstrated by the following exchange during a spring 1998 diabetes group session:

AKBAR, CWC AFRICAN BORN IN THE CARIBBEAN   In Chinese and other traditional medical systems there was a science of food based on the elements: fire, water, air, and earth. It was also subtlety in the medical system. In Indian and Chinese medicine, food is classified as either therapeutic or medical. We in the West have totally lost this science. Information can still be accessed but we need to do a lot of digging for it. Some cultures have not lost that connection.

SUSAN, CWC EUROPEAN CO-FACILITATOR   One way we can keep this knowledge alive is by listening to our bodies. Learn to listen to the body because the body *knows*. Our bodies still intuitively know what is good for them. I try to stay in touch with what my body tells me about what I am eating. For example, when I go canoeing in the Boundary Waters, I will know when it's safe to drink the water by asking is this life-giving for me. Also, when I went to Mexico I knew what water was safe to drink by doing the same thing. I have practiced it successfully so many times, I have no doubt that the system works for me.

CWC MEDICAL STUDENT   How do you practice?

SUSAN   You ask your body, not your mind which is full of all the TV commercials, Mom's advice—you have to filter through that stuff. It's like playing the piano—if you practice the scales enough times, then you just know. Anything you would put in your mouth, just ask if it's life-giving for your body . . . Bypass the mind; just ask the body.

I was listening to a radio program on NPR where some guys—I think they were anthropologists [looks and smirks at me]—were talking about how early people knew which plants were safe to eat. They said that it was trial and error. Somebody would eat something, then die, and everyone else would know not to eat it. It was not that at *all*!! People just knew from the natural environment. Sometimes our bodies know but we don't give ourselves the credit we are due for knowing our physical self. Our bodies just intuitively know as you grab the food whether it is good for you or not. Instead of letting the body know, you second thought it.

PETER, FILIPINO PARTICIPANT   But how do you *really* know?

SUSAN   The body knows because of the energy of food.

AKBAR   But what do you think blocks the knowledge?

SUSAN   You just need to practice, just like if you were learning to play the piano. You would start off with Mary Had a Little Lamb, not Mozart. The problem is that we were never even taught that we had a piano! Sometime in childhood, either through parents or school or TV we are somehow taught to like to eat things that are not in sync with what our body wants.

The session ended with everyone trying exercises to get more in tune with their bodies. A European facilitator showed an exercise using her arm that was demonstrated by a chiropractor. "You look at a particular food, and hold your arm out. If someone can push your arm down, then that means that you probably should not eat the food. Your body is having a negative reaction to it. But, if someone cannot push your arm down, it means that you should eat the food as your body is having a positive reaction to it."

Another European facilitator repeated her "Is this life-giving to my body" exercise. This time she made circles out of her thumb and forefinger, placing the right one in the left: "Look at a food, and if you can open your left thumb/forefinger circle, then the food is probably no good for you. If you cannot open it, the food is probably OK."

After this session, the homework assignment was for each participant to ask himself or herself two or three times a week before a meal, "Is this life-giving for my body?" and report on the body's response at subsequent meetings. This kind of reporting became formalized at each meeting with the daily check-in including each individual's experience in managing food cravings and blood sugar levels since the last diabetes group session. This body intelligence was thought to be particularly helpful to the diabetic in resisting the damaging food cravings for substances like refined sugar or excessive carbohydrates that not only further undermined health but could kill.

Much of the diabetes group healing effort focused on strengthening the individual's connection to the body's ancestral intelligence and practices around wellness—"getting people in touch with their bodies." However, the fact that this work was done in a social context was critical for the CWC cultural healing and embodiment process. It was not only *what* was eaten but *how* it was eaten that seemed to be critical to cultural healing. Even eating "real" or "ancestral" food in an inappropriate social context was seen as potentially promoting illness. In a diabetes group session, two European facilitators noted this:

SUSAN, CWC EUROPEAN CO-FACILITATOR   You can be in a culture with a high fat content for foods with no social connections, and will have a high rate of disease. But you can be in a culture with a high fat content for foods with strong social connections and a low rate of disease.

BONNIE, CWC EUROPEAN CO-FACILITATOR   In Western culture, you just focus on the diet—not the social [to cure a disease]. So it's not as simple as saying a particular food is bad for everyone.

In one session I began to notice—and this subsequently happened in several meetings—that there was a kind of eating silence, a noticeable pause in conversation early on in the meal during the diabetes group lunches. In one such session, the only sound was the rhythmic clanging of forks and spoons on plates and bowls as participants seemed to be intensely concentrating on eating what was a simple, typical meal—this time organic salad greens with organic dressing, bread and soup. Suddenly, one participant, who was getting up for seconds, broke the silence by saying, "You know, if I made this same thing at home, it wouldn't taste as good to me. Why do you think that is?" Making a circular motion with her hand around the table, another participant responded, with several other participants nodding in agreement as she spoke, "Because *we* are eating it together. Food always tastes better when you eat it with other people." According to many diabetes group participants, the group eating experience at lunchtime, including the socializing and informal sharing of stories about experiences with the dis-ease, had a healing effect.

This ritualized eating became at once an opportunity for contemplation to draw healing bodily practices from participants' ancestral memories and to build social networks among the diabetes group's diverse participants. Diabetes group meals provided another opportunity for the ritualistic types of pauses in group interaction, whether centered around a shared meal or conversation. Pauses and rituals were chances to slow down and listen to the ancestral wisdom inside the body of each person of African—and other—heritage.[6] Food ritual and the group eating experience linked the "two lands" at multiple levels: secular and spiritual (history and social relations), individual and community, Guatemalan and American, African and America, Filipino and American, or White and Black.

In addition to helping individuals slow down to contemplate embodied knowledge and build social networks with diabetes group participants, meals had a broader social role. Ritualistic eating and meeting experiences were deliberately facilitated by CWC leaders as part of its "philosophy of community." As explained to me by the medical director early on in the research process, "There's something about diabetes that increases the patient's dependence on doctors. What we want to do is give them a protective coating—a taste of community and culture that can strengthen their immune systems." In keeping with the CWC's broader mission to "unleash the power of citizens to heal themselves," the hope was that the "cultural wellness" modeled, experienced, taught, and, embodied during diabetes group sessions would enable participants to manage their diabetes without complete reliance on the conventional medical system. The group eating experience literally gave participants a *taste* of culture and its social manifestation in community.

Group support meetings, like the diabetes group, provided participants with an opportunity to "build community." "Community" was a core concept in the CWC's approach. For example, at various times during the course of research, the CWC incubated several nonprofit projects initiated by African Americans, Somalis, Ethiopians, and Africans born in the Caribbean.[7] The CWC African leadership saw these various programs as "creating a space to help African people to come . . . and learn how to work together; putting the different African instructors here so that people have to work together . . . working within the African concept of unity." The CWC African leadership saw itself as providing a surrogate home to people of African heritage. A territorial sense of Africa was thus displaced and absorbed into a notion of a diasporan community with a common and uniting experience of the African body in space and time as the basis of translocal identity. For example, Sara noted:

For many Africans who come here [to the Twin Cities]—like the Somalis and Ethiopians—the geographical community belongs to the city and their house just provides shelter. So, one of the biggest problems we had is that people didn't have any sense of loyalty to this place—the neighborhood—as home. They didn't care. But when we started to work with people to develop the people's theory, we asked them, "What would make this place feel like home?" And that's how this whole philosophy of community came up. The CWC's philosophy of community helps African people feel a sense of home here in Minneapolis.

CWC support groups like the diabetes group provided participants with a sort of laboratory for constructing community through supportive social interactions, if only in its bimonthly meetings. These support groups were seen as reducing the social isolation created by assimilation to "European" notions of individualism and the resulting breakdown of community hypothesized to make people sick, in the CWC's "people's theory." The hope was that this experience of community in the body or "home" spilled over from groups like the diabetes group to participants' lives outside the CWC.

A monthly class for CWC healers called the Medicine of Reconciliation helped to explain how the CWC practiced its concept of community. In these sessions the CWC's key African leader regularly emphasized that "the ultimate sign of healing is when someone could go out and build community." "Community" here referred to a sense of home that can be replicated and sustained regardless of actual place of residence and mutually supportive social relations, both with one's own "people" and, as a second step, with other people of differing cultural backgrounds. African "community" was the social manifestation of the harmonious state of being inside the body that resulted when mind (thought), body (action), and spirit (history and culture as realized in the social context of community) were in self-conscious balance.

The CWC's African leadership saw groups like the diabetes group as bridging the artificial dichotomies between the "individual" and "community" or "freedom" and "responsibility" considered so fundamental to European ways of knowing. The reconciliation that occurred was considered African in four senses. First, it promoted a fundamentally African epistemology in which the various creative forces inherent in nature were in harmonious balance. Second, for people of African heritage participating in the diabetes group, undertaking this cultural healing process had the additional effect of gradually activating and cultivating the internal strength to guide life decisions. Third, it built concrete social networks among diverse peoples. Fourth, it helped Europeans and other non-Africans adapt and apply what were considered fundamentally "African" ways of knowing to redress the drastic disjunction between mind/body/spirit promoted by their culture and history.

Another way that the CWC attempted to cultivate Africanness was through movement. Two CWC classes taught bodily movement techniques specifically intended to promote African community, African Soul Movement and Capoeira. Each of these groups met weekly for about two hours and included mostly American-born people of African heritage, although a few African immigrants also participated. Unlike many Invisible College classes and related support groups, neither of these classes included an ongoing, formal, facilitated discussion or classroom teaching format. Each of them focused on teaching particular bodily movements, with the teacher providing instructions and occasional commentary on the appropriate style or meaning of particular movements. Typically, for each class, the instructor would play music on a portable CD or cassette player and demonstrate various movements that the participants would attempt to copy in a type of call and response pattern. Movements were practiced as a group with emphasis placed on moving in unison with the teacher(s), other participants, and the music. Throughout the session, the instructor commented on movements, often providing encouraging statements or corrections of particular techniques.[8]

An example of African Soul Movement class dynamics was provided by a special "beauty seminar" for a group of young African American women in preparation for a debutante ball sponsored by a local chapter of a well-known national social organization for upper-income African American women. The following field notes passage provides a sense of how the body was engaged in internalizing Africanness.

CWC Africans demonstrated how to wrap head ties and wrappers, and the young women seemed truly engaged in the various ways one could tie and arrange them. I helped by doing some Yorùbá head wraps that I learned in Nigeria. After completing the demonstration, the women were invited to remove their shoes and join the instructor on the dance floor. The teacher played Nigerian high life music on a portable cassette player and instructed the women to line up in three long lines. With the music playing, the teacher, while dancing, introduced a sequence of movements: "Dance—African dance—is not about you. It is about being connected to creativity—being connected to the creator, each other, the music, the other dancers. By dancing together—in harmony—we are connected to the ancestors and are able to give them thanks . . . [To] take back the energy we have lost."

The women had initial difficulties. They seemed self-conscious—uneasy that they were not doing the movements correctly, or that their wrappers, which these young African American women were not accustomed to wearing, would fall off. However, most of them maintained the beat of the music. As the rhythms became faster and more complex, several of the women struggled with the movements. The teacher interjected, "These dances are working muscles that we have allowed to get lax." That was certainly my experience as some of the moves hurt, especially my back and back of the thighs. Several of the women focused on counting the steps, trying to mimic the teacher's movements, or holding on to their wrappers so that they would not fall off. Some would tease each other about a missed beat. They took a move and did a sort of contemporary African American youth hip-hop dance rendition of it and burst into laughter. The teacher encouraged them to "Move more freely—

loosen up with the flow of the music." After about ten minutes, the women danced with looser leg, arm, and hip movements as well as with flips of the hands and facial expressions to add their own style to the dance. No one seemed concerned about their wrapper. The room became quiet at this point; the students were not laughing or joking but had serious expressions, including furrowed brows with gazes fixed not so much on the teacher now but in front or at their feet. Several women now had their eyes closed and began to sweat, and I could hear the collective pace of breathing increase, matching the intensifying rhythms of this Yorùbá song that was playing. At this point, the CWC director abruptly ended the session as time had run out.

Class instructors had very clear and articulate philosophies about their work that informed their approach to teaching and were consistent with the CWC's broader mission of African community formation. In each of these classes the teachers considered themselves to be helping participants learn a way of moving the body that was distinctly African. Each class focused on teaching ways of moving the body that attempted to create group cohesion and, through particular rhythmic movements to "loosen up the body," to open the body to express the energy or spirit of the African ancestors. For example, in a session on women and leadership, a CWC African leader commented on the role of dance in inculcating embodied Africanness: "These silences allow us to hear the rhythms. Too much in our lives blocks the rhythms. It produces a kind of deafening and therefore our actions are distorted. It's kind of like dancing. It's a glorious thing for African people to get into the dancing—your rhythm is your own rhythm but it's also everyone else's rhythm. The music is always playing; you just have to tune in."

NEFERTITI, AFRICAN SOUL MOVEMENT TEACHER   We need to get back in touch with our Blackness, the collective ancestral memory that is written in our skins. We need to get in touch with the knowledge that our ancestors have left for us. My role is to help people of African descent get reintroduced to their natural rhythm and the source from which we come. The class deals with more than dance; it's about how we move through creation—helping us get back into the rhythm of the drum.

The ancestors that have gone before—that we need to be reconnected to. When I first started the class, I was thinking mostly of pregnant women and teaching them that they could still move. There's something unique to our particular heart beat—our vibrations—when we're together. We have to get comfortable with our sisterhood. When everybody is really dancing together in sync, it's just beautiful; it takes me back to the times when we were warriors. Then everyone knew the movement—the sound and call. And if something were about to happen, we would be able to hear the sound in sync and protect our tribe. But when we came to America, we started losing the rhythm.

When I first started dancing, I thought I could dance—you know like I knew how to dance to house music and stuff. But when I really started to study African dance with people from the continent, it was real hard. It was like my body felt trapped. It was like my body is not used to moving because the music is *so* polyrhythmic. I felt like I was dancing like a White girl. White people dance to their own beat; their rhythm is off. With me [when she first deliberately studied African dance], my hips—they were pretty good, but it was like my head and arms couldn't keep up in time. There was just too much going on. The rhythm is a little different, but we should be naturally able to do it because we are of African descent. We have to get back the dance and drum rhythm and remember how to move to a particular beat.

It's like how we move on the street. If you look at what's happening—all the stuff in the African community [social problems with Black people], it's like we're not in tune anymore. We're not in sync with our beat—with our sound. It's like we're operating on another frequency. We're not operating by our natural intuition and that's what's wrong with us—we're not in sync with the natural rhythm of the heart . . .

JCC   I don't hear you talking about this stuff in your class that much, though.

NEFERTITI   And I'm not sure people are ready to hear it, but, you know, as we get together more, I would like to bring this stuff up and talk about it more. Well, I want to but sometimes I'm not sure I have the words . . . Sometimes when I dance, there is conflict. Like sometimes for people in the group, it can be real self-focused and not connected to the energy of the ancestors . . . If there's not a collective spirit, then they compete. It keeps us at an individual level of performing instead of the African sisterhood that holds us together. It becomes like a more individual, technical performance; my intuition is less and I don't feel in sync.

The rhythmic movement in the group context of the class was thought to strengthen African identity. Not only learning the techniques of the dances, but the rhythmic movement instigated the energy of the African ancestors inside the body. Dance became an active metaphor and tool to model cooperative social relations. Movement was a tool for incarnating the Africanness inside the bodies of all people of African heritage.

The Capoeira teachers had a similar aesthetic of African movement.[9] They made a fundamental distinction between what they saw as a more authentic Africanized form of Capoeira and an appropriated Europeanized version. Korman, one of the teachers, explained that they try to teach and practice Capoeira from an

African-centered perspective, meaning respect for elders, cooperative resources, building good character, and negotiation . . . In the studio, Europeans just focus on the physical part of Capoeira; they dissect it, take it apart and focus only on one part. The White teachers come to commodify Capoeira. They don't try to teach it like the old masters where you had to know the philosophy from a cultural perspective. The White teachers often even try to hide the African roots of Capoeira; they just call it Brazilian. Here at the CWC, we can be honest about history and teach it from a holistic African perspective, including the music, philosophy, health, and diet. With White people in the class, they want to do their own thing. This is especially so with the White Americans, even more than the Europeans. In the U.S., it's like people work together by not working together. [The] focus is on what *I* want and how *I* want to do it; there always seems to be more conflict. When practicing with Black people, there's less cultural conflict. It's more like we're all moving together.

The aesthetic of unified movement in the African Soul Movement and Capoeira classes was more than a metaphor for shared identity. The rhythmic movement of the classes was a way of actually "working the spirit," as Murphy (1994) described the common principles of African diasporan ritual practice. In the CWC case, the spirit was the embodied spirit of African ancestors lying dormant inside the body. The movement activated the ancestors inside the body, making participants self-conscious of their heritage and creating an affective and visceral experience of what was considered African. Africanness was recognized as present in the motor behaviors practiced in bodywork classes and helped to create a surrogate African space and embodied experience of shared heritage. At least in the ritual space of the bodywork classes, territory was displaced by the body as the locus of African identity.

The CWC combined discourse with other sensory modes to produce embodied experiences of African community. CWC classes and various special events used verbal discourse and writing to teach its beliefs about identity and workings in the body. This process established the perceptual foundation for full embodiment of Africanness as represented by the mastery of a new set of bodily practices called wellness. Non-discourse-centered embodiment techniques included a range of explicit and subtle strategies designed to achieve what the CWC leadership defined as African ways of visualizing, orienting, moving, caring for, adorning, and "knowing" the body. Thought and spirit were considered literally inside the body, and therefore working on the body—sometimes generally called "bodywork" at the CWC—was an important point of entry in reconciling Africans with their heritage.

Various program activities, specifically the diabetes wellness group and

African Soul Movement and Capoeira classes, provided tools for participants to translate CWC epistemology and phenomenology into new ways of feeding, caring for, positioning, sensing, and orienting the body. Together they constituted a visceral and affective sense of Africanness.

The CWC process for inculcating its notions of Africanness into the body may be interpreted as an alternative theory of practice. CWC participants, as Bourdieu pointed out in the French context (1977, 1984), can be seen as unconsciously reproducing class relations through bodily practices and tastes associated with class position. The CWC leaders' notions of innate Africanness made the sociopolitical context that informed mainstream medical and health practices explicit, creating what can be seen as an alternative theory of bodily practice. The unconscious, habitual set of power relations that Jackson (1983) suggested in his theory of embodiment was deconstructed through CWC program activities. In the CWC leaders' theory of practice, assimilation was a kind of habitus, that is, a set of power relations that unconsciously instilled themselves in bodily dispositions. Unless one became conscious of this habitus, that is, "worked the body" through cultural healing, bodily practices unconsciously replicated distorted ways of knowing, and, by implication, power relations. As a result, African and other indigenous people in particular were no longer able to hear and meet their bodies' wellness needs and became socially, culturally, and physically sick. In a manner reminiscent of Foucault's notion of docile bodies (1980, 1982), CWC leaders saw assimilation as creating bodies that passively adopted conventional cultural notions and the existing power structure.

The CWC did not only create an opposing theory of practice. Its programs, with their almost ritualized quality (cf. Napier 2003), instilled alternative modes of bodily praxis. Whether these principles *really* existed and were shared across the various nationalities and ethnicities that comprised the CWC's African participants was not relevant. The ethnographic fact is that many participants came to believe that these bodily dispositions—the wisdom of the African ancestors about cultural wellness—existed, at some level of consciousness, inside their own bodies. Making this theory of bodily praxis clear and practicing it, the leadership believed, expressed and solidified their notions of Africanness. As a result, the body became the key vehicle through which Africa was experienced, sustained, and (re-)created.

The aesthetic of unified movement in bodywork classes had a special role in creating Africa. The rhythmic movement in the classes was a means of actually performing an African diasporan ceremony; students were in part "working the spirit" (Murphy 1994). In the CWC case, the spirit was the embodied essence and power of African ancestors containing shared African history and culture, dormantly residing inside the body. Exercising the spirit through bodywork was thought to awaken the African ancestors inside the body, producing an intimate experience of African social cohesion. Bodywork, along with the other CWC sensorial experiences, may be understood as helping participants move from a prereflective to a conscious level of awareness of this culturally constructed African identity. In the CWC theory of practice, the body knew; it was *socially informed* (Csordas 1990:7). The social context—"community" in CWC terms—transformed illness and suffering into new identities and empowered individuals to change their lives. In this context, stress, as manifested through the various lifestyle-related diseases such as diabetes and hypertension, which disproportionately affected CWC participants, became the basis for social transformation (Napier 2003:3–4 and 16). Cultural healing practices simultaneously worked on various levels of being: self-perception, physical body, and social relations—that is, mind, body, spirit. Dominant power structures, represented in unhealthy bodily practices, inhibited critical social action. Activating docile bodies to develop their innate ability for creative social critique and reconstruction healed the body and ultimately, perhaps, even the social order which it reflected.[10]

In many ways, the CWC approach to creating alternative body practices as a tool for cultural healing can be interpreted as a sort of grassroots theory of radical empiricism (Jackson 1989). It connected cognitive approaches to culture as rooted in the everyday lived experience of history, culture, and social relations among people of African heritage (Stoller 1989, 1997). It sought to devise a theory of human experience that consolidated conventional dualities between subject and object, mind and body, into a holistic theory of practice encompassing the human experience of culture, history, and social relations (see Ortner 1988).

The CWC, in attempting to promote the health of people living in a very diverse community composed of immigrants from around the world and Africa, as well as native-born Americans of various backgrounds, was faced in practice with many of the same issues confronted by anthropology: How do we understand (and in the CWC case, build) culture in a world where people do not necessarily share a sense of place? As is the case in the anthropological discourse on embodiment, the CWC's focus on the body as the intermediary agent and conduit of human experience provided a strategy for releasing Twin Cities African diasporan identity from the constraints of geographic territory. CWC bodily practices that put Africa—an idealized version of its history, culture, and social relations—inside the body enabled a delocalized sense of community identity that could be replicated wherever African people happened to be living. Africa was transformed from a place to a way of constructing and experiencing translocal community through the bodies of people living in diasporas—European, Latino, and others.

The CWC process for creating cultural practices, memory, and meta-traditions provided tools to produce embodied African community. Africa was more than an idea. It was a self-conscious state of being and way of knowing (mind) in which the mind/body/spirit were integrated into an ideally seamless continuum of experiential modalities that comprised the whole African person. Thought was bodily action, bodily action was thought, and both were guided by the residual historical energies of the ancestors (spirit). This embodied Africanness was an alternative technique for positioning the body in time (history) and space (place), thereby converting Africa into an imagined community and subjectively lived experience.

There was a unique and often deliberate interplay of various modes of sensing reality—visual, oral, gustatory, olfactory, and tactile—to promote CWC African embodiment dynamics (Howes 1991:7; Stoller 1987, 1989; Ohnuki-Tierney 1990). These sensorial modalities can substitute for territorially based communities in transnational contexts.

Healing the Spirit:
Embodying an African Historicity

For the CWC leaders and other active participants,[1] the body was under-stood as a sort of vessel that carried ancestral energy, perpetuating what was seen as core African cultural principles and practices over geographical space (place) and time (history).[2] The body was an active agent in the re-tention of Africanness. This embodied ancestral energy was the foundation of African community.

Multiple examples of the role of embodied African energy were provided by a weekly support group to promote women's leadership and explore the connections between spirituality and leadership. Called Leadership and Spirituality for Women, the sessions were regularly attended by about six women, three of whom would be described as "African" in the CWC's framework (including me, two other African Americans, and one woman from the Caribbean with African heritage) and three "European" women.

The sessions started at about 7 A.M. and ended at about 9 A.M. For the sessions, the room was darkened, incense burned, and a candle was lit and set in the middle of the meeting table. According to the African participant who facilitated these sessions, the candles and aromas "establish a peaceful atmosphere and help bring the ancestors to the room." There was an un-usual stillness in this otherwise bustling section of town as the daily routine for the office and surrounding neighborhood was just beginning. After reg-ularly attending these sessions for several months, an exchange between a European and African CWC leader during a particular class provided a crit-ical understanding of how the CWC perceived the transmission of "African culture" across time and space.

SUSAN, EUROPEAN LEADER[3]   I want to tell a story. There is this story about a
      little girl who scraped her knee in the playground and started to cry.
      She called out to her mother, who yelled, "Stop crying and act like a
      big girl!!!" So, just like that, [snaps fingers, suspends hands and
      pauses] the little girl stops crying—she cuts it off! Now what has
      happened is that that little girl has an unresolved issue that she car-

ries with her into adulthood. Anytime she's in a similar situation, she will remember this unresolved issue. This historical energy will hold part of her back in the past. It's like we each have this allocation of energy and if some of it is stuck in the past, we can't fully use our energy. We can't fully realize what it is we were meant to be.

JCC   I'm not sure if I know what you mean by "historical energy."

SUSAN   That's the baggage—all the stuff—unresolved stuff you carry with you from your personal history. It's not just spiritual; it also has a physical component. It sort of resides in your body and if you don't deal with it, it can make you sick.

JCC   Is this kind of historical energy what you mean when you talk about the history of your people?[4]

SARA, AFRICAN BORN IN AMERICA CWC LEADER   *Yes* [speaking emphatically while gently pounding the meeting table], they *are* related. But different traditions have different beliefs about how this actually works. One way of thinking about it is the whole notion of reincarnation. You see, I am part of a generation of all fifty-five-year-old African women wherever they may live throughout the world. My work [by the term "work" she means her life purpose, her spiritual goals—a term commonly used by CWC leaders] is to get in sync with all those other fifty-five- year-old African women and take on the role of elder to mentor those who are coming behind me and prepare for those who are coming after me.

Now, I may not complete my work in this lifetime. Any unresolved issues are passed on to the next generation. And I, and other members of my generation, may have to relive these issues until they're resolved. So, my personal historical energy and the historical energy of my people are interconnected. If I don't do my work, I'm leaving if for someone else of my people to deal with. Not dealing with it holds you back as a person and as a people. It stays with you.[5]

Another example, taken from a discussion at a local conference on African female circumcision, also clarified this notion of historicity. In the summer of 1998 the CWC cosponsored a two-day conference on African women's reproductive health, focused especially on the issue of female circumcision. This issue was of great concern to the local health care community, as Minnesota was one of several states that had outlawed it, but it was still practiced in many of the societies from which Twin Cities African immigrant women originated. While there was no official documentation that it was still practiced in Minnesota, there were multiple rumors that it was performed in the Twin Cities on African immigrant girls and young women. Female circumcision had also become a public health care issue as women who had had the procedure sought reproductive health care services. For example, one ethical dilemma for local health care professionals was whether a circumcised woman, after delivering a child in a Twin Cities hospital, should be sewn up again and if the health care professional should perform the procedure. Local African women told harrowing stories of humiliating treatment from local health care professionals, particularly in public clinic settings, as medical students were encouraged to examine the condition of their genitalia for clinical training, not clinical treatment purposes. Additionally, from the perspective of African activists, the legislature and the local health industry had not made sufficient efforts to engage African immigrant and refugee communities in deliberations about policy making in this area.[6]

The CWC saw the conference as an opportunity to both educate people of African heritage about the issue and give Africans, particularly women, a voice in local public policy making on this sensitive matter. The conference was facilitated by a nonprofit organization based in New York City with a substantially African immigrant and female staff that did advocacy education to prevent female circumcision and generally promote women's reproductive health. The first day of the conference educated Africans about female circumcision as a health issue. The CWC cosponsored the conference with two African immigrant nonprofit organizations in the Twin Cities. The sessions were facilitated by a Somali immigrant woman, a Sudanese immigrant woman, and a European woman born in America who had lived in Sri Lanka for several years and frequently referenced her parents' Irish immigrant roots in her presentation.

Female participants were evenly split between African American, Somali, and Ethiopian women with a few Nigerians and Kenyans, most of whom seemed to be well-educated English speakers between about twenty and forty years of age and working in health care, education, or nonprofit social service fields. However, about a third of the women were middle-aged, non-English-speaking Somali women, for whom the proceedings were interpreted. Most of the male participants were Somali community activists or social service professionals with one Caribbean man of African descent. Men and women met in separate rooms for most of the conference and came together at the end of the two days to devise the beginnings of a local advocacy and education agenda to address female circumcision in the Twin Cities. The conference included a very graphic slide presentation depicting the genitalia of women (not audience members) who had undergone various types of female circumcision procedures. The presenters described possible health-related and psychological complications. There were also a few, unplanned testimonials from African immigrant women, one Somali and one Yorùbá, who had experienced the procedure.

Generally, African immigrant women maintained that, in the words of an elder Somali woman through a Somali woman interpreter: "It's an old tradition, part of our culture. You made everybody proud when you did it. Anyway, there was no choice. When everybody does it, you don't know. You just go through it and go on with life. But I didn't want it for my daughters. It is not good for us anymore." One African American participant's question exemplified the response of many African American women to the presentation: "How can something so degrading to women happen on the continent?" During a break the second day of the conference, Baktre, a very active CWC African participant who was also a "women's spirituality consultant" and a social worker born in the Caribbean, discussed with me her feelings about the proceedings:

BAKTRE, AFRICAN WOMEN'S SPIRITUALITY CONSULTANT   I wonder how this female circumcision thing got started. I mean something must have happened for something so degrading to African women to happen. I would like to do some research to figure out how it started.

JCC   From my experience, it's very difficult to do fine-grained historical research to get at those kinds of questions in places in Africa that had mostly oral history. It's hard to get a sequence of events because the stories of the events change over the generations. You'd have to pull together the stories, whatever written accounts there might be, archaeological evidence too.

BAKTRE   Yeah, I know, but I think *we know*. Don't you? I think we *know* in our skin.

JCC   What do you mean?

BAKTRE   Well, you know I have visited parts of [East] Africa and Ghana. Ghana felt a lot like the Caribbean—I mean the swaying palm trees, the heat, the markets, and I liked it. But East Africa was different. I feel a connection with the soil—the people—like I know—*I know* that I have been there before. Like when I read Alice Walker's book, you know the one I'm talking about. I started it, I read it, and I read it all the way through without stopping, and then I just bawled like a baby when I finished it. I *knew*—I just *knew*—that I have experienced it [female circumcision] in Africa in another lifetime.[7]

CWC leaders had a conception of a kind of active historical "energy" that moved through time and was somehow imprinted into the body of people of African ancestry and concentrated in certain parts of the body, most notably the blood, the skin, or the heart.[8] The historical energy was both the combined accumulation of the collective experiences of African people over generations—"the history of your people"—and an individual African's experience of this history in his or her lifetime—"personal history" as referred to above. If this series of collective and/or personal historical incidents was comprised of resolved issues that promoted the development of the next generation of African people, then the energy was positive; if not, the energy was negative. According to the CWC leadership, for most people of African heritage this historical memory was latent and embedded in "Africans' collective unconscious."

This history was not only culturally specific—a person of African descent would not have been a person of European descent in another life—it was gender-specific as well. As stated by a woman in another Women, Leadership, and Spirituality session, "I know that there is a thread connecting me to all African women who have come before and all those who will come after me." So, in previous and subsequent lives, the spirit of women of African heritage would take on the bodies of other African women, either living in Africa or its diaspora. A current connection to African territory was not necessary to transmit this African historical consciousness. Embodied African historical consciousness existed and persisted as a result of any African ancestry, regardless of how remote. By holding history, the CWC African body also held time.

CWC leaders and active participants, particularly Africans born in America and Africans born in the Caribbean, believed that the African ancestors played a serious and active role in carrying African culture and guiding individual Africans to reconnect with their heritage. Although unseen, the ancestors were always present and if an individual was in touch with the "intelligence of the heart"—if a person developed their "natural prolific African spiritual capacity," she or he would be guided by this ancestral energy and apply its wisdom to everyday situations. According to Sara, "the intelligence of the heart is a kind of intuition informed by the wisdom of the ancestors—we need to be open to it to be guided by it. Being conscious of it is what makes us different from animals. This intelligence of the heart gives you a solid ground to stand on so that you can make good, right decisions."[9]

The ancestors were not only couriers of what were considered timeless principles of African culture, but they were also guides for the contemporary application of these principles in the daily lives of people of African heritage. The blood, skin, or heart were the physical loci for "sensing" African history and embodied knowledge. This embodied knowledge was spiritually transmitted over time and communicated today through the ancestors.

The ancestors were thought to connect contemporary people of African heritage with ancient wisdom,[10] but not all ancestors were equally capable of providing judicious heritage-based guidance. Individual ancestors retained the spiritual state they were in at the time they died. So, an African elder who died with unresolved issues would carry negative historical energy into the ancestral realm and not be in a position to provide wise spiritual guidance to the living. Conversely, those who died with most of their life issues resolved would be in a better position to provide spiritual guidance. For this reason, a person should always call a specific ancestor by name before seeking his or her ancestral wisdom. General calls might bring both negative and positive historical energy from the ancestors, thereby bringing confusion, not clarity to daily decision making. As explained by a woman of African heritage from the Caribbean, who was also the spirituality consultant quoted above, "I know that some of the ancestors are not part of my team." An insightful exchange between a European leader, two African CWC leaders (one born in the Caribbean and the other born in the United States) and me at a Leadership and Spirituality for Women session illustrated this component of CWC African historicity.

BAKTRE, AFRICAN CWC LEADER (born in the Caribbean)   I had the strangest experience yesterday. I was going to pick my children up from the airport. I was having a good morning—I mean I was just in my own space, and, suddenly, it felt like the room was getting smaller and I was walking down this narrow corridor. When I looked up, I saw this big woman—I mean she was *big* and she was *loud* and I could tell that she had *all* her ancestors with her. This woman and her ancestors were taking up all this room at the airport and I felt like my space was shrinking.

SUSAN, EUROPEAN CWC LEADER   Why I think some ancestors seem to take up so much room is because they died with unresolved issues. They were not present within themselves when they died, so they need more space. You have a genetic lineage and a spiritual lineage that is sensed, experienced, and understood through the body.

JCC   This is quite a coincidence. I spent all yesterday rereading my notes and trying to figure out everything I've learned about African ancestors through my work here. I started to write about it but couldn't finish because I still have questions. What's a genetic lineage; what's a spiritual lineage; and what's the difference?

SUSAN   Your genetic lineage is your physical inheritance. Your spiritual lineage is your soul inheritance. What we need to do is to bring our genetic [body] lineage in line with our spiritual lineage. We all are left to work out the unresolved issues of our lineage [our line of ancestors].

SARA, AFRICAN CWC LEADER (born in the United States)   This is not an individualistic notion of history. I am tied to all the African women who came before me and those who came after me. There are two types of ancestral energy. The first type—the spiritual lineage you mentioned—is related to finding truth and justice and it's feminine ancestral energy. The second type—the genetic lineage—is physical energy, and it's related to documenting in the sense of historical fact; it's male energy. This feminine and male energy are the two fundamental forces of creation and we must reconcile them within us.[11] This is our work [In this context, the term "work" meant spiritually guided life's mission, in CWC parlance].

JCC   What if a person of African descent is disconnected from his or her heritage? Would they know the presence of the ancestors?

SARA   Well, Jackie, you know, the term "ancestors" is really a term—an *anthropological* [in a sort of mocking but joking tone] term that we borrowed [all heads turn towards me and everyone laughs]. African people would not necessarily use the term "ancestor" but they may just refer to their deceased grandmother or something and seek her guidance.

But no, they [an "African" disconnected from his or her heritage] wouldn't know the presence of the ancestors. But they would sense some confusion. We must remember that the ancestors are not the only spirits in the room. There can be other disruptive spirits in the room. I am painfully aware that the ancestors are too at different levels. They die with all their unfinished *stuff*—their unfinished work. So, you must be specific about which ancestor you're calling. If you just say, "Let the ancestors come," you'll get the ones with the negative energy too.[12]

From the CWC perspective an important component of African notions of history was that it was intergenerational or collective, not individualistic like European notions of history. African notions of history focused on the impact of individual actions in the context of both past and future generations. An African individual could not escape the contemporary impact of the accumulated actions of one's ancestors. In the words of a CWC African elder, "No one is innocent. We all carry the victories and shortcomings of our ancestors."[13] As implied here, and emphasized in many other forums, "African intergenerational thinking" or collectivism and European individualism were thought to be opposing characteristics distinguishing African (also indigenous) and Western worldviews. Managing this "value conflict" was a primary objective in the CWC's work with people of African heritage and indigenous peoples. CWC African historicity balanced individual and collective historical experiences in its notion of ancestral energy, reincarnation, and memory.

Furthermore, the African historicity being constructed at the CWC proposed a distinction between two types of history. There was a more subjective and feminine sense of history—called a "spiritual lineage"—concerned with issues that lent themselves more to interpretation. History was also comprised of a sequential sense of historical facts considered more objective and masculine. Both senses of history were thought to be inherent in nature and in creative tension inside the body. Reconciling these two historical energies—the feminine/masculine, the African/European—was an essential goal of the African identity formation and cultural wellness process.

In CWC historicity, individuals were not simply the passive recipients of historical dynamics. Individuals had power to change and influence history. To some degree, personal history was constrained by the historical legacy of one's ancestors, that is, "the history of your people." At the same time, African people created their own history through their individual choices and actions.[14] History was comprised of a kind of energy—power—allocated to each person that should be used to promote social harmony. This energy was spiritual and transferred at birth from individual African to African. However, this personal historical energy was also linked to the collective history of one's people—past, present, and future. Failure to resolve personal issues prevented social harmony, creating negative individual and collective historical energy. Negative energy was carried from person to person and over generations until the various social issues were resolved.

CWC historicity suggested a theory of practice (Bourdieu 1977, 1984) to accommodate the interpenetration of personal agency and structural forces in history. It also proposed that these historical factors were manifest not only out in the world but were internalized in the body. Harmony in these embodied historical factors enabled African persons to remain attuned to bodily practices—"ancient cultural health practices," in CWC parlance—that sustained "cultural wellness" and "Africanness." An imbalance between personal agency and structural sociopolitical dynamics—your personal history and "your people's" history—disconnected people from their cultural heritage and related bodily practices. The breach in embodied historical energy produced illness and weakened African identity.

The CWC's programs converted African historical energy into actively embodied ancestral memory. CWC "African" leaders did not simply posit relationships between body (through blood, skin, or the heart), ancestors, and a sort of pan-African historical memory and cultural commonality. They maintained that the evidence for these connections was represented in everyday practices expressed by people of African heritage wherever they were born or happened to live. For example, Akbar, a prominent community African scholar born in the Caribbean and knowledgeable of various aspects of ancient Egyptian history and culture, explained:

AKBAR, CWC AFRICAN LEADER AND ELDER   Africans have gone through a total
     erasure. But the memory cannot be erased. This is difficult to understand because its almost totally outside the European paradigm

and conception of "history." There is a consciousness that is there that cannot be erased. It's more than Africans' combined history and culture—it's their memory of it. Part of the CWC's work is to activate this memory.

You know the story of the monkeys and the mangos. There was a monkey on an island who started washing mangos. He had done it for the first time. And then fifty to one hundred miles away, other monkeys will wash mangos, too.

We're not alone in this. Europeans have culture, too, but they try to deny it or pretend they don't know they have it. How else do you explain that they keep eating that lutefisk that they sell at Ingebretsen's? You just don't forget your culture because your people come here and you start calling yourself "John Smith" . . . [White people], by putting forward Christianity, they can pretend like Christianity has done away with their culture[s]—their Welsh heritage and so on. As if they have no ethnicity. It allows them to present themselves as just European and still carry this forward to this day.

JCC   Is this like a racial memory or a genetic memory?

AKBAR   No, I know those theories, and it's not like that. It's more like a collective unconscious; it's not a behavior or a learning. It's not like racial or genetic memory. It's more like the great things that we have done in the past. They left behind a certain practicality to it. For example, when pouring libation, you're calling on certain principles of the first time. Creation is based on it. It's a memory of the science of creation that our people have. Libation is a tradition that connects [you to it]. It's more of a spiritual philosophy.

"History" as a series of factual events is a European creation. Take, for example, an African naming ceremony. We recently did one for our new granddaughter . . . The naming ceremony is more than something that happened, an event or even a personal experience. The name of the child encapsulates history and past traditions in the child. After the ceremony, you could tell that the child took on a different aura. And the name will help the child take on a different aura throughout her life.[15]

The CWC's various classes, teaching methods, and other activities were designed to cultivate and introduce these African bodily practices as primary tools for reactivating dormant, embodied Africanness. The life histories collected in the course of this study were replete with reports of what I call African diasporan epiphanies—moments of sudden insight whereby various CWC participants, mostly women, reported discovering unexpected commonalties in bodily practices—what the African elder cited above called "things that we have done in the past that . . . have left behind a certain practicality to it." For example, the CWC's key African leader and two other African women, one born in Zaire and the other in Ethiopia, told the story of a social gathering that exemplified this component of the CWC's historicity.

Last summer a woman, a scholar, who does quite a lot of anthropological-type research among Nubian and Egyptian village women—this is an African [actually this woman would be described as African American by most people] who lives in California and has lived for some time in Nubia—anyway she came to Minnesota to do a presentation at the Twin Cities Art Museum [a pseudonym] on the tension between Nubian and Egyptian women as part of their exhibit on ancient Nubia. Her work was initiated by her desire to understand Muslim women in their cultural context. I knew someone who knew her. You know how you as a Black person come from out of town to do some work for a majority institution but you have no local connections with your own community. So, I invited her over for dinner at my house with some other African women—about thirteen in all—from all over. There were a couple of African women born in Zaire, Ethiopia, Ghana, Kenya, the Caribbean, and America. Well, you know, initially this woman, the scholar was a little cautious and testy. . .

Well, anyway, we started talking about this question of Africanness. The sister who is the Nubia scholar reminds me a little bit of you. She said things like, "You can't just say you are African because people don't see you as African." She was always talking about the diversity of Africans. But I say, yes, we are a diverse people. But there are some common threads. We will see them wherever *we* are. There is a certain sameness there. Anyway, my way of dealing with this issue is to approach it from a base of sisterhood—to promote relationships between African women that are respectable, protective, inspiring, watchful, noncompetitive. So, I asked a question to get the women to start telling stories. I asked, "What are some of the basic things you do now that you bring from your childhood, the way you were raised? For example, how you carry yourself in a kitchen—our domain." And somehow we started talking about chickens—how we prepare chickens [we both laugh].

Mitzi[16] from Zaire started talking about learning to ring the chicken's neck and how she didn't want to do it. Although she was initially squeamish about it, she eventually learned it. And today Mitzi knows all the cultural things she needs to know about taking care of a household that will continue with or without men—the cooking, cleaning. The private lives of families—the work of women—organizing the space, the prayers, the clothes, how to dress, how to feed and care for our bodies. Our people are in trouble when the women are in trouble—when our domains have been invaded.

Well, back to the chickens. What I remember most is somehow we kept coming back to the chickens. And as we talked about it, we all suddenly realized that all these African women—from all these different places—were taught to cut up chicken the very same way—into fourteen pieces. I don't remember all the specifics, but you know what some people call the thigh and leg—well, there's no separate name for them—it's just all called the leg. For everybody, the leg, thigh and hip make up three pieces. Although we all prepare the feet differently, you don't throw it away. Everyone cuts the breast in the exact same way, so that the wishbone is intact. And at some point during the meal, the person who gets the biggest piece [of the breast], gets to break the wishbone. Everybody buys whole chickens—not chicken parts. To this day, I never buy chicken parts. When you're frying, you have to cut up your own chicken. This was so profound because it was so very *practical*! And, for everyone, by the time you're nine or ten years old, this knowledge is passed on to you. Not in an artificial kind of way, but in a natural way as part of what you learned in the course of the day.[17]

This sense of historicity—where history was seen as a kind of energy that lives and moves through the individual and social body producing common, continuous, although largely unconscious everyday practices across the African diaspora—explained how people of so many diverse backgrounds—Somali, Liberian, Amharic, Oromo, Yorùbá, African American, and Jamaican—could all be considered African, although living in America. This historical energy carried not only a common African essence. This energy also was a subconsciously embodied memory connecting every person of even partial African ancestry, whether they recognized it or not. These everyday cultural practices transcended time and place or nationality and provided empirical evidence of the unity of "African" culture.

In anthropological terms, the CWC's African historicity claimed that history was more than the accumulation of sequential historical events and facts. It also represented a kind of habitus in which individual actions and behaviors—personal agency—were unconsciously informed by the accumulated actions of one's predecessors—the African ancestors—and the contemporary social environment, which together instill unconscious bodily dispositions and techniques (see Bourdieu 1977, 1984; M. Jackson 1989). Culturally appropriate health and wellness practices were a component of these African bodily practices; they were imprinted on the body's ancestral memory. Reawakening dormant African bodily practices not only strengthened shared African identity, it was also absolutely essential to promoting health and wellness. Thus, many of the CWC's classes, support groups, and special events were deliberately designed by the leadership to make participants conscious of their embodied ancestral African bodily practices and develop them so that they may be self-consciously applied in their everyday living.

The CWC was often called upon to facilitate meetings to build community consensus around community-wide issues. A CWC African leader's recounting of a very difficult meeting involving African as well as European community members further elucidated the relationship between CWC African historicity and embodiment processes. A conversation about the issue of race brought particular discomfort. It was presented as an example of the daily role of ancestors in the Women, Leadership, and Spirituality meeting. What was most striking in this conversation was the belief that the ancestral world reflected the state of interracial relations present at the times of their death, and that the living could influence the relations of ancestors.

SARA, AFRICAN CWC LEADER (born in America)   Yesterday, I was probably
naive. Well, not naïve, but if you're operating at an intellectual or
egotistical level, you might miss what is hidden—the spiritual. There
were two types of ancestors at work yesterday and not all of them
were about reconciliation—some were about destruction. Some of
the African ancestors are still struggling with the pain of the brutal-
ity they suffered. Some of the European ancestors are still dealing
with their stuff too. If you recognize that you can call on the ancestors who are at a more advanced level to work with the others [an-
cestors], you can help them [the ancestors] work it out. If you don't,
then there will just be confusion.

The African CWC leader added that "Part of our work is for me to understand my people's traditions for understanding this stuff and your people's [European's] traditions for understanding this work. Then we should
share it. The problem was that this work is not being done. It's usually presented in terms of race." The CWC notion of embodied historical energy
was seen as replacing "race" as a concept and as a more constructive framework for addressing racism.

Despite the focus on the body as the conduit of history and identity, the
CWC's African leadership did not see itself as promoting a "racial" conception of identity. They saw themselves as promoting a more constructive
"cosmological" perspective—"how my people and your people deal with
creation" as expressed by the CWC African leader quoted above. Such a
cosmological perspective included understanding culturally specific notions of spirituality, history, the transmission of culture, and the role of the
body—the connections between mind, body, and spirit. In this approach
the body was seen as having a central mediating role in integrating various
poles of opposition considered inherent in nature and the cosmos:
personal/social or agency/history, mind/body, masculine/feminine,
African/European, Black/White. Application of this more holistic, cosmological perspective was seen as a constructive strategy for understanding
racism and promoting improved relations between people of African and
European heritage.

The CWC maintained that racism, along with sexism, was an outcome of
the tendency of "rational" Western cultures to disdain and subjugate everything that was seen as irrational. For example, according to Susan during a
staff planning for the community discussion on racism:

The "European" worldview is dualistic; it fragments and separates to analyze and
classify. It separates in order to conquer. In contrast, the indigenous or "African"
worldview is more holistic, spiritual, and harmonious. It seeks ways to build relationships—ways to integrate. The Europeans' culture of rationality produces a hatred for the nonrational—women or any culture that is seen as nonrational is

devalued. Once you promote a more holistic way of thinking that focuses on the place of connection and unity, then the whole notion of race and racism becomes ridiculous—there's no place for it [racism] in this way of thinking [holistic/African/spiritual/indigenous]."[18]

Until "the work is done to understand racism from a cosmological perspective," reconciliation across the various "communities," "cultures," or "between my people and your people" is not possible.[19] "Europeans haven't really looked at their own worldview . . . Europeans have to reconcile what happened in their culture and try to heal its effects. Indigenous peoples have a spiritual way of knowing what Europeans have tried to destroy. This has to be reconciled before they [Europeans] can expect to get along with any other culture. They have to recognize their history for what it is and deal with it . . . There's no basis to talk about forgiveness or guilt or any of that until we deal with this. In fact it's not even the issue."[20]

The CWC saw its work as promoting cultural wellness practices as tools for helping various communities understand and share their cosmology. This sharing was considered a prerequisite to "building community" both among people of African heritage and other community [ethnic] groups. "Africans need to look at this pursuit of Whiteness—the glorification and worshiping that is so outside yourself. It takes you on a journey that continually destroys your divinity."[21] Because they were considered more "spiritual," this work of defining and teaching "the cosmology of your people" as a means of promoting community reconciliation was considered a role for women in particular—African women in their community and European women in their community. The Women, Leadership, and Spirituality class was designed by the CWC's African leadership to help women explicate and personally apply the "cosmology of their people" and guide reconciliation within their community as a first step to create better relations between the African and European.

So, in the CWC's historicity, racism was more than a social construct. It was a negative historical energy that was inscribed into the bodies of both African and European peoples. In this approach, racism became a cultural health issue. Society's persistent failure to address racism as an embodied historical product perpetuated this negative energy, thereby hindering racial reconciliation. Positioning racism as an embodied historical energy was another means of displacing race as the primary determinant of African identity. In addition to devising a shared basis for understanding historical dynamics, CWC notions of historicity provided a conceptual framework and strategy for addressing racism. As implied by the above accounts, storytelling and journaling were essential tools to, as the leadership described it, to "help people hear the wisdom of the ancestors." Storytelling and journaling incarnated notions of African history. Sara, a CWC African leader, used open-ended questions to elicit storytelling. She and another male African leader described this combination of open-ended questioning and elicitation of stories as classical African teaching tools that helped "bring out the African within us." I observed her using and describing this teaching and embodiment strategy with Africans and others in multiple participant observation contexts. For example, in an African Parenting class she explained, "In the ancient African tradition, we find our spiritual center through storytelling. Africans teach through stories. This is in part the function of what's called old wives tales. Writing in our journals becomes a way of documenting our experiences—our own stories—so that we can learn from them. The stories help to teach us the old practices in the African tradition. They connect our real-life stories to the stories of ancient Africa. [The stories]—the old practices—will give you clear instructions so that you can make the right decisions."[22]

Akbar, another CWC African leader born in the Caribbean who was very active in the CWC, explained the centrality of eliciting personal stories through asking open-ended questions to develop "the African's sense of self." " The African process of teaching is based on a very different pedagogy. You ask the student questions to draw out the knowledge they already have inside."[23] The knowledge is "already inside" because it was thought to lie dormant inside the body of every person of at least partial African ancestry.

Members of a diabetic support group, both people of African heritage and others, frequently spoke of the therapeutic effect of "just talking about one's life and experiences. It helps bring out the knowledge I already have inside about how to deal with the disease."[24] A leader recounted how the healing role of discussion groups and storytelling was formalized through the notion of a "talking circle" or a "healing circle"—a frequently used CWC technique. A Dakota Indian woman in one of the community planning meetings that led to the formation of the CWC explained that in her tradition, people formed "talking circles" as a sort of connected dialogue in which a group of people "sits and listens to someone for hours. Listening actually becomes part of the healing strategy because you have a chance to tell your own story; you feel important, validated, understood, and supported."[25]

In describing her work with a very emotionally distraught "African" of multiracial heritage" a CWC African born in America leader described how she used an "African style of leadership" to work with this participant. "I use leadership as a tool to guide people to an understanding of how to reconnect with their heritage. It is a form of leadership rooted in my own culture and traditions. I understand that my role is not to fix the problems but to help them surface the problem they can't see and help them to fix it themselves." At a Medicine of Reconciliation session designed to teach various CWC constituents how to work with others to promote health and wellness, the CWC founder and director advised participants to use open-ended questions to "empower clients" to devise their own cultural health strategies. She also cautioned them to be conscious of how their own cultural biases can influence the questions they may or may not ask.

You need to develop questions to ask. As a counselor or health care professional, we are taught to have all the answers . . . One of the best ways to work is to come up with questions that encourage the person to come up with their own solutions, especially when that person comes from a different tradition. We don't use questions enough. Let's let the person [client] be in charge . . . Where I'm coming from will influence how I ask questions . . . Even if we are asking questions, the questions might be biased and lead the person in another direction. That's not necessarily bad, but we do need to recognize that we have biases.[26]

Aida, an Ethiopian immigrant, community activist, and business owner of Amharic and Tigrean heritage, explained the founder-director's leadership style as an elder, emphasizing the importance of open-ended questioning and storytelling in her CWC interactions:

AIDA   What struck me most in these meetings is how Mother Zenia worked. She asks questions, not just to know the answers but to teach—to show the knowledge is inside. To remind me that it may not even be the right time to know the answer. She has been very supportive . . . I admire Mother Zenia so much—her stamina, her quiet strength. Although it was sometimes difficult [the work], I rarely heard her complain. I have found an elder who is giving me a sense of direction. She helps me recognize who I am as an African woman. A sense of being came.

JCC   How would you say that has happened?

AIDA   Through the relationship—the way we talked about things, the questions, the stories. In just describing my experience [to Mother Zenia], I then felt calmer.

Aida, in her late thirties, had escaped war in Ethiopia with her sister on foot as a youngster, where she ended up in a Kenyan refugee camp. She lived in Egypt and West Africa before arriving to Minnesota where she is a community activist and some one whom I jokingly call the Mother Teresa of the Twin Cities' African community. A whirlwind of activity, she has helped many Africans with a wide range of social service issues. She abhorred describing herself as a "refugee"—a term which she adamantly felt was dehumanizing.

Thus storytelling was experienced as a way of producing clarity about identity; making explicit the dormant knowledge of essential Africanness thought to be inscribed in the body.

The Map to Wellness was another technique used by CWC leaders to ask questions that elicited stories to help participants identify and problem-solve core life issues and to promote what the CWC calls "cultural health practices." Much of the work around African identity formation was done in these private sessions. The medical director, who was a physician and African born in Haiti, conducted most of these sessions and the technique was applied with CWC participants of various ethnic backgrounds. The Map to Wellness sessions were two to four hours long and resulted in a graphically presented diagnosis of the psychological and lifestyle impediments to "cultural wellness." In follow-up Map to Wellness sessions, the participants developed a plan, a "map," that included strategies to help them achieve cultural wellness for themselves and significant others. These were private, generally one-on-one counseling sessions, although couples or families sometimes participated. Because they were private as opposed to group counseling sessions, I was not generally permitted to attend them. However, participants did comment on the personal impact of these sessions, often stressing the powerful healing role of storytelling, just talking, and having someone to listen intently. Hara, an Ethiopian woman who had been in the United States for about ten years, explained her experience with the Map to Wellness technique:

I have been . . . born again. It helped me to really see my culture as an African woman. Because growing up, I did not really have good connection with my culture. Christianity back home really pulled us away from our culture. I did not go to traditional ceremonies because they were considered evil. It helped me to see the true role of the woman. I now know that it is not the role of a woman to be humiliated, abused—it's not really a part of our culture, but the men would say that it is part of Oromo culture . . . My culture really values *family*. In valuing family, there has to be a competent element to help keep us together. The husband must understand that a family must provide mutual understanding, love, and respect. That's the role of the CWC. It helps African women figure out their role here.[27]

Again, storytelling, this time accompanied by graphic depictions of cultural identity, was experienced by an African woman as a powerful tool for defining her identity.

In another parenting class the topic was the importance of journaling for personal growth as "African" women. Sara, who facilitated these meetings, explained:

Journaling is critical because it helps us come to terms with the truth. The word is powerful once it is written down; it forces you to deal with things. The most important thing for balancing all the different roles we take as African women—wife, mother, community workers—is keeping our energy level high . . . You need to know how to make priorities in your day so you have time to rest. If you understand your energy level, you need to know how to adjust life so that you don't feel stressed—like your spiritual life is being pinched. Keeping a journal will help you track your feelings and your energy level so that you know how to adjust it. It will help you discover your internal sources of renewal . . . It [journaling] will help you know yourself. Because if you don't know yourself, you can be many other people.[28]

Leaders encouraged all African participants, as well as others, to maintain journals, and provided notebooks for those who were just beginning to keep a journal. Many African CWC participants made copious notes in their journals during CWC sessions and special events. Several participants who were Africans born in America and had been working with a CWC African elder for some time had voluminous journals documenting all aspects of their "coming into their own as African women." These journals were rich documents for recounting personal experiences of coming to terms with one's "African" identity, but they were not accessible to me during the course of field research because of their intensely private nature. The focus on storytelling, note taking, journaling, and diagramming as techniques for healing and establishing identity facilitated my role as a native participant observer, but in some contexts, especially early in the study, it complicated matters. The CWC's key African born in America leader sometimes expressed misgivings about my taking notes in certain sessions, even though other African participants, and non-Africans in the case of ethnically diverse classes like the Women, Spirituality and Leadership sessions, were encouraged to keep a journal:

SARA, CWC AFRICAN LEADER   I know that you are doing research and although I see you writing notes in parenting class, I just see you as a parent. "Research" makes me uncomfortable because it's based on *objective* Western ways of knowing. In the African tradition you learn from experience, not through doing research. Is there any effort of Black anthropologists to develop a truly "African" anthropology— one based on African principles? Would your work at the CWC contribute to an "African" anthropology?

JCC   I don't know if there is a distinctly "African" anthropology emerging. I know that in anthropology, people speak of, for example, a "British or French anthropology" that they think have different perspectives that come out of their unique national traditions. But, there is a lot of debate and controversy in anthropology about whether we can truly call anything "African" because of the cultural differences among Africans living in Africa and throughout the world. And really that's what I'm trying to study with the CWC—how, who, and what is "African"; how it's defined and expressed, particularly with the growing numbers of Africans from the continent living in the Twin Cities.[29]

This conversation made an implicit analogy between the "Western" as "objective" and the "African"—included in the general rubric of "indigenous cultures" in many discussions—as more "holistic" or "spiritual," that is, as valuing subjective, lived experience and intuition as a more legitimate means of understanding and learning. Storytelling, sometimes elicited through open-ended questioning by a CWC leader and recorded through journaling, were seen as African forms of learning and healing through lived experience and as more effective ways of understanding African issues than the "objective" methods of "Western research" that are part of anthropology. Another example from the above discussion demonstrates my method of dealing with the occasional discomfort about my note taking and my practice of a form of research (anthropology) that was sometimes perceived as Western:

JCC   We anthropologists basically try to get at people's personal stories and put them all together to understand a bigger issue like how identity and culture are created among people of African descent— what I'm studying here. Yes, we are supposed to be objective, but in a sense I think of it as different from what you're saying.

When I, and some other anthropologists use the term "objective," we don't mean that we can somehow stand back and have a purely unbiased—not influenced by our own training or background—our point of view on a very personal human issue like identity. What we mean is that we will try hard to be conscious of how our background influences our interpretation of what we see and hear, and include all perspectives—whether we personally disagree or agree with them or not. One way we maintain this discipline is by trying to write down exactly what different people say and do as well as things about the atmosphere of, for example, a meeting room. That's why I sometimes ask people if I can use a tape recorder.

In addition to writing down exactly what I hear people say or do, I write down what I think about what I see people say or do. We do this because we know that what a person hears or sees is also influenced by their background—they'll pay attention to certain things but not others, and sometimes not even realize they're doing it. So, that's why you always see me writing. To present a truly balanced picture of what it is to be "African" here, I need to write down the stories I hear, and I need to journal to make sure I can separate out what I really think versus what other people think.

SARA, CWC AFRICAN LEADER   That's all fine and I know what you're saying, but when we having a class or something I still can't help but think of you as a participant. If I thought of you as just a researcher, this would be hard for me. If you were just a researcher and you were not experiencing any personal growth as a result of your research here, there would be no point in your doing it and I wouldn't support it.

So, it would help if you wouldn't take notes in the leadership class. I want you to focus on your own stories and what you get out of it.

JCC   OK, I respect your wishes. I won't write notes during the class. Instead, I'll write about what I learned after the class is over.[30]

This leader's initial ambivalence towards my writing in classroom or support group contexts emphasized the centrality of lived experience in creating and embodying CWC African historicity, in contradistinction to what was considered objective, Western knowledge. The CWC leadership's perception of the core distinctions between European and African ways of knowing prompted a regular discourse about the nature of research and the ways of knowing that should be used by a researcher who was "African." These ongoing discussions enriched my understanding of the CWC's strategies for embodying Africanness.

The self-conscious negotiation of my roles as an African American native anthropologist was a constant issue in the research, although it became less important as the CWC's leadership was exposed to ethnographic and life story interviews as core research methods in the study, the various interview guides I developed, and my notes from CWC committee meetings. Over time, the leadership saw these methods as complementing their focus on the use of stories and journaling as tools to "bring out the African within." For example, later on in the research, as I was walking down the hall after one of our monthly research briefings, the executive director casually mentioned: "I think this anthropology stuff—collecting and respecting stories for understanding—is the way we want to do research at the CWC. It's a way for us to have a voice in telling the story of how we do our work and why we do it."[31]

The act of telling and writing stories was seen as a multisensory method for inducing consciousness of innate Africanness, that is, embodiment. Stories, whether spoken or written in the form of class notes, journals, or maps to wellness, were thought to induce a sort of whole-body introspection in which participants became conscious of their knowledge and literally began to feel the presence of the ancestors inside their bodies. Stories helped reconnect mind, body, and spirit (or thought, action, and ancestral history)—an integration considered critical in embodying Africanness. Cultural healing and Africanness occurred when these three parts of being were reconciled. For example, participants who were gaining embodied insights during these sessions, frequently proclaimed, for example, "My heart feels light," meaning they were experiencing a moment of wholeness and harmony—the epiphanies which come as the African inside one is viscerally experienced.

During journaling, the physical act of writing also was thought to make conscious, as a participant stated above, "the knowledge already inside."

Because writing self-consciously engaged the mind and body simultaneously, it was seen as a particularly effective tool for embodiment. It produced a kind of feedback loop whereby latent ancestral wisdom literally flowed from the heart, skin, and blood through the arm and hand then back to the mind, promoting consciousness of personal connections to a collective African historical experience inside the body. Writing had the additional advantage of creating an "objective" record of a person's Africanized historical experiences. Participants were encouraged to study the stories in their journals, as the leadership believed that it would further strengthen innate African history and consciousness.

The CWC created a cultural conception of history and helped participants embody it in order to promulgate its notions of African community. The CWC's approach to African history—considered an expression of the African collective spirit—created community. A shared African identity requires a common historical experience among the profoundly different backgrounds represented by constituents. The experience and cultivation of history were considered integral to "being African," regardless of national or ethnic origins.

Approaches to historicity in the ethnohistorical literature are very helpful in understanding the CWC's approach to history. One of the most fundamental contributions of ethnohistory in the twentieth century is a conceptual framework for understanding how history is culturally specified in both non-Western and Western societies (Cohn 1980; Boyarin 1994). A trend in both anthropology and history is a more adjectival use of the term "ethnohistory" that focuses on the comparative study of how societies conceptualize, experience, interpret, and construct the past, as well as how these written and oral constructions interact with political, economic, cultural, and social processes over time (Krech 1991; Faubion 1993). This places the term in the same general category as ethnobotany or ethnopharmacology.[32] While ethnohistory still tends to focus primarily on non-Western or marginalized societies, the approach is also very useful in understanding the cultural specification of historical processes in institutional cultures, the middle class, and elites (e.g., Wallace 1980).

Ethnohistory in the sense suggested above has a particularly important role as anthropology attempts to understand contemporary cultural phenomena.[33] It provides a framework for examining how culturally specific traditions for organizing and managing diversity are changing in globalized and transnational contexts (e.g., Appadurai 1996; Hannerz 1996). An ethnohistorical perspective is also important because the construction of new histories is central to identity formation (see Faubion 1993). Although not necessarily presented as ethnohistory, some of the most intricate studies of nation building examine the process whereby conceptions of the past are created in conditions of pluralism, and how they affect contemporary political processes and ethnicity (see Anderson 1983; Alonso 1988; Connerton 1989). In addition to emphasizing how history is perceived and constructed at the group level, other studies also analyze how individual historical consciousness and memory are created and represented, using oral narrative as a window into how a society understands and adapts to changing social realities (Basso 1995).

The sense of historicity espoused by the CWC African leadership involved three interrelated concepts: the central role of the ancestors—indeed, the general "role of spirits in the world"; reincarnation as generated through transmission of historical energy and memory inside the body; and the notion of a holistic "African" cosmology that integrated thought, individual action, history, and community.

The CWC not only taught this cultural conception of history, it also instilled it in participants' bodily images and practices through deliberate use of group storytelling and journaling as tools of cultural recall. Personal stories expressed everyday practices which were interpreted as representative of timeless aspects of African culture. They provided the historically based, empirical evidence for shared African community across time and geography. Storytelling was considered an ideal embodiment tool because the process of reflection and writing or speaking in a social context was thought to engage all aspects of being.

The personal stories told in CWC classes could be seen as miniature life histories. They connected individual life stories with the construction of collective historical memory. The psychologist Jerome Bruner referred to the individual life story as a "cognitive achievement" that reflected the particular models a culture makes available for describing a life course (1987:13). This notion was very helpful in understanding how individual life stories elicited through CWC storytelling and journaling were engaged in the construction of both collective memory and CWC African historicity.

In the process of eliciting stories and group discussion, the CWC leaders posed open-ended questions that promoted discussion of similarities in life experiences, particularly those of women. CWC participants shared details of their lives that highlighted broad common ties. CWC leaders commented on stories in a manner that emphasized similar practices and experiences. In the CWC's culture, these life stories were interpreted by its African leaders as evidence of the commonalty of experience—particularly at the level of mundane, everyday life—of diverse African peoples. Indeed, the banality and intimacy of these practices were considered compelling evidence of the resilience of essential, embodied Africanness. Thus, a collective memory of embodied historical experience was constructed from the reported similarities in personal experiences of CWC participants as they engaged in classes and support groups.

After several sessions, participants gradually began to self-consciously define their common Africanness as the underlying reason for such similarities across the experiences of women with seemingly very different backgrounds. Often at some point in these classes, women would experience what I call "embodied epiphanies"—sudden insights into their African identity, particularly as expressed in what one participant called "her womanly culture," aspects of grooming, home, health, and child care, as well as other related techniques which involved bodily action. In this way, defining and highlighting similarities in everyday practices and bodily techniques, from the CWC leadership perspective, the "African within" was cultivated. It reconnected participants to their innate ancestral wisdom, promoting consciousness of collective African history and, therefore, cultural healing. In this process the body, not territory, became perceived and viscerally experienced as the locus of African community.

The social construction of collective memory is an essential component of identity formation (see Halbwachs 1980). The CWC's programs and activities provided a social context for creating a translocal African collective memory. Through a process of ongoing negotiation and adjustment between individual participants and the CWC's African leadership, a particular "master narrative" of African history was being formed (White 1978). This master narrative was not so much an interpretation of particular historical events but a theory of how African history operated that could accommodate participants' diverse historical backgrounds and experiences.

The narrative focused on the primacy of the African body as the mediator and vehicle to change, experience, and interpret historical events. As White argues, "every historical narrative has as its latent and manifest purpose the desire to moralize about the events of which it treats" (1987:14). It also gives meaning and provides guidance about behavior, and in the CWC case, promotes cultural wellness or, in the leadership's words, how to "stay African while living in America." The CWC's notion of history provided a way of interpreting the diverse pasts of the Twin Cities African diaspora that enabled it to propose a shared identity and future to its diverse participants.[34]

For the CWC, history was personalized and not just the impact of distant sociopolitical forces over time. Africans and other people who might be considered subjugated (for example, women) were also individual agents of their own history, not simply the passive recipients of dominant historical forces. Thus, the CWC's theory of history could be seen as articulating, albeit in its own culturally specific way, the dialectical relationship between sociopolitical structure and human agency that drives history and social relations (Giddens 1979). It provided a pivotal role for individual agents—in this case the African person—to construct history while recognizing the force of structural factors.

The detachment of historical events from African territory not only delocalized community, it also had the effect of delocalizing temporality. Time and space were compressed into the body. Interpreting a historical event was a matter of determining how it was experienced in the body. A historical event, for example, transatlantic slavery—the "whole Middle Passage thing" in one participant's words—would automatically contribute residual positive or negative energy to contemporary African people wherever they lived. Unless the negative historical energy was deliberately redressed by contemporary African people, it would continue to disrupt the natural, harmonious energy flow, producing social discord and disease in future generations of African people. Thus, the CWC's notion of history not only established African identity, it consolidated historical time into the body.

Following Bourdieu (1977, 1984) and M. Jackson's (1983) work on embodiment, the CWC's approach to history may be seen as a sort of bifurcated theory of practice that proposes that "Africans" adopt certain unconscious bodily techniques from both the dominant society and from their heritage. Two habitus, rather than a single one, are involved. These bodily techniques include everyday practices, in the CWC's terms, as well as ways of caring for the body, thinking about the body, and understanding and experiencing the world, including its history. In the process of assimilating into European culture, and because of practices of cultural domination, as stated above by a CWC African leader, "the African has been silenced," that is, disconnected from the embodied voice of the ancestors and their wisdom. The CWC attempted to teach a historicity that provided an alternative framework for interpreting African cultures and history, thereby making this complex of inert bodily practices self-conscious. The CWC's theory of practice could also be seen as providing the basis of an alternative historicity which privileged thought and action, that is, the whole person as the mediator of historical experience.

At the CWC the fundamental basis of history was energy—or power. CWC historicity, in keeping with its mission to empower "citizens to heal themselves," unleashed participants' innate ability to shape their lives, historical events, and the social order. The idea of embodied history subverted dominant notions of race, culture, and the subordinated role of Africans and African Americans in the power structure (cf. Comaroff 1985). In the CWC's model, everyone's history and, by implication, culture, was experienced through the body. This enabled the CWC to propose a notion of African identity in primarily cultural terms, as opposed to dominant North American racial constructs. Furthermore, it suggested an equalization of African and European relations by proposing that the body mediated culture and history for all people. By co-opting both African and European ideas of experience, the CWC's notion of African historicity positioned the body as the locus of social critique and, significantly, as a potential tool of political action.

Epilogue to a Diasporan Journey

My diasporan journey through Powderhorn was ending, but it seemed like the community was in the throes of a new beginning. Lake Street had an air of heightened energy and possibility. Although several businesses had closed since I started my work here, several new ones had opened. There was a new tailor shop owned by a Somali man who reminded me of the fashion magicians that I knew in West Africa in the 1980s. Like them, he could sew "Italian" suits and indigenous African clothing with equal ease and quality—all without the use of any patterns! The African bookstore, owned by a Kenyan immigrant, moved to the back of a new and popular reading salon in an adjoining community, where the African diaspora was meeting for coffee, lectures, debate, and conversation. The salon was owned by a bicultural woman of Yorùbá and African American heritage who had lived in Nigeria for several years. There was even a new Creole restaurant and catering business, owned by African Americans with Louisiana roots, that had a diverse clientele from the various diasporas that comprised the area. Gumbo some how seemed like a natural accompaniment to this neighborhood's American stew.

Business at the Mercado Central, the new Spanish market, was booming, and the relocated African grocery store and record shop seemed to be thriving in their new Lake Street locations. Two new community facilities—an expansive, well-equipped, and community-friendly YWCA and a new community development agency—had opened up in the same period. The Sears site's redevelopment, although stalled for several years, seemed to be on a path towards rebirth. The building's development plan was debuted to the community in a ceremony with much fanfare and press coverage attended by hundreds of people from the neighborhood and Twin Cities region. Even Colin Powell, right before his appointment as secretary of state and in his capacity as leader of his national community volunteer initiative, America's Promise, attended the event and was its keynote speaker. One of the new community centers in the neighborhood was named in his honor. While attending the event at the end of my research for this study, I briefly wondered if these new organizations would, in fact, compete with some of the more established organizations, such as the CWC, for participants and funding. However, given the tremendous diversity and still persistent poverty of this community, unfortunately there seemed to be plenty of demand for all of the innovative services available. Despite the new sense of hope and possibility encouraged by the physical and economic revitalization of parts of the neighborhood's major commercial strip, the 2000 Census and public health statistics showed even increasing levels of social challenge, as newcomers from United States and world communities arrived here to start a new life.

This dynamism, increasing diversity, and the related need for services spilled over into the CWC's programs and even its spatial organization. Class and community support group offerings had more than doubled by the end of my research and writing in 1999. English-as-a-second-language classes taught by Latino participants were added to the offerings, and a variety of women from diverse European, African, Native American, and Asian backgrounds were taking on prominent leadership roles. The organizational structure was becoming more specialized with the addition of a financial manager and an evaluation program, reflecting the new demands produced by the growing list of funders that supported this creative organization.

The CWC's offices continued to add artifacts reflective of the various backgrounds of its pluralistic participants and staff. While African decor was still very evident, it seemed much more subtle in the CWC's material culture. The addition of more office furniture for new staff, along with new statuary and textiles, gave the CWC a more cluttered feel with fading evidence of its original design. It felt very much like the home of a well-traveled grandmother who, over the years, had lived life fully and quickly, leaving very little time for redecorating. The neighborhood's and the CWC's accelerating dynamism and quick response time to change had also taken its toll on me physically and emotionally. After almost flunking out of the often rigorous Capoeira class and some other bodywork classes; having participated in what seemed like countless interviews and community meetings; and after the emotional drain of balancing the various cultural worlds that crisscrossed this study, I faced two exhausting tasks. I needed to resettle my life and pull the intricate strands of the CWC experience into a story that could help to inform both anthropology and nonprofit sector practice. Then September 11 happened . . . The Twin Cities, especially its African immigrants and Muslims, like the rest of the country, are still reeling from its aftershocks.

Minnesota's large Somali community, most of whom are Muslim, has come under great scrutiny as America's War on Terror unfolds.[1] Several Twin Cities-based Islamic charities suspected of funding terrorism are under investigation and have had their assets frozen and their leaders arrested by the federal government. Somali-owned check-cashing businesses, which have been critical in providing financial assistance to relatives living in war-torn Somalia, have been closed.[2] Hate crimes against Somalis across the state have increased, including the spraying of Ku Klux Klan-style racial epithets on businesses in St. Cloud and in Rochester, two Minnesota cities outside the Twin Cities metropolitan area. Furthermore, several Twin Cities Somalis, most of whom have lived productive lives in the Twin Cities without criminal incident for a number of years, are being detained in a Seattle-based federal facility for visa violations. Their deportation sentences are being appealed as their legal counsel argues that to return them to a country in civil war without a political or justice system would be inhumane. Until 2000, Minnesota had among the most vibrant economies in the country. These new community conflicts are not generally the norm for Minnesotans who have actively helped Africans resettle in this state and are probably exacerbated by the recent economic downturn.

This post-September 11 strife has been complicated by several community incidents in the Twin Cities over the past two years, most notably the police shooting of a mentally disabled Somali and the separate police shooting of an unarmed African American youth—both in Minneapolis. The Somali community, many of whom, of course, had fled the war violence of their homeland, were shocked and confused. In 1999 a mentally disabled woman, who happened to be White, was also shot by police, leading to the formation of a specialty unit to help officers peacefully resolve community disputes involving residents with mental health issues. The incident involving the Somali man led to an effort by some African American and Somali nonprofit sector leaders to collaborate around police violence issues. The Minneapolis police committed to redoubling efforts to productively resolve such disputes and in 2003 began federally mediated community meetings with various segments of the Black community to promote better relations. African immigrant nonprofits, especially Somali ones, made a concerted effort to organize their constituents to be counted in the 2000 Census. Somali nonprofit leaders and community volunteers were trained to administer census questionnaires and explain them to residents who were often suspicious of government. Many Somali leaders felt that the census severely undercounted their community. The 2000 Census, police-community relations, the post-September 11 response, the 2002 midterm election, especially the loss of Senator Paul Wellstone, who was an ardent advocate for Somalis, and the general economic decline have had the effect of politicizing the African immigrant nonprofit sector. A partial outgrowth of these trends is a new crop of African immigrant-led nonprofits, several of which explicitly address African diasporan diversity issues.

Since just 2001, a Somali legal advocacy group and another community organizing group have formed to advocate for their civil rights. Another group, co-lead by a Yorùbá immigrant and a Somali immigrant, provides general social services and also makes explicit efforts to reflect the diversity of the African diaspora in its programs and governance. Another agency, created by a Somali high school student concerned about the increasing conflicts among African diasporan students, has a mission to promote positive relations between African and African American youth. A chapter of an international mutual aid society of African diasporan women married to Nigerians has also been formed in the Twin Cities. A diasporan leadership development nonprofit has also emerged to help Africans promote peaceful conflict resolution and community development in both the United States and abroad. Other new African immigrant mutual aid and nonprofit organizations focus more on direct social service issues of immediate concern to their particular community. More such groups are likely as African immigrants grow in political understanding and ability to navigate America's social systems. Many Twin Cities Africans are living in fear of racial and religious profiling. Outreach and collaboration with persons of diverse backgrounds and shared interests is more than a philosophical issue; it is an undeniable matter of survival.

This study started with a fundamental question in contemporary African diasporan anthropology: Who is "African" in a global ecumene? The ethnographic data demonstrated that the answer to this question was not a simple matter of determining if the anthropologist can establish a factual "African" historical, biological, or geographical origin for the participants who defined themselves as such in the local cultural context being studied. The answer was in dynamic flux. It was influenced by unpredictable convergences in broader sociopolitical and economic factors and the actions of various historical agents. "Who was African" at the CWC was not coterminous with the locations in Africa or people recently originating from places in Africa. The notion of who was African was extended across continental or national boundaries into a creative, transnational discourse on African diasporan identity.

CWC participants had differing answers to the question, "Who is African?" The leadership was proactively creating and promoting a shared, alternative construct of translocal African identity taken from competing models presented by different segments of the CWC. Although the CWC leadership constructed a deliberate mission and programs to create and promulgate a shared African identity, the ethnographic data show that there were debates among participants about how "African" identity should be defined and expressed. The answer to the question "Who is African" also depended, in part, on the actor's position within the complex global flow of cultural meanings into which the CWC was linked. To understand the dynamics of African diasporan identity formation, this study described and analyzed the parameters of these debates among African CWC participants as well as the leadership's ideological and programmatic efforts to create a commonly shared identity among them. The ways in which these notions had been problematized, deconstructed, and reformulated by CWC leaders and participants provided several interesting insights into translocal cultural processes and the anthropology of contemporary cultural complexity.

Within the limitations of conventional models of integrated, geographically bound cultural wholes, the African diaspora in North America is an anomaly. Anthropological approaches that privilege spontaneous cultural reproduction do not accommodate examples such as the CWC, which mix and connect the identity formation processes of both African immigrants, who have very recent and current social networks to people on the African continent, with those of African Americans and others who self-consciously construct their own African identity. The CWC example is more in line with approaches that emphasize the role of agency (see Giddens 1979) and the invention of tradition (see Hobsbawm and Ranger 1983), which privilege conscious and unconscious cultural re-creation (also see Brandon 1993; Mudimbe 1994; Barnes 1997).

The CWC case demonstrates that culture is blurred in multiple ways. People who define themselves as African are from various backgrounds—Oromo, Tigrean, Amharic, Somali (various clans), Yorùbá, Hausa, Grenadan, Haitian, African American, biracial (mostly "Black" and "White" parentage, among others). While these groups could claim some sort of original (however remote and/or partial) African geographical or biological ancestry, African identity has taken on a more expanded meaning at the CWC. It has become a category—embodying a particular aesthetic and epistemology of meaning and being—which even people without African ancestry espouse and attempt to emulate and practice. As is the case with North American culture more generally, particularly when factoring in the global impact of travel and communications technology, conventional categories of "African" and "European" are conflated and compressed; the African is American; the American is African; the periphery is in the center (Hannerz 1996).

In the context of African diasporan cultural processes in North America, the CWC case is not unusual. A discourse on transnational identity has been a constant part of African American history in North America, expressed, in part, through various explicitly pan-African movements (e.g., Waters 1990). The classic underlying questions of African diasporan studies—Who is [*really*] African?; How "African" are African Americans?; How "American" are Africans?—are not helpful in analyzing the CWC's strategies to define identity. The more appropriate question is: How do the people who in some way define themselves as "African" construct their own identity?

Applying contemporary models of global cultural dynamics to the findings of this study suggests several new directions for African diasporan anthropology. First, "African," particularly in the contemporary flow of transnational cultural interchange through migration and the media, is best seen as a constructed and imagined community (Anderson 1983) as opposed to a definitive geographically bounded cultural entity. Here "imagined" is *not* used to imply that the CWC's notions of African identity are in any way less "authentic" than those of people born, socialized, and living on the African continent. This study, like that of Gupta and Ferguson (1997a), argues that *all* ethnocultural categories are socially constructed in a political and historical context. The local sociopolitical context at issue here is the CWC and how it constructed a translocal African ethnocultural category through sociopolitical negotiation.

Second, Hannerz's (1996) construct of a habitat of meaning is useful in understanding African diasporan cultural dynamics. Here culture is not defined in geographical terms. Global cultural flows are seen as creating intersecting collective systems of meaning called "habitats," which are shaped and acquired in social life.[3] The CWC's African identity definitions and processes are among several intersecting "habitats of meaning" (cf. Hannerz 1996) operating in a metropolitan region that, because of its centrality in the global economy and increased immigration of African people and others, has become a translocal site. The African habitat of meaning created by the CWC is not integrated, shared, distributed, or tidily coterminous with a distinct geographic area or population. It is evident from various media accounts and ethnographic data from Africans who have decided not to participate in its work that the CWC does not monopolize the process of creating a pan-African identity. Instead, the CWC is an institutional agent, one among a diverse array of agents, for example, other nonprofits, social institutions, corporations, the state, public health agencies, individual actors, and others, engaged in creating and managing the variously distributed habitats of meaning in the Twin Cities' African diasporan population. The CWC, along with many other institutions, has an intermediary role as a nonprofit funded by philanthropic and, to a lesser extent, government and other private resources in creating and managing the complex flow of cultural meanings to and from the Twin Cities African diaspora. It therefore provides an important window on how transnational cultural processes operate, even though it does not represent the totality of African identity thought in this respect.

In attempting to map the social organization of diversity, Hannerz (1996:69–72) suggests that we consider four frames through which transnational cultural processes flow: routinized microlevel social relations, the state, the market, and movement. By movement, he is referring to a "highly deliberate, although often decentered handling of meaning, a matter of persuasion and proselytizing in relationships between those converted and those not yet converted" (1996:70). The CWC's African identity formation processes, and indeed many nonprofits working to revitalize diverse communities, may be understood from such a frame. The CWC is an institution composed of leaders deliberately constructing new meanings (in this case "African") from the disparate shreds and patches of delocalized identity that characterize its largely diasporan constituents. A more comprehensive translocal ethnography of diasporan identity in the Twin Cities would require examination of other institutional sites where "African" identities are also being shaped.

CWC African community formation dynamics are also an example of what some analysts refer to as the intensified, self-conscious "culture-making" activity that characterizes contemporary global cultural dynamics (Appadurai 1996). Off-the-shelf identities with neat, conventional associations between place and ancestry are increasingly complicated by transnational flows of meaning and people. In such circumstances, people often find themselves in the position of remaking collective systems of meaning in new locations that remain interlinked into worldwide social, political, and economic networks. Led by Africans born in America, that is, "African Americans," CWC participants from various Ethiopian, Somali, Nigerian, Afro-Caribbean, and other ethnocultural groups are attempting to construct a shared African identity out of this difference.[4] The CWC is a translocal conduit in producing, organizing, and managing the creation of a shared sense of "African" identity from the diverse streams of historical, political, and cultural experiences that form the diaspora, including African immigrants, Afro-Caribbean immigrants, and African Americans living in the Twin Cities. The CWC privileges specific cultural practices that are considered "African" at the same time that it tries to offer models of culture to support its cultural health and wellness agenda. Robertson (1992:34, 41) suggests that cultural production may be intensifying as people try to make sense of an increasingly complex world. The CWC African leadership exemplifies this process as it reflects on and reconstructs the meanings associated with key "metacultural" concepts such as culture, health, African, the body, and race—all of which are core concepts in the anthropology of complexity.

Construing "Africa" as a habitat of meaning that may take on various geographical manifestations in the global flows of culture has several methodological implications. Essentially, this perspective suggests that social networks that span several continents may be more critical as the locus of cultural processes than actual geography at a given point in time. This is not to suggest, as I think some approaches do, that place is indefinitely relegated to secondary importance as a site for identity formation. However, the meaning of place and other markers of identity should be problematized. Thus, ethnography focused on key agents in diasporan networks is one approach to studying the construction of African transnational culture. In this approach, for example, traders working across Harlem, New York and Dakar, Senegal, might form one conduit in a two-way traffic of knowledge and cultural innovation; or adherents of the Yorùbá religion in Brooklyn, Bahia (Brazil), and Ilé-Ifẹ̀ (Nigeria) would be another. This option of multisite ethnography can be logistically complex and not feasible for many researchers. Another strategy, adopted here, is to identify a diasporan crossroads—a particular translocality—that because of its position in the global cultural flow concentrates and amplifies broader transnational processes. This approach, while not necessarily providing conclusive generalizations about the emerging culture of a particular translocality, does contribute to efforts to devise theoretical and methodological frameworks for transnational anthropology.

Scholars are increasingly applying an embodiment perspective in a wide array of research topics. Comaroff (1985) examines the role of bodily practices in reproducing and reformulating cultural identity, representing historical consciousness, and expressing cultural resistance, particularly in conditions of major social change and inequality (also see Lock 1993). A large group focuses on the body as a site for cultural change and resistance (see Mullings 1984; Buckley 1985; Vaughan 1991; Feierman and Janzen 1992; Fontenot 1994; Moore 1994:27). Still others propose that embodiment move from being primarily a microanalytic technique to a broadly applied paradigm for the analysis of culture and history (Jackson 1983, 1989; Stoller 1989, 1997; Csordas 1990:39; Bourdieu 1984, 1977; Napier 2003).

Studies in ethnoaesthetics also demonstrate an increasing interest in embodiment (Sieber 1973; Hebdige 1979; Silver 1981; Ridless 1984; Hardin 1988). Efforts, especially in literary analysis (Gates 1984, 1988; Soyinka 1976, 1984), to identify an "atlantic," "transatlantic," or "black aesthetic" (Gilroy 1993) that have resulted from the various kinds of cultural interchanges in the African diaspora[5] also demonstrate this growing interest in embodiment. This search for an African diasporan aesthetic, however, departs from culturally deterministic models of essentialized, syncretic cultural process as exhibited, for example, in negritude (Senghor 1977) or Afrocentric theory (Asante 1987). Instead, these contemporary approaches explore the interpenetration of political economy, history, and ideational and social systems with emphasis on the role of the body in the often unconscious reproduction of certain elemental cultural principles.

For example, studies of African diasporan musical forms are particularly instructive in these efforts to identify African diaspora aesthetics. Several scholars are documenting the multicentric interchanges and mutual influences between African diaspora and continental African musicians that have produced popular African music such as Fela Ransome Kuti's Afro-jazz and Caribbean reggae and have contributed to the development of global popular music. An example is "world beat" music (cf. Zindi 1985; Brown and Tucker 1986:221; Erlmann 1991).

As these authors suggest, the body has become an important site for the study of contemporary diasporan processes as well as a useful framework for identity issues.

CWC Africanness is not a cognitive identity expressed in semantic categories; it is an affective, multisensorial, visceral means of rearticulating self into society and history. Embodiment provides a conceptual framework for interpreting how the CWC is creating alternative constructs of race, culture, and history. It enables an understanding of how African territory can become localized in the African body in the context of a competing North American habitus of race and Blackness. It also provides a framework for explaining how the CWC's cultural process is informed by the broader sociopolitical context, without contorting the emic experience into conventional categories in the study of African diasporan identity. Instead, the meanings and associations of these various ways of conceptualizing and organizing African peoples can be problematized as part of the research task.

New approaches to community are helpful in understanding African diasporan cultural formations. The CWC's "African habitat of meaning" is not just an idea or an aesthetic, it is also a social network, albeit a shifting one. The intersecting "scapes" that form the CWC's social networks can be seen as comprised of several different types of postcommunity (Appadurai 1996; Ortner 1997a). I have already discussed how the CWC is a translocal community in that it is primarily based in one place but draws in and sends out social networks that extend throughout the world. It is also an imagined or invented community in two senses. Some "African" members, many of whom have never been to Africa, imagine themselves as part of an essentialized "African" culture and actively construct social activities to help build a living social network to actualize this ideal. These imagined communities can be based on constructed memories of a distant and unknowable African past. CWC African immigrant participants, including their second-generation immigrant children, also have a "community of the mind" in the sense that their affiliation is based more on memories of their common origin, even though they may not have visited their home countries for years. The CWC, because of its neighborhood location, also had an element of Ortner's "neo-communities." Many participants live in the Powderhorn neighborhood while others live in other Twin Cities areas. However, the CWC's activities draw them together on a regular basis to interact with others who participate in its social network, including multiple "ethnic" groups.

In this period of "postcommunity," the CWC might also be considered a "neo-tribe" in Maffesoli's (1996) sense of social networks that mimic anthropological tribes in that they have some level of shared identity. From this perspective, the CWC is attempting to create neo-tribes at several levels: a supra-African neo-tribe and a Powderhorn one. Neo-tribes are developing in response to the breakup of mass culture and are organized around sociality—just being together—and a sort of identity-building ethic, whereby creating and sustaining the neo-tribe is an end in and of it-self. In many ways, the proliferation of interest-based nonprofit organiza-tions can be seen as an example of this phenomenon. The CWC's program activities are very much like the initiatory rituals and membership stages that Maffesoli attributes to these neo-tribes. He does not establish a neo-tribe as a hard and fast social structure. Reflecting the contested and delo-calized identities of the postmodern period, CWC Africans are members of several different and partially overlapping neo-tribes: CWC African, African American, Yorùbá, Somali, Wiccans, cultural healers, and so on.

Social networks are a fundamental base of new communities. To fully un-derstand these communities, it is critical to accommodate the lived experi-ence of the people who create them. In the absence of shared systems of meaning coterminous with clearly defined territory, postcommunities may find other bases to at least experience commonality, if only situationally. The CWC leadership recognizes the overlapping and potentially conflict-ing identities that African diasporan and other peoples experience. They have created an intimate means of inventing and experiencing community that connects the personal, cultural, and social through the process of heal-ing "dis-ease" and promoting wellness—a universal human need and con-cern.

For them the body is a tool for integrating the fractured and multiple identities that are such a common experience in a so-called postmodern world. In addition to helping to explain the specificity of the CWC case, embodiment may have broader application for other aspects of the African diaspora. A persistent problem in anthropology has been the extent to which various cultural representations, particularly among African Ameri-cans, represent "more authentic" spontaneous and unconscious retentions, conscious cultural constructions, or some essentially noncultural, that is, uniquely "racial" adaptations to oppressive North American sociopolitical conditions.[6] Embodiment shows a way to accommodate both conscious and unconscious production of all cultural processes, including diasporan vari-ants, without reverting to either neoracist (Balibar and Wallerstein 1991; Harrison 1995) or Afrocentric theory. Again, the CWC provides examples of how the model can help explain such dynamics.

CWC participants may be seen as having embodied, at various levels, a North American habitus involving dominant notions of race and Blackness as well as health and wellness. Participants are not necessarily aware of themselves as having embodied these notions, but the leadership has de-vised particular theories of health and wellness, and epistemologies of African identity which it self-consciously teaches to participants to change their notions of self to become more "African," or in their words, "wake-up the African within." The embodiment framework not only helps to articu-late the CWC's notion of African identity lying dormant inside a European-dominated body, it also helps to explain what Merleau-Ponty (1962, 1964) would call the process of objectification. In this study, some pre-objective, affective feeling of illness is re-defined by the leadership as a disconnection between the self, society, and an uncultivated African identity inside the body. Applying Napier (2003:18), the CWC's "people's theory," underlying epistemology, and related ritual activities in its program and classes provide a set of models, metaphors, and visceral experiences that productively transform stress and resulting illness into new identities and lifestyles.

The CWC's leadership deliberately designs it programs and spatial environment to re-create and help instill notions of Africanness in which various mind/body dualisms—defined as "European"—are collapsed to create a holistic sense of health and wellness embracing individual, community, and society. The power of the CWC's identity formation process cannot be fully explained from an objectivist, intellectualist standpoint. It also cannot be adequately explained as an "ethnic" effort to redefine African cultural identity to increase the scale of Black political influence in the Twin Cities. Most participants and leaders do not see their involvement as in any way political. Csordas (1990:21) suggests that "the body is an irreducible principle, the existential ground of culture and the sacred." Stoller (1997) calls for a scholarship—a way of knowing and telling—that acknowledges and respects the body's sensuous experience of social life. In the CWC case, the body is positioned as a tool to reconstruct power relations with dominant society (cf. Comaroff 1985:124). These cultural processes are at once unconscious and self-conscious. The "African" diasporan body is crafted as an mnemonic scheme displacing dominant North American notions of race, territorially based culture, and Blackness as the locus of identity.

The CWC is one of several locally based nonprofits across the United States engaged in what is now called "comprehensive community revitalization." These initiatives are described by different terms and may have different emphases, for example, "community building," "building social capital," "strengthening social infrastructure," "promoting civic engagement," or "civic investing." However, regardless of the terminology or their specific strategic focus, all such efforts essentially attempt to leverage more concrete community development activities like health care, housing, economic development, or social services to engage community residents, and other key stakeholders, into long-lasting change—"revitalization"—of a particular geographical area, often an economically depressed or declining urban neighborhood with a multiethnic resident base, increasingly comprised of both native-born North Americans as well as immigrants and refugees from throughout the world (Gardner 1991; Connell 1995). Some of these initiatives are organized along the basis of neighborhood geography and are called "neighborhood-based." Others are focused on "communities of interest" and are not necessarily exclusively geographically based but may emphasize a particular ethnic constituency, for example, Latinos or Asians. Such groups are referred to as "identity-based" community-based development organizations. Still others, which involve immi-grants who maintain active ties with their countries of origin, define their community of interest in transnational terms, for example, a group in the Boston area that promotes community development in that city as well as the Dominican Republic (Levitt 1997) or the Opportunities Industrializa-tion Center focused on inner-city, largely African American job training, which has an international arm that provides similar services in Africa.

Whether their primary focus is housing, jobs, or health care, these proj-ects are struggling in practice with a mirror image of the same issues fac-ing sociocultural anthropology's study of contemporary sociocultural dynamics: How do we understand and—in the case of community devel-opment organizations—change the local impact of global economic and social dynamics? What is "neighborhood" or "community" in an increas-ingly global economy? How do we strengthen a sense of community in American urban settings where residents might have allegiances through-out the world, or have different models for conceptualizing and mobilizing diversity? Is place or "neighborhood" even the right frame of reference for local development efforts, when residents actually live at least regionally and, often, translocally?

Structurally, urban-based comprehensive revitalization projects are often situated in the interstices of where the global and local sociopolitical, eco-nomic, and cultural processes meet. One of the core underlying issues with which these projects must deal—whether the economic development proj-ect focuses on affordable housing, job training, or community organiz-ing—is the potential conflict of collective ideational systems and practices for mobilizing people and resources presented by the new mix of immi-grants and other newcomers. Some of these initiatives, such as the one studied here, meet underlying issues of diversity and identity formation head-on and attempt to devise deliberate programming to help define and position cultural identity to build community. Because of their deliberate, largely self-conscious efforts to address these issues and the fact that they are often supported by philanthropies that work transnationally, such proj-ects concentrate and highlight translocal cultural processes that sociocul-tural anthropologists are attempting to study and theorize.

Some scholars maintain that we are entering a postnational global order whereby, with the increasing impact of transnational migration, the media, and multinational corporations, the nation-state has a declining role in or-ganizing and managing cultural diversity (Rosenau 1990). Several scholars also suggest that the non-governmental sector is taking on an increasingly important function in managing the global flow of ideas, people and capi-tal (Appadurai 1996:168, 190–91; Levitt 1997). As Fisher (1997:441) notes, "the global growth of the 'nongovernmental sector' intersects with issues of vital concern to anthropologists. Study of these changes not only enriches our understanding of local and translocal connections that enable and constrain flows of ideas, knowledge, funding, and people, but also invites us to reconsider both conventional notions of governance and Foucaultian ideas of governmentality and how technologies of control affect both the personal and the political, and help us examine changing relationships among citizenry, associations, and the state." While anthropologists have paid some attention to the analysis of such initiatives in international development contexts (e.g., Ferguson 1994; Escobar 1995; Weisgrau 1997), an anthropology of community development in the United States, and of the nonprofit and philanthropic sector in general, is just emerging (Odendahl 1990; Odendahl and O'Neill 1994; Fisher 1997).

Observers of American culture have long recognized that nonprofits and informal civic associations may be a distinctive component of American political culture (Bellah 1985; Tocqueville 1994). They are at the core of civil society—the social loci falling between the state and the private sphere which, while overlapping with both, often provides a basis for formation of alternative discourses and, sometimes, political resistance (Joseph 1995; Sanday 1998b). As an outgrowth of civil society, almost by definition, grassroots community revitalization groups such as the one studied here bring together a wide range of voices and are an important component of how public debate about social problems is being formed. This study therefore contributes to emerging anthropological efforts to understand the "independent sector's" function in transnational identity and community formation.

This study indicates some ways in which ethnographic research in the independent sector can help inform key theoretical issues. Throughout African diasporan history, the nonprofit or voluntary sector has been an important forum and nexus in political resistance and in the construction of alternative, often transnational, cultural identities. From the founding of the African Methodist Episcopal Church in the eighteenth century to the 1960s' Black Power movement, various contemporary pan-African cultural movements, churches, mutual aid associations, schools, and other grassroots organizations, along with academic scholars, have created a rich discourse in defining how people of African descent might articulate their cultural identity vis à vis Africa and America. The serious anthropological study of various pan-Africanist movements, including both the historical and the new African diasporas, many of which are engaged in multiple ways in the nonprofit or voluntary sector, has a largely untapped potential for contributing to the anthropology of cultural complexity. The convergences between African diasporan cultural dynamics and the nonprofit/philanthropic sector have created a cultural sphere that can greatly contribute to the study of contemporary global cultural dynamics. An underpinning of new social science models of community is that these formations are somehow particular to the postmodern period. Clearly this is not the case with the African diaspora in the Americas; there is a centuries-old discourse on transnational community, and there has been deliberate community and political action since the nineteenth century to actualize these visions of identity. Contemporary culture theory and postcommunity models would be very helpful in enriching our understanding of the African diaspora in the premodern period. Several scholars (e.g., Kopytoff 1987; Fardon 1987; Chambers 1996) have begun to apply such approaches with interesting results.[7]

This study also underscores some of the ways an anthropology of the African diasporan nonprofit sector might contribute to current efforts to promote research-driven ethnography in applied settings (Sanday 1976, 1998b; Ferguson 1994; Cernea 1994; Moore 1994; Forman 1995; Ahmed and Shore 1995; Reed 1997), particularly focused on transnational phenomena. Policymakers, funders, and nonprofit practitioners are often searching for new language and conceptual models to move beyond the confines of "neighborhood" as the focus for revitalization in communities comprised of transnational, diasporan constituents as well as native-born North American majority and minority residents. In addition to documenting creative identity formation strategies in new communities, anthropologists can also demonstrate the potential for regressive and oppressive tendencies that can arise from nonprofit sector or any other efforts that reify or racialize culture. The dynamics of community and identity formation is of increasing concern to a wide range of publics with interests in community development and social justice issues.

The immediate relevance of ethnographic research on community revitalization movements to nonanthropologist policymakers and others present particular challenges. While our work always occurs within a political context, the researcher must remain ever vigilant about the political implications of the research. As indicated in this book, great pains were taken to explain the purposes, scope, and limitations of the research to participants. Furthermore, foundations and public funders are paying increasingly more attention to evaluating program outcomes, especially for newer nonprofits like the CWC that are experimenting with innovative strategies. In many ways, academic anthropological research makes judgments about issues specific to the topic being studied, in this case how identity formation takes place in a segment of the Twin Cities African diaspora. Therefore, throughout the fieldwork and in this study it has been important to emphasize that these judgments do not constitute an assessment or evaluation of the CWC's capacity as a "community building initiative." Ultimately the researcher has very little control over how his or her research findings, whether they are in an applied or a conventional setting, such as a village, are politically appropriated. My conscientious attempt to put controls in place to prevent misinterpretation of the data, while ensuring that the study is useful for a wide range of public audiences, is a common challenge faced by anthropologists doing basic research in applied settings such as the nonprofit sector.

The CWC, and other initiatives like it, has a cultural mix that, while it is becoming more common, is only beginning to be documented or theorized in the Africanist or African diasporan anthropological literature. The CWC draws on the diverse African immigrant and refugee populations represented in the Twin Cities. There are particular anthropological research traditions surrounding each of these groups in the anthropological literature. However, as Holtzman and Foner (1999) point out, in the North American context, where particularly refugees are minimum wage workers at the lowest rungs of the class order and are often segregated within communities with the highest concentrations of poverty and disaffected native-born "ethnic" communities, classical interpretations of culture and identity are either irrelevant or, at best, inadequate. A particular challenge, emphasized in this study, is identifying what is useful from conventional depictions of, for example, the Yorùbá or Nuer in the anthropological literature and determining how to combine it with original ethnographic data. This process involves a careful deconstruction of often-taken-for-granted models into which we are socialized from our earliest days of training. Updating our understanding of contemporary Nuer life, for example, in the context of the Sudanese civil war and African refugee experience is an important intermediate step in making conscious and appropriately applying the classical models in the anthropological literature. Although I initially did not expect this to be the case, my experience of aspects of contemporary Nigerian life during conventional ethnohistorical fieldwork in Nigeria was important preparation in translating classical approaches for the contemporary issues in this study.

Although current theory presents a wide range of options for conceptualizing issues in the anthropology of transnational cultural issues, none of them quite accommodates the very complex socio-economic and cultural diversity represented by cases such as the CWC which involves African, Asian, and Latino immigrants and refugees, native-born African Americans, Asian Americans, and Whites, along with donors who represent some of the most powerful private and public institutions in the region. No one model can accommodate this astounding complexity. The need to blend conventional and contemporary approaches across disciplines may represent a common challenge for researchers attempting to theorize about transnational identity issues from the types of diasporan and other diversities now increasingly represented throughout North American metropolitan areas.

Embodiment, because it attempts to take a step back from the epistemological assumptions inherent in many current approaches to ethnicity, panethnicity, and diasporas, may offer a useful alternative research paradigm. It refocuses attention and takes seriously the participants' lived experience—the actual process of creating identity and culture in these very unique circumstances—and uses these data to inform theory, rather than retrofitting this complexity into comfortable old notions that either do not fit the conditions of transnational communities or are being very deliberately reconstructed by members of these groups. At the same time, it takes note of the fact that participants' subjective experiences are unavoidably influenced by structural factors. By problematizing the linkages between subjective experience and sociopolitical dynamics, an embodiment research paradigm can help point out some of the culturally creative ways people are responding to shifts in the global economy in their daily lives. It can provide an even deeper grounding of theory than that facilitated by standard participant observation methods in ethnographic research.

A participatory research approach is a natural, albeit not necessary, extension of an embodiment perspective on transnational identity formation processes. Engaging participants in the definition of the research problem as well as in feedback and reflection in the course of analysis may help to uncover "culture in the making." In this study, it was particularly helpful in highlighting the very nuanced ways that new identities are being formulated through community initiatives. It helped me move from a focus on "ethnic" identity formation at the study's early formative stages to a more thorough appreciation of embodiment practices and cultural variation in ways of conceptualizing and organizing cultural diversity, core issues in the CWC's work. Systematic and regular participant feedback on interpretations of the data and aspects of research design, for example, interview guides, instead of detracting from the objectivity of my research, pointed out even more subtleties in the CWC's cultural agenda. Such participatory research practices were a critical corrective to the imposition of very powerful epistemologies that underlie mainstream approaches to culture and identity formation in both public discourse and anthropology. However, this level of participation also requires an intensive level of reflection; for example, copious journaling was a discrete complement to field notes, to sort out how the research itself might have been influencing participants' construction of identity as well as to provide an additional control on the urge to impose convenient models of identity (e.g., "race," ethnicity, "African"), which may or may not have been ethnographically accurate in such intensely transnational circumstances, where people, particularly leaders, might have read the same ethnographies as the researcher and were deliberately reconstituting anthropological and other models for the express purposes of managing identity.

This study focuses primarily on how the CWC's identity formation processes can inform anthropological theory. However, because of its focus on African diasporan identity formation through the nonprofit or voluntary sector, this study also potentially indicates how anthropology might inform both theory and various public debates about community development issues. Key research topics might include, for example, alternative ways to define "community" in revitalizing areas comprised in part of residents with active ties to many countries; ways to create shared experiences and ideas of identity in translocal communities; various cultural issues that might impact the effort to "build community" in translocal circumstances, for example, differing notions of history, culture, or conceptualizing and organizing diversity; how the voluntary sector can serve as a training ground to develop community organizing skills that transfer across "ethnic" communities; how to create experiences that provide a surrogate sense of "home" for displaced people; how to create supportive social networks that can be used to promote healing of physical ailments; how medical practitioners might adapt their practices to more effectively work with diverse healing systems evident among refugee or immigrant as well as minority clients. While this study does not assess the CWC's effectiveness in addressing any of these issues, it does document how these issues might be approached and may be relevant for practitioners addressing similar concerns in other communities.

It is almost a truism in current anthropological discourse to say that contemporary global cultural dynamics are bringing together images, peoples, institutions, and symbols in unpredictable permutations for which conventional theory is largely unprepared. In many ways, this study's circuitous, interdisciplinary journey through the African diaspora—and the underlying interplay between anthropological theory and community development practice—is an artifact of these unusual convergences—and disjunctures—in the contemporary global ecumene. Although this study's research strategy may commit what amounts to heresy in some anthropological circles, unusual times often require unusual measures. A transnational anthropology of cultural complexity may entail just such an eclectic blending and extension of social science theories, methods, and "area studies" outside their conventional boundaries—geographic or otherwise. As an intermediate space crosscutting the scapes of various public spheres (Appadurai 1996), the nonprofit philanthropic sector represents a research site that American anthropology cannot continue to ignore as it searches for ways to understand contemporary global cultural dynamics and continue the tradition, started in the earliest days of anthropology, of pursuing research in the public interest.

Appendix A: Research Design, Methods, and Documents

Research Design

The fieldwork and writing for this study was conducted over a twenty-eight-month period from April 1997 through August 1999. The fieldwork and writing process was divided into three periods, although data collection, analysis, and writing tasks overlapped at different stages of the study.

PRELIMINARY FIELDWORK (APRIL 1997 THROUGH DECEMBER 1997)

Although I had already met many of the principal CWC participants in other non-research-related activities, during the first period I explained the proposed study; attended relevant meetings and sessions; identified an initial fieldwork methodology, including first-round ethnographic interviewing guides and research protocols; strengthened rapport and trust with CWC participants; and finalized a study proposal acceptable to the CWC. I maintained a full set of field notes and journal entries which became critical as I proceeded with data analysis in the study's later phases.

CORE FIELDWORK (JANUARY 1998 THROUGH DECEMBER 1998)

I began regular attendance at various CWC community and other meetings and relevant program sessions during the second period. I lived only ten minutes away in a neighborhood adjacent to the communities served by the CWC, making full-time participation in CWC activities manageable. On average, I spent forty-two hours per week in direct CWC participant interaction, including observing and interviewing of various sorts during CWC business day and evening and weekend classes or other special events. I spent about thirty hours per week writing and analyzing field notes.

WRITING AND DATA ANALYSIS (JANUARY 1999 THROUGH DECEMBER 1999)

During the third period, my work shifted to interpretation and writing. To maintain a connection to the CWC, I occasionally attended special events and class sessions, amounting to more than an average of about one hour per week. My goals were to identify theoretical models to interpret the data; collect relevant statistical data on community demographics available from various public agencies; review media accounts that illuminated the broader sociopolitical context in which the CWC operated; meet with key community stakeholders, particularly funders who supported the CWC's work; and write the actual study.

Ethnographic Data Collection and Analysis Techniques

Throughout the research process, I used a wide range of data collection and analysis methods. The CWC's program and other activities provided a rich array of ethnographic and historical sources for the proposed research. I used four basic sources: oral history, written materials, ethnographic evidence, and interpretations of material culture and spatial aesthetics. CWC participants, nonparticipants, teachers, and volunteers provided oral history and ethnographic evidence. I conducted both formal individual interviews and group interviews of participants in the context of CWC classes and support groups. Participants also conducted tours of the CWC's premises, at which time they provided commentary on its material culture and spatial aesthetics. I also collected much ethnographic evidence from participants during participant observation in CWC program interactions and conversations.

FIELD RESEARCH AND ETHNOGRAPHIC EVIDENCE

The CWC's class and special event calendar changed each quarter. However, there were certain kinds of program activity that remained fairly constant despite changes in specific class offerings. I conducted research in five of these: (1) individual health assessment and counseling sessions, as permitted by participants; (2) group-oriented nonprofit workshops, training sessions, and classes; (3) board-related and planning committee meetings; (4) nonprofit-sponsored community and family events; and (5) nonprofit staff and board meetings with other community stakeholders, for example, funders, mainstream physicians, or municipal planning and health commission representatives.

ORAL HISTORY

The CWC had not developed formal oral traditions or a written history, but I elicited stories of key events in the nonprofit history from clients, staff, board, volunteers, nonparticipating constituents, and funders. From these historical accounts, I learned how various CWC subgroups depicted and interpreted the nonprofit's philosophy, mission, and services and how

these related to the identity-building process. I also interviewed participants and nonparticipants from each African diasporan group to elicit life
histories focusing on migration stories, personal conceptions of identity,
community, and the CWC's role in their lives. Particular attention was paid
not only to documenting chronologically the various groups' migration
and CWC participation histories, but understanding notions of historicity
and identifying how these notions may have been changing, and how this
process was informed by broader power and economic structures.

WRITTEN DOCUMENTS

Written documents included minutes and other meeting documents
from CWC committees and the board of directors. Attention was paid to
the written meeting proceedings and reports of African diasporan-related
committees and classes. Also, various program mission, narrative and
graphical documents, and evaluation reports proved indispensable in analyzing the CWC's discourse on identity, health, and wellness. Various reports, produced by universities, governmental public health and planning
agencies, and nonprofit research organizations provided critical sociodemographic and population health data relevant to this study. Additionally,
media accounts from both mainstream and ethnic newspapers provided
critical perspectives, especially on the broader sociopolitical and economic
environment (Schneider 1999).

Finally, I produced copious field notes, including verbatim accounts of
participant conversations, descriptions of nonverbal behaviors and other
contextual matters (e.g., sketches of room layout for special events); analyses of these ethnographic data; and transcriptions of taped interview sessions. Because of the CWC's emphasis on storytelling and journaling about
personal experiences, I kept not only field notes but also a detailed personal journal documenting my reactions and reflections. As a "native anthropologist" this journaling became critical to help ensure that I was
consistently sorting out the diverse emic and etic perspectives and opinions
about "African" identity—especially in the many instances when a particular perspective conflicted with either my personal or Africanist academic
points of view.

MATERIAL CULTURE INTERPRETATIONS

The CWC's material culture—its interior design, selection and place-
ment of artifacts, smells, lighting, sounds—were all deliberately configured
by its leaders to produce an environment that was conducive to producing
African identity and cultural healing. Thus, great attention was paid to the
details of the interior and surrounding environment. The CWC's spatial
layout and ambiance were recorded in sketches, photographs (Appendix

B), written descriptions and interpretation, and participant and nonparticipant commentaries that were all included in field notes.

Participatory Research Methods

The study utilized participatory fieldwork methods, which included collaboration with the CWC staff to present and describe the study in a manner accessible to its participants. We developed general research protocols, including a confidentiality and informed consent policy and forms that all interviewed participants had the opportunity to review and sign. We compiled a "research binder" left in a very public and accessible location in the CWC reception area that could be reviewed by CWC participants. The research binder included a one-page description of the study, devised in collaboration with the executive director and medical director, a copy of the informed consent form, and a clear statement of ethics indicating how the study's findings would be disseminated.

I did a mass mailing to all CWC African participants, including a cover memo from myself and the executive director with an attachment describing the goals, general procedures, expected outcomes, and information-sharing strategies of the study. All CWC African diasporan participants as well as staff and board members were sent a copy of the project description, and the study's purpose was reexplained as I attended CWC participant meetings. CWC participant and staff feedback, commentary, and my responses to them are included as ethnographic data in this study. This interaction provides critical insights into how the diverse ethnic and social backgrounds of CWC participants influence the African identity formation process. Other components of the participatory research method used in the study included collaboration with the CWC staff to present and describe the study in a manner accessible to its participants.

TABLE A.1. SAMPLE OF CWC PROGRAM SERVICES
FROM THE SPRING 2000 PROGRAM CALENDAR

Program Division	CWC Classes and Other Services
Core Member Activities	• Map to Wellness: Systematic holistic health assessment process • Circle of Healing: Social support network to help heal illness • Birthing Team: Support network for pregnant women • Doula in Training: Training for prospective midwives • Foot care, massage, chiropractic, acupuncture services
Health Institute	• Capoeira • Yoga • Tae Bo • Earth Dance: Learn and embody feminine version of the Lord's Prayer • Healthy Menopause • The Old Days' Home Remedies • Citizens Health Action Teams • Moving from Dis-ease to Wellness • Seasons & Rhythms: Support group for people of African heritage with depression, tension, pressure • Conscious Conception: Prepare our bodies to invite a divine soul to enter us • European Women, Death and Dying • African American Parenting • European Parenting • Gay and Lesbian Community Health Action Teams
Invisible College	• Personal and Professional Coaching • Community building, cultural interpretation, support network formation services from Invisible College medical doctors, cultural healer, and social worker • African and African American Elder Consultations • African Council of Elders

Program Division	CWC Classes and Other Services
	• African Spirituality, Heritage and Culture: A Paradigm of Knowledge
	• European Cultural Council
	• Indian Women's Resource Center
	• Lao Mothers and Daughters
	• Culturally Based Leadership Support for Europeans
	• European Celebrations/Rituals
	• Special Events with Tjanara Goreng Goreng, an Australian Aboriginal Healer, Educator, and Dancer
	• Blending the Traditional and Conventional Medical Practices
	• Imhotep Science Academy: Science program for black students to promote careers in sciences and deepen their personal identity as Africans
	• African Student Alliance
	• Coalition of African Women
	• Latino Growers Association
	• Guatemalan Latino United Efforts (GLUE)
	• Latinas' Support Group
	• Leadership and Spirituality for Women
	• Cultural Immersion and Community Immersion: Customized program for institutional clients
	• Healthy Powderhorn Farmers Market

Appendix B: Cultural Wellness Center and Powderhorn Photographs

Figure B.1. CWC Reception Desk: Linking the Two Lands. Bruce Silcox, Photographer (Minneapolis).

Figure B.2. CWC Reception Area: Creating African Home in America. Bruce Silcox, Photographer (Minneapolis).

Figure B.3. The Ancestors Are with Us. Bruce Silcox, Photographer (Minneapolis).

Figure B.4. An Altar Honoring European Women. Bruce Silcox, Photographer (Minneapolis).

Figure B.5. Sculpture and Textiles: Evoking African Spaces. (Note tapestry with Celtic design on the right wall.) Bruce Silcox, Photographer (Minneapolis).

Figure B.6. Masking: Conjuring African Memory. Bruce Silcox, Photographer (Minneapolis).

Figure B.7. Invisible College Session: Studying "Ancient Wisdom." Bruce Silcox, Photographer (Minneapolis).

Figure B.8. The Invisible College: Cultivating Indigenous Knowledge. Bruce Silcox, Photographer (Minneapolis).

Figure B.9. Capoeira: (Body) Working the Spirit. Bruce Silcox, Photographer (Minneapolis).

Figure B.10. Capoeira: Building African Community. Bruce Silcox, Photographer (Minneapolis).

Figure B.11. African Soul Movement: Recalling Ancestral Rhythms. Bruce Silcox, Photographer (Minneapolis).

Figure B.12. Community Masking and Puppetry Studio. Bruce Silcox, Photographer (Minneapolis).

Figure B.13. Annual Community Festival Participants. Bruce Silcox, Photographer (Minneapolis).

Figure B.14. Creating Home at the Annual Community Festival. Bruce Silcox, Photographer (Minneapolis).

Notes

Preface

1. For convenience, I generally spell "Black" with a capital "B" to refer to United States-born Americans of African ancestry as an ethnic group. However, ethnographic chapters attempt to express participants' notions of identity. Therefore, in instances where a participant preferred it, "black," "black American," and so forth are spelled in lower case.

Prologue

1. African American participant in a Twin Cities regional conference on African refugees, March 27, 1998.

2. Immigration and population estimates are from 1996 and are derived from two sources: a working paper prepared by Barbara Ronnigen, Minnesota Planning Division, State Demographic Center, St. Paul, Minnesota, and a study conducted by the Federal Reserve Bank (Minneapolis). Ronnigen's report combines data from the Immigration and Naturalization Service, public schools, and state human service agencies to estimate the size of various new populations. The report emphasizes that estimates probably undercount populations because secondary migration from other United States cities is not generally captured in these highly mobile communities. In 1996, the Twin Cities' seven-county metropolitan region's population was about 2.6 million, a 9 percent increase over the 1990 census. Together, the cities of Minneapolis and St. Paul have about 700,000 residents. The foreign-born population is relatively small but included a larger proportion of recent immigrants than most metropolitan areas in the United States (Federal Reserve Bank of Minneapolis 1999, 4–5).

3. Lake Wobegone is a fictional Midwestern community created by Garrison Keillor for his regular radio show.

4. Dirk Johnson, Ethnic Change Tests Mettle of Minneapolis Liberalism, *Wall Street Journal* October 18, 1997, A1.

5. See Gilliam 1992; D'Amico-Samuels 1992; and Feldman 1994 for analyses of the racialization of social problems in mass media.

6. According to the 1990 Census, unemployment rates were highest among American Indians at 16 percent, African Americans at 15 percent, and Chicanos and Latinos at 8 percent.

7. The former director of the University of Minnesota's Institute on Race and Poverty, john powell, spells his name with lowercase letters in all his publications. This preference is reflected when his name is cited in this study.

8. For example, according to a study by the Foundation Center, a national research group and think tank on the philanthropic sector, in 1997 Minnesota had the second-highest level of philanthropic giving in the country. According to the Minnesota Council on Foundations, the state has three of the largest foundations in the United States and, because of the large number of multinational corporations based here, a very strong tradition of corporate philanthropy as well.

9. Transnational refers to economic, political, and cultural processes that link persons and institutions into social relations that transcend national boundaries (Appadurai 1996). "Transnational" refers to these broader global dynamics. The term "translocal" focuses on the interaction of a particular location, such as an urban neighborhood, within this global flow of meaning.

10. "Culture" as used here is not being applied in the conventional sense of a geographically bounded, integrated system of meaning and values corresponding to particular people, but is used in the more processual sense proposed by Hannerz (1996).

11. Orthography for Yorùbá words is derived from Roger C. Abrahams, *Dictionary of Modern Yorùbá* (London: University of London Press, Ltd., 1958). Also, a special thanks to my friend and colleague, Dr. Mojúbàolú Olúfúnké Okome of the Brooklyn College, City University of New York, who provided further assistance with contemporary colloquial forms of the language.

12. Although African diasporan studies is an interdisciplinary field, this study focuses primarily on the work of professional sociocultural anthropologists. The work of other disciplines is considered to the extent that they inform African diasporan anthropology in North America. The long and controversial study of African Americans by early twentieth-century physical anthropologists is not considered her.

13. Research methods in the study of nonverbal behavior established by Birdwhistell (1970) and Hall (1992) were also an integral component of this study's fieldwork methodology.

Chapter 1. "Africa" in Minnesota

1. Unless otherwise noted, this description of the CWC's spatial environment and design are excerpts from my journal.

2. In an advertisement in a neighborhood paper, Ingebretsen's described itself as an "old world marketplace of fine Scandinavian foods, imported gifts and needlework . . . We have everything you need to bring your Scandinavian heritage to life." As indicated in the introduction to this study, many of Minnesota's original European immigrants were Scandinavian. Americanized versions of Scandinavian culture were sustained by a range of cultural institutions, including the Swedish American Institute located in Minneapolis and various summertime cultural festivals.

3. This arts group performs community theater. It is best known for organizing an annual community festival for which it produces large papier-maché masks. These masks attempt to combine the masking traditions of the many cultures represented in the neighborhood. (See Appendix B for photos of these masks, work in the annual festival, and a storefront studio where some of the masks are made.)

4. Many of the classes which provided data for this study were part of the Invisible College (IC), a CWC unit devoted to bringing out, teaching, and applying "indigenous ways of knowing."

5. Historically, anthropology has had some impact on the development of pan-Africanist culture theory. For example, in his preface to *Black Folks, Then and Now* (1939: vii), Du Bois wrote, "Franz Boas came to Atlanta University where I was teaching in 1906 and said to a graduating class: 'You need not be ashamed of your African past;' and then he recounted the history of black kingdoms south of the Sahara for a thousand years. I was too astonished to speak. All of this I had never heard and I came then and afterwards to realize how . . . silence and neglect . . . can let truth ultimately disappear or . . . be unconsciously distorted."

6. As is common in the literature (see Whitten and Szwed 1970; Mintz and Price 1992) the term "African American" is used here to refer to people of African descent living in the Americas. The term is used interchangeably with the term "African diaspora in America or the New World." The term "African Americanist studies" refers to the scholarly documentation and analysis of African diasporan history and culture in the Americas. "African diasporan studies" is a more inclusive term which may refer both to the Americas and other regions of the world to which African peoples have migrated at different historical periods. "Culture" as used here is not being used in the conventional sense of a geographically bounded, integrated system of meaning and values corresponding to particular people, but is used in the more processual sense proposed by Hannerz (1996).

7. Combination of Jamaican and American nationalities.

8. While Melville Herskovits was not the first or only scholar to engage in such research, (see Price-Mars 1983; Hurston 1935, 1938; Woodson 1936; Du Bois 1939) he can be credited with helping to establish the foundation whereby African diasporan studies would eventually be seen as an acceptable area of anthropological study in the academy.

Chapter 2. Ethnographic Grounding

1. Whites (called "Europeans" by the CWC leadership) included both United States-born and foreign-born persons of descent from the countries and ethnicities native to the European continent. Blacks (called "Africans" by the CWC leadership) included both United States-born and foreign-born persons with descent from the countries and indigenous ethnicities of Africa. At the CWC most Black participants were African American, Afro-Caribbean, Somali, Amharic-Ethiopian, Oromo-Ethiopian, Tigrean-Ethiopian, Yorùbá-Nigerian, Igbo-Nigerian, Hausa-Nigerian, Liberian, and Eritrean. Asians included persons mostly from Vietnam, Laos, and China as well as the Hmong—a nomadic group originating in Southeast Asia. Most Latinos were Chicano with Mexican ancestry or Guatemalan.

The 2000 Census estimated that there were about 13,000 Somalis living in Minnesota. Although this figure was commensurate with the number of Somali-speaking school children enrolled in Minnesota public schools, Somali community leaders suspect that census figures underestimated their number. With the growth of the community over the past two years, government demographers estimate that anywhere from 25,000 to 30,000 Somalis in Minnesota live primarily in the Twin Cities metropolitan area, with significant numbers in the Rochester area. According to Somali leaders, this figure would still be an underestimation, given the baseline undercount in the 2000 Census.

2. As a general rule, this study describes ethnographic events and other related activities in the past tense, as they occurred during the course of ethnographic research. I use the present tense for the analysis of these ethnographic data and for references to anthropological and other scholarly literature.

3. See Table A.1 in Appendix A for a listing of classes and support groups from one of its program calendars.

4. See Table A.1 in Appendix A for a representative listing of CWC classes from a program calendar.

5. The CWC's African constituent base alone represents at least ten different national and/or ethnic groups.

6. CHI is a pseudonym for the CWC's precursor organization. This account of the CWC's organizational history is based on participant interviews and a CWC program calendar article, "How the CWC Was Born," June-August 1998, p. 3.

7. In the CWC's parlance, a "cultural healer" was someone who was not formally trained in mainstream medical practices but was thought by staff or some segment of the community to have mastered knowledge and application of the healing traditions of a particular culture. Of the three cultural healers on the CWC's staff, two were European and one was an African woman born in the Caribbean. However, at some level, given the CWC's broader cultural healing focus, all full-time staff were considered cultural healers.

8. In the lexicon of the nonprofit and philanthropic sector, a "self-help group" would be a mutual aid association formed by the members of a particular ethnocultural group that is not necessarily formally incorporated or recognized as an eligible tax-exempt organization according to government policies.

9. On average, I would loosely estimate that about 20–30 percent of the CWC's volunteer base was male.

10. As a relatively new organization, the CWC was just developing a reliable database of participant socioeconomic information. There were about two hundred participants, and seventy were identified as African or African American by the leadership. However, this list did not represent the broader network of African or African American and other supporters who participated in the CWC's work in some fashion. My own statements about CWC constituent sociodemographic characteristics were drawn from both publicly available sociodemographic statistics and from my direct exposure to participants in interviews, participant observation, or other ethnographic research settings and are not necessarily conclusive.

11. The CWC, however, can be classified as a particular type of community development group called a "community revitalization" nonprofit. Such revitalization groups do not necessarily work on diversity issues, although those defined by community development scholars as "identity-based" may explicitly address these concerns in their community development agendas. A principle conclusion of this study is that grassroots nonprofit groups like the CWC have been an innovative forum for the creation of alternative metacultural constructs throughout North American African diasporan history, warranting more serious anthropological study.

12. This approach also builds on Van Maanen's (1988:127) notion of a critical tale (see also Lamphere 1992: 17). It additionally applies models in the classical social network ethnographies (see Mitchell 1956; Turner 1957; Hannerz 1980; Johnson 1994) to transnational ethnography.

13. Urban Colation and Minnesota Department of Health, Spring 1997.

Chapter 3. "Three Parts African"

1. This third component of Africanness—the CWC's articulation of an "African way of knowing"—warrants an extended discussion and is more fully explored in Chapter 6.

2. Some CWC African diasporan participants used the term "black American" to refer to the skin color of a particular American. Other CWC participants were offended by the use of lowercase "b" because, to them, it was "racial" as it only focused on skin color. For the purposes of this study's ethnographic chapters, black is spelled with a lowercase "b" when it is used solely to describe a color as in a person's skin tone.

3. Discussion with CWC African elder and leader, August 25, 1998.

4. African Soul Movement teacher, April 4, 1998.

5. February 27, 1998, in field notes, p. 50.

6. Discussion with CWC "African born in America" participant, August 6, 1998, field notes, p. 492.

7. Ibid.

8. Interview on September 28, 1998, field notes, p. 582.

9. CWC "African born in America leader" and elder, August 25, 1998, field notes, p. 525.

10. Meeting with CWC "African born in America" elder, June 12, 1998, field notes, p. 250.

11. For CWC African American leaders who describe themselves as "Africans born in America," African ancestry is not a passive, remote historical charter for identity. The leadership has devised a particular historicity that articulates an idea of how African ancestors intervene both in the body and in contemporary social relations (see Chapter 7).

12. Discussion with CWC African elder, August 25, 1998, field notes, p. 493.

13. The Health and Wellness Committee was one of four CWC standing committees. It helped to direct CWC health practices policy and was composed of about eight people, including professional health practitioners and community members.

14. Interview, August 4, 1998, field notes, p. 401.

15. Interview, August 14, 1998, field notes, p. 450.

16. African American Diabetes Wellness Group participant, August 28, 1998, field notes, p. 510. This participant was insistent on a lower case spelling of the term "black."

17. CWC African born in America, March 29, 1998, field notes, p. 178.

18. Interview with CWC "African/African American" participant, September 28, 1998.

19. African elder and CWC leader, February 27, 1998.

20. CWC class, April 17, 1998, field notes, p. 268.

21. The term "African American" was used occasionally by CWC "Africans born in America" when speaking to a ethnically mixed group or other audiences that may become confused by their uncommon inclusion of all people of African heritage in the term "African." However, these participants, as indicated throughout the study, prefer the term "African" to other possible ethnocultural labels.

22. Medical student workshop on African culture, July 8, 1998, field notes, p. 399.

23. Interview at CWC on August 11, 1998, field notes, pp. 393–95.

24. Interview excerpt, June 6, 1998 in field notes, pp. 476–79.

25. Literally, the "sons and daughters of Oduduwa." Oduduwa is considered the progenitor of the Yorùbá people. The association organizes a well-attended Yorùbá cultural festival in the area. MIND, Minnesotans Involved in Nigerian Development, is a Twin Cities-based mutual aid association for Nigerians. The Igbos in Minnesota have a mutual aid society that annually presents Igbofest, a cultural festival.

26. Several CWC African immigrant participants used the word "tribe" to refer to their African ethnic origins. I used the terms in quotes here to describe CWC participants' usage of the term. I refrain from using the term to analyze CWC identity

formation because of the well-documented ambiguities and potential pejorative connotations of the term.

27. I deliberately refrain from classifying these physical indicators as "racial," as the CWC leadership has a different understanding of "race" from that which is popularly or anthropologically understood.

28. Discussion with CWC "African born in America" participant, August 6, 1998, field notes, p. 489.

29. Life history interview with Selassie at a neighborhood restaurant, March 19, 1998, field notes, pp. 119–21.

30. Life history interview with CWC Ethiopian immigrant leader, June 1998, field notes, p. 366.

31. Ibid.

32. Life history interview with Akin, June 10, 1998, field notes excerpts from pp. 468, 472, 478.

Chapter 4. Organizing Across Diasporan Crosscurrents

1. See Schneider (1999:763) for discussion of ways in which media accounts can be used to see if themes evident in a particular setting are echoed in the wider society.

2. Rosalind Bentley and Chris Graves, "Killer Sought As Taxi Driver Is Mourned," *Star Tribune*, March 10, 1998, A1.

3. In recent years landmark class action legal suits by the NAACP have addressed increasing segregation and poverty concentration. In a 1995 case, settled in winter 2000, the NAACP sued that stated policies had concentrated poverty in the inner city, making an adequate education impossible for children there. Many of those children were children of color. In 1998 the NAACP won a class action suit against the federal Department of Housing and Urban Development and local government agencies for supporting the concentration of public housing complexes in the largely low-income and African American area of North Minneapolis. The settlement includes the construction of new, lower density housing in low-income areas as well as affluent parts of the city and the suburbs. Also, see Chapter 2 for a socioeconomic profile of the Powderhorn community and changing demographics in Minnesota.

4. Kimberly Hayes Taylor, "Somalis in America: Working Through a Clash of Cultures: Efforts Are Being Made to Ease Tensions Between Somali and African-American Students," *Star Tribune*, March 22, 1998.

5. Letter to the editor, Scott W. Johnson, *Star Tribune*, Sunday, March 25, 1998, A10.

6. "Black" here refers to native-born African Americans.

7. Brandt Williams, "Somalis Build Community, Bridges in Minnesota," *Insight News*, April 6, 1998, 23, no. 11, 1.

8. A CWC conference on female circumcision and the subsequent formation of a coalition to continue public education and influence public policy on the issue was an example of how nonprofit sector diasporan collaboration can build capacity for joint political action.

9. According to 1990 Census data, four out of ten African Americans in urban Minnesota lived in poverty.

10. *Journal of Blacks in Higher Education*, Winter 1996/1997.

11. One prominent example, not studied here, is an economic development nonprofit and foundation run by an African American church leader who was born

in Sierra Leone. The organization, in addition to creating several innovative business projects, runs an annual rites of passage program which involves taking African American youth on a tour of Ghana.

12. Kimberly Hayes-Taylor, "Conference Celebrates States Ties to Africa," *Star Tribune*, October 4, 1998, B1.

13. Ibid.

14. The Midwest Black Publishers Coalition, based in Minneapolis, formed in 1991 to offer large advertising markets to potential clients (*Insight News*, "Uniting the African Family," June 8, 1998, 1). Also, Stoller (1996) examines the role of African diasporan tourism in Ghana in creating transnational economic exchanges and influencing identity formation on both continents.

15. Frank Anokye, *Insight News*, August 26, 1998, 1.

16. There were indications that the coalition's marketing efforts may have been somewhat successful. For example, several months after the first delegation visited, African American nonprofits, church-based groups, and mutual aid associations had organized orientation programs of several months to prepare for PANAFEST. Ghanaians living in the Twin Cities helped to provide language instruction and introduction to the culture of Ghana.

17. Excerpts of discussion with CWC "African" leader, a Yorùbá born in Nigeria, June 10, 1998, field notes, pp. 462 and 479–81.

18. For example, the Yorùbá immigrant quoted above applied CWC African diversity models in several other community activities. One such setting was Ẹgbẹ́ Ọmọ Odùduwà, a Twin Cities Yorùbá mutual aid association, where he initiated a series of joint activities with CWC African leaders. He was also part of a committee that planned a graduation recognition ceremony for seniors at an area high school with the highest concentrations of Africans and African Americans. The original planning committee for this event became the Pan-African Elders Council, thus extending CWC models of identity.

19. Discussion at CWC conference, August 22, 1998.

20. CWC "African" elder, July 7, 1998, field notes, p. 345.

21. Excerpt from ethnographic interview with Amina, August 25, 1998, field notes, pp. 508–10.

22. CWC continental African participant, June 1998, field notes, p. 508.

23. Conference participant comment, August 6, 1998, field notes, p. 532.

24. CWC African elder, March 13, 1998, field notes, p. 99.

25. The pseudonym "Selassie" is used for the founder and director of this agency. Although he is identified by name in the cited *Star Tribune* article, to maintain confidentiality his name is not used in this study.

26. See Chapter 4, above for a life history interview excerpt with Selassie that provides background on the formation of this project.

27. Kimberly Hayes Taylor, "Pain of African AIDS Crisis Touches Minnesotans: Groups Take Initiative for Education Overseas," *Star Tribune*, July 4,1998, A1.

28. Several CWC African immigrant leaders maintained active social and financial ties with Africans throughout the world. So arguably these participants could have become agents in communicating and applying the CWC's diversity models in other cities with sizable African settlements. However, tracking these most far-reaching flows of transnational cultural exchange is not feasible in this study. The focus here is on mapping the contours of transnational cultural dynamics through the CWC and its African agents.

29. Earlier formulations of ethnicity (cf. R. Cohen 1978, Keyes 1976; Barth 1969; A. Cohen 1969) developed as an alternative to conventional units of analysis in anthropology such as tribe or village. Although there is some variation in the differ-

ent approaches, essentially ethnicity was seen as the process whereby individuals living in a political unit defined themselves as cultural collectivities to compete for power and resources with other groups (Williams 1989). Recently this approach to the organization of diversity has been critiqued for its focus on concrete and distinctive cultural boundaries, as well as its inattention to the role of the state and ideology in intergroup competition, translocal processes of identity formation, and self-identification of identity (see Barth 1984; Fardon 1987; Appadurai 1990; Bhabha 1990).

30. See Chapter 7 and the Epilogue for a discussion of how models of community are being elaborated to accommodate transnational cultural phenomena (e.g., Anderson 1983; Ortner 1997b).

31. While Appadurai's technoscapes are not addressed here, it should be noted that the telephone and internet, specifically electronic mail, have probably created diasporan cybercommunities also engaged in the organization of diversity on a transnational scale (see D'Alisera 1999).

Chapter 5. The African Body Resistant

1. "Community Health Initiative" is a pseudonym for this precursor organization.

2. "CWC, How the CWC was Born," in *Summer Program Schedule,* June-August 1998, 3.

3. CWC director, February 13,1998, field notes, p. 32.

4. From People's Theory program graphic, see Appendix C.

5. CWC, "Principles of Community/Cultural Health Practices," December 1996 and Winter 1997.

6. CWC, February 1997, program flyer used to market its services.

7. Ibid.

8. See CWC, "Cultural Health Improvement and Management" service description brochure, March 1997.

9. CWC Individual Services Description, March 1997.

10. CWC, Summer Program Calendar, 1998, 1.

11. In such contexts, the terms "indigenous" or "people of color" and "African" were often used synonymously.

12. See Chapter 7 for a description and analysis of the CWC's techniques for embodied cultural healing.

13. McKnight and Kretzmann's (1993) influential asset-based model of community development is an example.

14. These social connections were not emotional ties but in many cases were instrumental in that they involved the common practice of providing financial support to one's family and friends still living in Africa or other continents.

15. From a life history interview session, March 19, 1998, with CWC "African" leader, field notes, pp. 171–72.

16. "European" leader, April 11, 1998, at CWC community forum on racism.

17. "African born in America" leader, June 15, 1998, field notes, p. 278.

18. Capoeira is an Afro-Brazilian martial art. *Orisha* is the generic term used for Yorùbá deities in the Africanist literature.

19. "African born in America," interviewing session, July 1998, field notes, p. 315.

20. Interview with active CWC "African" participant, March 1998, field notes, pp. 185–86.

21. CWC staff planning meeting for a community forum on racism, April 5, 1998.

22. See Comaroff (1991, 1985) for examples of how the ritualized political resistance inherent in Tshidi Zionism responded to South African subjugation through colonial public health policies, particularly its regimens of hygiene, bodily restraint, and healing.

Chapter 6. Healing the Mind

1. The terms "mind/body/spirit" and "knowing/being" as opposed to "mind, body, and spirit" are used to denote the CWC's notion of unity in these ways of being.

2. Staff meeting, April 5, 1998, field notes, p. 194.

3. Community forum on racism, April 10, 1998, field notes, p. 214.

4. Although CWC "European" identity formation was not the primary focus of this study, it should be noted that the CWC had a wide range of special classes and support groups for this constituency. For example, the CWC developed the Resource Center for European American Cultural Health that, among other things, helped participants discover "the heritage of ancient wisdom of European peoples . . . balance our cultural values of individual and autonomy with a sense of community." From a CWC program brochure, fall 1998.

5. Community forum on racism, April 10, 1998, field notes, p. 220.

6. Also see later in this chapter for an analysis of CWC's cosmological approach to political action.

7. Interview with CWC medical director, May 16, 1998.

8. The chalice metaphor was frequently used in CWC sessions on racism to portray its cosmological approach to social action.

9. CWC, August 16, 1998, field notes, p.450.

10. CWC, Women and Leadership session, September 15, 1998, field notes, p. 550.

11. CWC, Women and Leadership session, September 15, 1998, field notes, p. 550.

12. CWC African elder, June 15, 1998, field notes, p. 284.

13. Dr. Jonas (pseudonym) was a physician and director of a major public health program affiliated with a Twin Cities hospital. In addition to helping the CWC build partnerships with the mainstream medical system, she was also a user of its services. In fact, several of the region's most prominent community leaders and philanthropists used CWC services.

14. The medical director was an African physician born in the Caribbean.

15. Following the title of Asante's (1990) book, *Afrocentricity*, this term is used instead of Afrocentrism. As is common knowledge among many Twin Cities African and African American participants (see Chapter 4), a transnational marketplace in the trade of "African" goods has emerged based, in part, the promotion of idealized notions of Africa. Stoller (2001:70–78) analyzes this so-called Afrocentric marketplace in New York City. The growing diversity and specialization of the Twin Cities African diasporan nonprofit sector suggests that for-profit entrepreneurs are not the only agents involved in this activity. I would not, however, suggest that this activity is driven by Afrocentricity. Not all sellers and certainly not all consumers are interested in expressing or promoting idealized notions of Africa. Some, for example, Randall Robinson's TransAfrica Forum, focus on addressing economic development and political issues, not on promoting Afrocentricity as conceived by Asante and in other scholarly analyses (Walker 2001). My research among African and African American hair braiders and their clients suggest that some customers

were interested in espousing "African pride" through their hairstyle and fashion choices (Copeland-Carson 1992). But others saw their braided styles as an apolitical personal preference based on the coif's convenience and ability to make the hair grow faster, allowing for loose, flowing styles that were described as white by some Afrocentric braiders.

16. For example, Leonard Jeffries, former chair of City University of New York's Black Studies Program and prominent Afrocentrist, claims that Black people ("sun people"), because of higher levels of melanin, are, in addition to their other attributes, culturally superior to White people ("ice people").

17. See also the CWC's preferred "cosmological" strategies for addressing contemporary race relations.

Chapter 7. Healing the Body

1. See Chapter 1 for a description of the CWC's spatial environment.

2. CWC elder, June 18, 1998, field notes, p. 461.

3. "Unleashing the power of citizens to heal themselves" was the CWC's general mission.

4. A study conducted by the Urban Coalition and the Minnesota Department of Health (1997) reported that communities of color in Minnesota had significantly higher levels of health problems, including higher infant mortality rates, diabetes, hypertension, and AIDS/HIV than did the state's White population.

5. "Cultural food" was a CWC synonym for "ancestral food" or "real food."

6. See Chapter 8 for an extended discussion of conversational pauses as ancestral moments.

7. The CWC did not exclusively incubate African projects. There were also several similar collaborations with European, Hmong, Chicano, Latino, and American Indian partners.

8. This section's data is based is drawn from my participation in some African Soul Movement and Capoeira classes, as well as interviews and more informal discussions with the teachers and some participants in various CWC contexts.

9. The Capoeira class was taught by an African American husband and wife team who study the *orisha* of Yorùbá religion.

10. It is important to note here that although the leadership's intent was to cultivate Africanness inside the body, this study does *not assess* of the extent to which the CWC approach was successful. Not all participants who would be defined as "African" by the leadership espouse its African ways of knowing/being.

Chapter 8. Healing the Spirit

1. The African American leaders, in particular, had a pivotal role in guiding African identity through the CWC. Other CWC participants did not articulate such an intricate view of African diasporan historicity. As demonstrated in Chapter 3 of this study, the body was the primary referent for African identity among CWC Africans born in America, continental Africans, or African Americans; however, the CWC's leaders had a much more elaborate theory which gave direction to both formal and informal programs.

2. See Chapter 6 for a description of the CWC's articulation of these core African cultural principles and practices.

3. This person is also a well-known natural healer in the community and former CWC board member and is now working at the CWC. Active CWC participants preferred the term "European" to "White" in reference to people whom they would define as having primarily ancestors from a European country. The term "White" was used primarily when specifically discussing issues of racism.

4. The term "your people" was frequently used at the CWC to refer to what anthropologists would describe as an ethnic group. It is often used in the context of understanding and describing the "history of your people" or the "culture of your people" as a prerequisite for effective interracial reconciliation and is often used synonymously with the term "community" as in the "European community in Minneapolis."

5. Women and Leadership Session, June 24, 1998, field notes, pp. 322–24.

6. This session led to the spin-off of a CWC-sponsored African women's health care advocacy group that continues to operate in the Twin Cities. It includes African American and Afro-Caribbean women as well.

7. Alice Walker's *Possessing the Secret of Joy* (1993) is a partially fictionalized account of female circumcision in Africa.

8. These are the same parts of the body (see Chapter 3) that are also thought to carry latent African identity or consciousness.

9. CWC African elder, March 11, 1998, field notes, p. 82.

10. The CWC has an ongoing Ancient Wisdom Series which presents monthly seminars on "well-being, healthy lifestyle and healing through preserving culture and being connected to heritage. Presenters are from African, Asian, European heritage" (CWC summer 1998 program catalog). From about January through fall 1998 the series presented various speakers to devise a "cosmological" perspective on racism—a spiritual solution that instead of looking at interracial relations, defines humanity's relationship to creation.

11. As noted in the introduction to this study, for all the its constituent ethnic groups, the most active CWC participants tended to be women. Many of the CWC's identity theories, notions of historicity the body deal with issues of defining and reconciling womanhood in the context of health, contemporary community, history, and gender relations.

12. February 1998, Women and Leadership session.

13. CWC African elder, September 17, 1998, field notes, p. 486.

14. Note here that the term "individual" was frowned upon in CWC discourse, as it was thought to suggest Western individualism, considered to be a major cause of illness in the "people's theory." The preferred CWC term for individual is "person." "Individual" is used here to refer to one person, not to suggest that the CWC espouses a philosophy of individualism.

15. CWC African leader and elder, June 15, 1998, field notes, pp. 266 and 280–81.

16. Pseudonym.

17. Discussion with African CWC leader and founder, August 26, 1998.

18. Exchange between two CWC European leaders and the African director at planning meeting for community forum on racism, March 24, 1998, field notes, pp. 125–26.

19. In keeping with its rejection of what was deemed as mainstream political constructs, the CWC used the terms "your people," "my people," or "our people" instead of "races" or "ethnic groups."

20. All quotations in this paragraph are from an exchange between a CWC African leader and two CWC European leaders during the planning meeting for community forum on racism, March 25, 1998, field notes, pp. 137–39.

21. CWC African elder, planning meeting for racism forum, March 24, 1998, field notes, p. 140.

22. CWC founder and African elder, February 27, 1998, field notes, pp. 81–82.

23. June 15, 1998, field notes, p. 282.

24. Diabetic Support Group member, June 9, 1998, field notes, p. 243.

25. CWC director at seminar for University of Minnesota medical students on cultural healing practices, March 25, 1998, field notes, p. 142.

26. July 16, 1998, Medicine of Reconciliation class.

27. Life history interview with Ethiopian immigrant woman, June 1998.

28. CWC founder and African elder, African Parenting class, August 14, 1998.

29. Conversation with CWC director/founder/African leader, March 13, 1998, field notes, p. 96.

30. Discussion between JCC and African director of the CWC, March 13, 1998, field notes, p. 97.

31. June 15, 1998, field notes, p. 265.

32. There is little justification for the continuing designation of ethnohistory as a distinct subfield; most of its perspectives and methods have become conventional wisdom in both anthropology and history. Arguments for retaining ethnohistory as a distinct subfield (Farriss 1988) focus on its use of historical methods on subjects of traditional focus in anthropology. However, historical methods are in such wide use in anthropology, and so many historians use ethnographic methods (Ohnuki-Tierney 1990:2–4), that this does not seem to sufficiently qualify ethnohistory as a distinct subfield. The use of historical methods by anthropologists—as is current common practice—has almost become a fundamental standard of high quality ethnography (Fernandez 1990).

33. Use of historical methods and comparative examination of the historicities of different interest groups, including elites, is a common tool for applied anthropologists documenting organizational cultures in corporate, public, or nonprofit institutions (see Spradley 1980; van Willigen 1986).

34. See Fentress and Wickham (1992:xi) on the social construction of history in identity formation processes.

Epilogue

1. Minneapolis's major daily, the *Star Tribune*, has done extensive coverage of the impact of September 11 on the state's Somali community. For example, see Kavita Kumar, "Seattle's Fledgling Somali Community Takes Heart, Lessons from Minneapolis," *Star Tribune*, January 13, 2003. Also see Eric Black, "Profile: Omar Jamal, Director of Somali Justice Advocacy Center," *Star Tribune*, January 6, 2003.

2. One such business owner was arrested and then exonerated.

3. Also see Chapter 5 for a presentation of Hannerz's model of global cultural processes.

4. Gupta and Ferguson (1997a) call this "people-making" and "place-making."

5. Also see Appadurai's (1996:169) discussion of alternative forums for cultural production using the example of the formation of a "Black Public Sphere Collective."

6. Even Mintz and Price's (1992) most recent revision of their creolization model still privileges unconscious and spontaneous cultural reproduction as somehow more authentic.

7. Detailed historical studies of American slavery are beginning to question another key component of conventional syncretic models of African diaspora culture

in the Americas (Apter 1991): that in seventeenth-to-nineteenth century America, West and Central African peoples were too heterogeneous to share fundamental cultural features that could be used as baseline to analyze African American cultural development. For example, using documentary evidence and linguistic analysis, historian Douglas Chambers's (1996:100–134) detailed research on eighteenth-century Virginia posits a largely Igbo cultural origin for African slaves in this region. He and other scholars (e.g., Hall 1992; Thornton 1992) maintain that there were "culturally distinct zones" in particular periods and regions of the transatlantic slave trade that can be identified and used to better pinpoint the African impact on African American culture and American society in general. It is noteworthy that recent Africanist analyses (e.g., Kopytoff 1987) using detailed historical, linguistic, and archaeological evidence are proposing that a distinguishable African, even "pan-African," cultural complex did exist at particular historical periods. These cultural patterns were not timeless or neatly integrated but did inform the parameters of debate during periods of cultural change and internal continental and, I would say, by extension, perhaps intercontinental and diasporan migration. With the increasing sophistication of historical anthropological methods, it will be interesting to see if the field somehow returns to Herskovits's original premise that a distinct West African cultural pattern forms the baseline of African diasporan cultural reproductions in some North American regions, at least for certain documentable historical periods.

Furthermore, the relatively new journal *Diaspora* and a new online journal, *Ìrìnkòrindò: A Journal of African Migration,* provide important new forums to revise analyses of African diasporan history still based on conventional notions of culture. "Ìrìnkòrindò" is Yorùbá for incessant wanderings or travels.

Bibliography

Books and Articles

Abrahams, R. C. 1958. *Dictionary of Modern Yorùbá*. London: University of London Press, Ltd., 1958

Abu-Lughod, J. 1991. Writing Against Culture. In *Recapturing Anthropology*, ed. R. G. Fox. Santa Fe, New Mexico: School of American Research Press.

Ahmed, A., and C. Shore, eds. 1995. *The Future of Anthropology: Its Relevance to the Contemporary World*. London: Athlone.

Ajayi, J. F. A. 1970. Bishop Crowther: An Assessment. *Odu* 4:3–17.

Ajayi, J. F. A., and M. Crowder, eds. 1985. *History of West Africa*, 3rd ed. Harlow, England: Longman.

Alba, R. D. 1990. *Ethnic Identity: The Transformation of White America*. New Haven, Conn.: Yale University Press.

Alleyne-Dettmers, P. 1997. A Case Study of Global Compression in the Notting Hill Carnival. In *Living the Global City: Globalization as Local Process*, ed. J. Eade. London: Routledge.

Alonso, A. M. 1988. The Effects of the Truth: Representation of the Past and the Imagining of Community. *Journal of Historical Sociology* 1, no. 1:33–57.

Amin, S., ed. 1974. *Modern Migrations in Western Africa*. London: Oxford University Press.

Anderson, B. 1983. *Imagined Communities*. London: Verso.

Anderson, G. 1974. *Networks of Contact: The Portuguese and Toronto*. Ontario: Wilfrid Laurier Press.

Appadurai, A. 1981. The Past as a Scarce Resource. *Man* 16, no. 2:201–19.

———. 1986. Theory in Anthropology: Center and Periphery. *Comparative Studies in Society and History* 28:356–61.

———. 1990. Disjuncture and Difference in the Global Economy. *Public Culture* 2, no. 2:1–24.

———. 1996. *Modernity at Large: Cultural Dimensions of Globalization*. Minneapolis: University of Minnesota Press.

Appiah, A. 1992. *In My Father's House: Africa in the Philosophy of Culture*. New York: Oxford University Press.

Apter, A. 1991. Herskovits' Heritage: Rethinking Syncretism in the African Diaspora. *Diaspora* 1, no. 3:235–60.

———. 1992. *Black Critics and Kings: The Hermeneutics of Power in Yorùbá Society*. Chicago: Chicago University Press.

Aradeon, S. B. 1989. Transborder Cultural Interaction: The Case of Hausa Mosque Styles on the Nigeria/Niger Border. In *Borderlands in Africa: A Multi-Disciplinary and Comparative Focus on Nigeria and West African.* Lagos, Nigeria: University of Lagos Press.

Aronowitz, S. 1973. *False Promises: The Shaping of American Working Class Consciousness.* New York: McGraw-Hill.

Asante, M. 1987. *The Afrocentric Idea.* Philadelphia: Temple University Press.

Asiwaju, A. I., ed. 1985. *Partitioned Africans: Ethnic Relations Across Africa's International Boundaries, 1884–1984.* New York: St. Martin's Press.

Auge, M. 1978. Status, Power and Wealth: Relations of Lineage, Dependence and Production in Alladian Society. In *Relations of Production,* ed. D. Seddon. London: Cass.

Baer, Hans. 1984. *The Black Spiritual Movement.* Memphis: University of Tennessee Press.

Balibar, E., and I. Wallerstein. 1991. *Race, Nation, Class: Ambiguous Identities.* New York: Verso.

Banfield, A. W. 1969. *Dictionary of the Nupe Language.* Farnborough, Eng.: Gregg. Original edition 1914.

Banton, M. 1957. *West African City.* London: Oxford University Press.

Barker, M. 1990. Biology and the New Racism. In *The Anatomy of Racism,* ed. D. Goldberg. Minneapolis: University of Minnesota Press.

Barley, N. 1983. *Symbolic Structures: An Exploration of the Culture of Dowayos.* Cambridge: Cambridge University Press.

———. 1987. *Plague of Caterpillars.* Harmondsworth: Penguin.

Barnes, J. 1984. *Flaubert's Parrot.* London: Jonathan Cape.

Barnes, S. T. 1986. *Patrons and Power: Creating a Political Community in Metropolitan Lagos.* Bloomington: Indiana University Press.

———. 1997. *Africa's Ògún: Old World and New.* Bloomington: Indiana University Press.

Barth, F. 1984. Problems in Conceptualizing Cultural Pluralism. In *Prospects for Plural Societies,* ed. D. Maybury-Lewis. Washington, D.C.: American Ethnological Society.

———. 1989. The Analysis of Culture in Complex Societies. *Ethnos* 54:121–42.

———, ed. 1969. *Ethnic Groups and Boundaries.* Boston: Little Brown.

Basch, L., G. N. Schiller, and C. Szanton-Blanc. 1994. *Nations Unbound: Transnational Projects, Postcolonial Predicaments, and Deterritorialized Nation-States.* Langhorne, Pa.: Gordon and Breach.

Bascom, W. 1951. Social Status, Wealth, and Individual Difference Among the Yorùbá of Southwest Nigeria. *American Anthropologist* 53, no. 2:490–505.

———. 1962. African Arts and Social Control. *African Studies Bulletin* 5, no. 2:22–35.

———. 1969. *The Yorùbá of Southwestern Nigeria.* New York: Holt, Winston, and Rinehart.

Bashi, V., and A. McDaniel. 1997. A Theory of Immigration and Racial Stratification. *Journal of Black Studies* 27, no. 5:668–82.

Basso, E. 1995. *The Last Cannibals: A South American Oral History.* Austin: University of Texas Press.

Bauman, Z. 1992. *Intimations of Postmodernity.* London: Routledge.

Bean, F. D., et al. 1989. *Opening and Closing the Doors: Evaluating Immigration Reform and Control.* Santa Monica, Calif.: RAND and Urban Institute.

Bellah, R., et al. 1985. *Habits of the Heart.* Berkeley: University of California Press.

Bendor-Samuel, John. 1989. *The Niger-Congo Languages.* Boston: Lanham Press.

Berry, S. S. 1978. *Cocoa, Custom, and Socio-economic Change in Rural West Nigeria.* Oxford: Clarendon.

Bhabha, H. K., ed. 1990. *Nation and Narration.* London: Routledge.

Birdwhistell, R. L. 1970. *Kinesics and Context: Essays on Body Motion Communication.* Philadelphia: University of Pennsylvania Press.

Boas, F. 1934. The Outlook for the American Negro. *The Shaping of American Anthropology, 1883–1911: A Franz Boas Reader,* ed. G. Stocking. New York: Basic Books. Original edition of article 1906.

Bohannan, P. 1957. *Justice and Judgment Among the Tiv.* London: Oxford University Press.

Bourdieu, P. 1963. The Attitude of the Algerian Peasant Toward Time. In *Mediterranean Countrymen: Essays in the Social Anthropology of the Mediterranean,* ed. J. Pitt-Rivers. Paris: Mouton.

———. 1977. *Outline of a Theory of Practice.* Translated by R. Nice. Cambridge: Cambridge University Press.

———. 1984. *Distinction: A Social Critique of the Judgment of Taste.* Cambridge: Cambridge University Press.

Bowen, Eleanor S. [Laura Bohannon]. 1964. *Return to Laughter.* New York: Doubleday.

Boyarin, D., and J. Boyarin. 1993. Diaspora: Generation and the Ground of Jewish Identity. *Critical Inquiry* 19:693–725.

Boyarin, J., ed. 1994. *Remapping Memory: The Politics of TimeSpace.* Minneapolis: University of Minnesota Press.

Bradbury, R. E. 1957. *The Benin Kingdom of the Edo-Speaking People of Southwestern Nigeria.* London: International African Institute.

Brandon, G. 1993. *Santeria from Africa to the New World: The Dead Sell Memories.* Bloomington: Indiana University Press.

Broderson, A. 1957. National Character: An Old Problem Re-examined. *Diogenes* 20:84–120.

Brokensha, D., M. M. Horowitz, and T. Scudder, eds. 1977. *The Anthropology of Rural Development in the Sahel.* Binghamton, N.Y.: Institute for Development Anthropology.

Brown, J., and B. Tucker. 1986. *James Brown: The Godfather of Soul.* New York: Macmillan.

Bruner, E. 1996. Tourism in Ghana: The Representation of Slavery and the Return of the Black Diaspora. *American Anthropologist* 98, no. 2:290–304.

Bruner, J. S. 1987. *Actual Minds, Possible Worlds.* Cambridge, Mass.: Harvard University Press.

Bryce-LaPorte, R. S. 1972a. Black Immigrants: The Experience of Invisibility and Inequality. *Journal of Black Studies* 1:29–56.

———. 1972b. Black Immigrants in the United States: A Comparison with Native Blacks and Other Immigrants. *Industrial and Labor Relations Review* 47, no. 2:265–84.

Buckley, A. D. 1985. *Yorùbá Medicine.* London: Clarendon.

Burawoy, M., et al. 1991. *Ethnography Unbound: Power and Resistance in the Modern Metropolis.* Berkeley: University of California Press.

Burnham, P. 1980a. *Opportunity and Constraint in a Savanna Society: The Gbaya of Cameroon.* London: Academic Press.

———. 1980b. Raiders and Traders in Adamawa: Slavery as a Regional System. In *Asian and African Systems of Slavery,* ed. J. L. Watson. Oxford: Blackwell.

Busia, K. A. 1951. *The Position of the Chief in the Modern Political System of the Ashanti.* London: Oxford University Press for the International African Institute.

Butcher, K. F. 1994. Black Immigrants in the United States: A Comparison with Other Blacks and Other Immigrants. *Industrial and Labor Relations Review* 47, no. 2:265–84.

Castro, M. 1989. *The Politics of Language in Miami.* Miami, Fla.: Greater Miami United.

Cernea, M. 1991. *Putting People First: Sociological Variables in Rural Development.* New York: Oxford University Press for the World Bank.

———. 1994. *Making Development Sustainable.* Washington, D.C.: The World Bank.

Cerroni-Long, E. L., ed. 1995. Insider Anthropology. *National Association of Practicing Anthropologists, Bulletin 16.* Arlington, Va.: American Anthropological Association.

Certeau, M. 1984. *The Practice of Everyday Life.* Berkeley: University of California Press.

Chambers, D. B. 1996. "He Is an African But Speaks Plain": Historical Creolization in Eighteenth Century Virginia. In *The African Diaspora,* ed. A. Jalloh and S. E. Maizlish. Arlington: University of Texas Press.

Chatterjee, P. 1986. *Nationalist Thought and the Colonial World: A Derivative Discourse?* New York: The United Nations University and Zed Press.

Clifford, J. 1988. *The Predicament of Culture: Twentieth Century Ethnography, Literature and Art.* Cambridge, Mass.: Harvard University Press.

———. 1994. Diasporas. *Cultural Anthropology* 9, no. 3:302–38.

Clifford, J., and M. Fisher, eds. 1986. *Writing Culture: The Poetics of Ethnography.* Berkeley: University of California Press.

Cohen, A. 1969. Custom and Politics in Urban Africa: A Study of Hausa Migrants in Yorùbá Towns. Berkeley: University of California Press.

Cohen, R. 1978. Ethnicity: Problem and Focus in Anthropology. *Annual Review of Anthropology* 7:379–403.

Cohn, B. S. 1980. Anthropology: The State of Play. *Comparative Studies in Society and History* 22, no. 1: 198–221.

———. 1987a. The Census, Social Structure and Objectification in South Asia. In *An Anthropologist Among the Historians and Other Essays.* Delhi and London: Oxford University Press.

———. 1987b. *An Anthropologist Among the Historians.* Delhi: Oxford University Press.

Colson, Elizabeth, and Max Gluckman, eds. 1951. *Seven Tribes of British Central Africa.* Manchester: Manchester Press.

Comaroff, J. L. 1982. Dialectical Systems, History, and Anthropology: Units of Study and Questions of Theory. *Journal of Southern African Studies* 8, no. 2:143–72.

———. 1985. *Body of Power, Spirit of Resistance.* Chicago: University of Chicago Press.

Connell, J., et al. 1995. *New Approaches to Evaluating Community Initiatives: Concepts, Methods, and Contexts.* New York: Aspen Institute.

Connerton, P. 1989. *How Societies Remember.* New York: Cambridge University Press.

Crane, D. 1972. *Invisible Colleges: Diffusion of Knowledge in Scientific Communities.* Chicago: University of Chicago Press.

Csordas, T. J. 1990. Embodiment as a Paradigm for Anthropology. *Ethos* 18, no. 1: 5–47.

Curtin, P. 1969. *The Atlantic Slave Trade: A Census.* Madison: University of Wisconsin Press.

———. 1975. *Economic Change in Pre-Colonial Africa: Senegambia in the Era of the Slave Trade.* Madison: University of Wisconsin Press.

———. 1992. *Cross-Cultural Trade in World History.* Cambridge: Cambridge University Press.

D'Amico-Samuels, D. 1992. A Not So Hidden Disgrace: What Talk About Literacy Says About Race. *Transforming Anthropology* 3, no. 1:8–12.

Depres, Leo A. 1984. Ethnicity: What the Data and Theory Portend for Plural

Societies. In *Prospects for Plural Societies*, ed. D. Maybury-Lewis. Washington, D.C.: American Ethnological Society.

Derman, W., and L. Derman. 1973. *Serfs, Peasants, and Socialists: A Former Serf Village in the Republic of Guinea*. Berkeley: University of California Press.

Desmond, C. J., ed. 1982. *The Cambridge History of Africa*. Vol. 1, *From the Earliest Times to c. 500 B.C.* Cambridge: Cambridge University Press.

Devisch, R. 1985a. Approaches to Symbol and Symptom in Bodily Space-Time. *International Journal of Psychology* 20:389–415.

———. 1985b. Symbol and Psychosomatic Symptom in Bodily Space-Time: The Case of the Yaka of Zaire. *International Journal of Psychology* 20:289–616.

Dillard, J. L. 1970. Non-Standard Negro Dialects: Convergence or Divergence? In *Afro-American Anthropology: Contemporary Perspectives*, ed. N. E. Whitten and J. Szwed. New York: Free Press.

———. 1973. *Black English: Its History and Usage in the United States*. New York: Vintage Books.

Drake, S. C. 1982. Diaspora Studies and Pan-Africanisms. In *Global Dimensions of the African Diaspora*, ed. J. E. Harris. Washington, D.C.: Howard University Press.

Du Bois, W. E .B. 1939. *Black Folk, Then and Now: An Essay in the History and Sociology of the Negro Race*. New York: H. Holt and Company.

———. 1990. *The Souls of Black Folk*. New York: Vintage Books/Library of America. Original edition 1903.

Durkheim, E. 1947. *The Division of Labor in Society*. Translated by George Simpson. Glencoe, Ill.: Free Press. Original edition 1893.

Eade, J., ed. 1997. *Living the Global City: Globalization as Local Process*. London: Routledge.

Ehret, C., and M. Posnansky. 1982. *The Archaeological and Linguistic Reconstruction of African History*. Cambridge: Cambridge University Press.

Epstein, A. 1969. *Politics in an Urban African Community*. Manchester: Manchester University Press.

Erlmann, V. 1991. *African Stars: Studies in Black South African Performance*. Chicago: University of Chicago Press.

Escobar, A. 1991. Anthropology and the Development Encounter: The Making and Marketing of Development Anthropology. *American Ethnology* 18, no. 8:658–82.

———. 1995. *Encountering Development: The Making and Unmaking of the Third World*. Princeton, N.J.: Princeton University Press.

Espiritu, V. L. 1992. *Asian-American Panethnicity: Bridging Institutions and Identities*. Philadelphia: Temple University Press.

Evans-Pritchard, E. E. 1940. *The Nuer*. Oxford: Clarendon.

———. 1949. *The Sansusi of Cyrenaica*. Oxford: Clarendon.

Eze, E. 1997. *Postcolonial African Philosophy: A Critical Reader*. London: Blackwell.

Fabian, J. 1983. *Time and the Other: How Anthropology Makes Its Object*. New York: Columbia University Press.

Fardon, R. 1987. African Ethnogenesis: Limits in the Comparison of Ethnic Phenomena. In *Comparison in Sociology*, ed. L. Holy. London: Blackwell.

———. 1988. *Raiders and Refugees: Trends in Chamba Political Development, 1750 to 1950*. Washington, D.C.: Smithsonian Institution Press.

———. 1990. *Localizing Strategies: Regional Traditions of Ethnographic Writing*. Edinburgh and Washington, D.C.: Scottish Academic Press and Smithsonian Institution Press.

Farriss, N. M. 1983. Indians in Colonial Yucatan: Three Perspectives. In *Spaniards and Indians in Southeastern Mesoamerica*, ed. M. MacLeod and R. Wasserstrom. Lincoln: University of Nebraska Press.

———. 1984. *Maya Society Under Colonial Rule.* Princeton, N.J.: Princeton University Press.

Faubion, J. D. 1993. History in Anthropology. *Annual Review of Anthropology* 22:35–54.

Feierman, S. 1990. *Peasant Intellectuals.* Madison: University of Wisconsin Press.

Feierman, S., and J. M. Janzen, eds. 1992. *The Social Basis of Health and Healing in Africa.* Berkeley: University of California Press.

Feldman, A. 1994. On Cultural Anesthesia: From Desert Storm to Rodney King. *American Ethnologist* 21, no. 2:404–18.

Fentress, J., and C. Wickham. 1992. *Social Memory.* Cambridge, Mass.: Blackwell.

Ferguson, J. 1994. *The Anti-Politics Machine: "Development," Depoliticization, and Bureaucratic Power in Lesotho.* Minneapolis: University of Minnesota Press.

Fernandez, J. W. 1990. Tolerance in a Repugnant World and Other Dilemmas in the Cultural Relativism of Melville J. Herskovits. *Ethos* 18, no. 2:140–64.

———, ed. 1991. *Beyond Metaphor: The Theory of Tropes in Anthropology.* tanford, Calif: Stanford University Press.

Fisher, R. 1997. *Building Communities and Community.* Essays on Philanthropy, no. 27. Bloomington: Indiana University Press.

Fisher, W. F. 1997. Doing Good? The Politics and Antipolitics of NGO Practices. *Annual Review of Anthropology* 26:439–64.

Foner, N., ed. 1987. *New Immigrants in New York.* New York: Columbia University Press.

———. 1996. *Changing Identities: Vietnamese Americans, 1975–1995.* Boston: Allyn and Bacon.

Fontenot, W. L. 1994. *Secret Doctors: Ethnomedicine of African Americans.* Westport, Conn.: Bergin and Garvey.

Forde, C. D. 1954. *African Worlds.* London: Oxford University Press.

———. 1956. *Efik Traders of Old Calabar.* London: Oxford University Press.

Forman, S., ed. 1995. *Diagnosing America: Anthropology and Public Engagement.* nn Arbor: University of Michigan Press.

Fortes, M. 1945. *Dynamics of Clanship Among the Tallensi.* Oxford: Oxford University Press.

———. 1949. Time and Social Structure: An Ashanti Case Study. In *Social Structure: Essays Presented to A. R. Radcliffe-Brown,* ed. M. Fortes. Oxford: Oxford University Press.

Fortes, M., and E. E. Evans-Pritchard. 1940. *African Political Systems.* Oxford: Oxford University Press.

Foster, R. J. 1991. Making National Cultures in the Global Ecumene. *Annual Review of Anthropology* 20:235–60.

Foucault, M. 1980. Body/Power. In *Power/Knowledge: Selected Interviews and Writings 1972–1977,* ed. C. Gordon. New York: Pantheon.

———. 1982. *The Archaeology of Knowledge and the Discourse on Language.* New York: Pantheon.

Frazier, E. F. 1939. *The Negro Family in Chicago.* Chicago: Chicago University Press.

Fried, M. 1968. On Concepts of "Tribe" and "Tribal" Society. In *Essays on the Problem of Tribe,* ed. J. Helms. Seattle: University of Washington Press.

Gans, H. J. 1962. *The Urban Villagers: Group and Class in the Lives of Italian Americans.* New York: Free Press.

Gardner, John. 1991. *Building Community.* Washington, D.C.: Independent Sector.

Gates, H. L. 1988. *The Signifying Monkey.* New York: Oxford University Press.

Gates, H. L., ed. 1984. *Black Literature and Literary Theory.* New York: Methuen.

Giddens, A. 1979. *Central Problems in Social Theory: Action, Structure and Contradiction in Social Analysis*. Berkeley: University of California Press.

Gilliam, A. 1992. Towards a New Direction in the Media "War" Against Drugs. *Transforming Anthropology* 3, no. 1:19–233.

Gilroy, P. 1987. *There Ain't No Black in the Union Jack*. London: Hutchinson.

———. 1993. *Black Atlantic: Modernity and Double Consciousness*. London: Verso.

Glazer, N., and P. Moynihan. 1965. *Beyond the Melting Pot*. Cambridge, Mass.: MIT Press.

Gluckman, M. 1941. *The Economy of the Central Baratose Plain*. Rhodes-Livingston Papers, no. 7. Livingstone, Northern Rhodesia: Rhodes-Livingstone Institute.

———. 1958. *Analysis of a Social Situation in Modern Zululand*. Rhodes-Livingstone Institute Papers, no. 28. Livingstone, Northern Rhodesia: Rhodes-Livingstone Institute.

Gold, Steven. 1995. *From the Workers' State to the Golden State: Jews from the Former Soviet Union in California*. New Immigrant Series. Boston: Allyn and Bacon.

Goode, Judith, and Joanne Schneider. 1994. *Ethnic and Racial Relations in Philadelphia: Immigrants in a Divided City*. Philadelphia: Temple University Press.

———. 1958. *The Developmental Cycle in Domestic Groups*. Cambridge: Cambridge University Press.

———. 1966. *Succession to High Office*. Cambridge: Cambridge University Press.

———. 1967. *The Over-Kingdom of the Gonja*. In *West African Kingdoms in the Nineteenth Century*, ed. C. D. Forde and C. Kayberry. London: Oxford University Press.

Gordon, M. 1964. *Assimilation in American Life: The Role of Race, Religion and National Origins*. New York: Oxford University Press.

Gottlieb, A., and P. Graham. 1993. *Parallel Worlds: An Anthropologist and a Writer Encounter Africa*. New York: Crown Publishers.

Gramsci, A. 1971. *Selections from the Prison Notebooks of Antonio Gramsci*, ed. and trans. Quintin Hoare and Geoffrey Nowell. New York: International Publishers.

Gray, J. 1989. *Ashe: Traditional Healing and Religion in Subsaharan African and the Diaspora*. New York: Greenwood Press.

Greenberg, J. H. 1973. *Languages of Africa*. Hague: Mouton. Original edition 1963.

Greene, V. 1975. *For God and Country: The Rise of Polish and Lithuanian Ethnic Consciousness in America, 1860–1910*. Madison: State Historical Society of Wisconsin.

Griaule, M. 1948. *Dieu d'eau: Entretiens avec Ogotemmel (Conversations with Ogotemmelli: An Introduction to Dogon Ideas)*. London: Oxford University Press for the Oxford International Institute.

Gupta, A., and J. Ferguson, eds. 1997a. *Culture, Power, Place: Explorations in Critical Anthropology*. Durham, N.C.: Duke University Press.

———. 1997b. *Anthropological Locations: Boundaries and Grounds of a Field Science*. Berkeley, Calif.: University of California.

Gutkind, P. C. W., and I. Wallerstein, eds. 1976. *The Political Economy of Contemporary Africa*. Beverly Hills, Calif.: Sage.

Gutman, H. G. 1976. *The Black Family in Slavery and Freedom, 1750–1925*. New York: Vintage Books.

Guyer, J. 1980. Food, Cocoa and the Division of Labor by Sex in Two West African Societies. *Journal for the Comparative Study of Society and History* 22:355–73.

Gyeke, K. 1997. *Tradition and Modernity: Philosophical Reflections on the African Experience*. New York: Oxford University Press.

Halbwachs, M. 1980. *Collective Memory*. New York: Harper and Row. Original edition 1950.

Hall, E. T. 1969. *The Hidden Dimension*. Garden City, N.Y.: Anchor Books. Original edition 1966.

———. 1973. *The Silent Language*. Garden City, N.Y.: Anchor Press. Original edition 1959.

———. 1974. *Handbook for Proxemic Research*. Washington: Society for the Anthropology of Visual Communication.

———. 1976. *Beyond Culture*. Garden City, N.Y: Anchor Press.

———. 1989. *The Dance of Life : The Other Dimension of Time*. Garden City, N.Y.: Anchor Press/Doubleday. Original edition 1983.

Hall, G. M. 1992. *Africans in Colonial Louisiana: The Development of Afro-Creole Culture in the Eighteenth Century*. Baton Rouge: Louisiana State University Press.

Handler, R. 1988. *Nationalism and the Politics of Culture in Quebec*. Madison: University of Wisconsin Press.

———. l998. Raymond Williams, George Stocking, and Fin-de-siècle U.S. Anthropology. *Cultural Anthropology* 13, no. 4:447–63.

Handlin, O. 1974. *Boston Immigrants: A Study in Acculturation*. Revised edition, New York: Atheneum.

Hannerz, U. 1969. *Soulside*. New York: Columbia University Press.

———. 1980. *Exploring the City*. New York: Columbia University Press.

———. 1987. The World in Creolization. *Africa* 57:546–59.

———. 1992. *Cultural Complexity*. New York: Columbia University Press.

———. 1996. *Transnational Connections: Culture, People, Places*. London: Routledge.

Hardin, K. 1988. Aesthetics and the Cultural Whole. *Empirical Studies of the Arts* 6, no. 1:35–57.

Harris, J. E. 1971. *African Presence in Asia: Consequences of the East African Slave Trade*. Evanston, Ill.: Northwestern University Press.

———, ed. 1982. *Global Dimensions of the African Diaspora*. Washington, D.C.: Howard University Press.

Harrison, F.W. 1995. The Persistent Power of "Race" in the Cultural and Political Economy of Racism. *Annual Review of Anthropology* 24: 47–74.

Harrison, I. E., and F. W. Harrison, eds. 1998. *Pioneers in African-American Anthropology*. Champaign: University of Illinois Press.

Hart, K. 1985. The Social Anthropology of West Africa. *Annual Review of Anthropology* 14:243–72.

Harvey, D. 1989. *The Conditions of Post-Modernity: An Inquiry into the Origins of Culture Change*. Cambridge: Blackwell.

Hebdige, D. 1979. *Subculture: The Meaning of Style*. London: Methuen.

———. 1990. *Cut 'n' Mix: Culture, Identity and Caribbean Music*. London: Routledge.

Helm, J., ed. 1968. *Essays on the Problem of Tribe: Proceedings of the 1967 Annual Spring Meting of the American Ethnological Society*. Seattle: University of Washington Press.

Helmreich, S. 1992. Kinship, Nation and Paul Gilroy's Concept of Diaspora. *Diaspora* 2, no. 2:243–49.

Herskovits, Melville. 1930. The Culture Areas of Africa. *Africa* 3:59–77.

———. 1937. African Gods and Catholic Saints in New World Negro Belief. *American Anthropologist* 36:635–43.

———. 1938. *Dahomey, An Ancient African Kingdom*. 2 vols. New York: Augustin Press.

———. 1941. *Myth of the Negro Past*. Boston: Beacon Press.

———. 1947. *Trinidad Village*. New York: Knopf.

———. 1962. *Human Factor in Changing Africa*. New York: Knopf.

———. 1966. *The New World Negro: Selected Papers in Afroamerica Studies*. Bloomington: Indiana University Press.

———. 1971. *Life in a Haitian Valley*. New York: Doubleday Anchor. Original edition 1937.

Herskovits, M. J, and F. S. Herskovits. 1934. *Rebel Destiny: Among the Bush Negroes of Dutch Guiana.* New York: McGraw-Hill.

———. 1936. *Suriname Folklore.* New York: Columbia University Press.

Herskovits, M., and W. Bascom. 1959. *Continuity and Change in African Cultures.* Chicago: Chicago University Press.

Herzfeld, M. 1987. *Anthropology Through the Looking Glass: Critical Ethnography in the Margins of Europe.* New York: Cambridge University Press.

Hill, P. 1972. *Rural Hausa.* Cambridge: Cambridge University Press.

Hobsbawm, E., and T. Ranger. 1983. *The Invention of Tradition.* Cambridge: Cambridge University Press.

Holloway, J. E., ed. 1990. *Africanisms in American Culture.* Bloomington: Indiana University Press.

Holtzman, J., and N. Foner. 1999. *Nuer Journeys/Nuer Lives: Sudanese Refugees in Minnesota.* Boston: Allyn and Bacon.

Hopkins, A. G. 1973. *An Economic History of West Africa.* London: Longmans.

Howe, S. 1999. *Afro-centrism: Mythical Pasts and Imagined Homes.* New York: Verso.

Howes, D., ed. 1991. *The Varieties of Sensory Experience : A Sourcebook in the Anthropology of the Senses.* Toronto: University of Toronto Press.

Hudson, B. A., and W. Bielefeld. 1997. Structures of Multinational Nonprofit Organizations. *Nonprofit Management and Leadership* 8, no. 1:31–55.

Hurston, Z. N. 1935. *Mules and Men.* Bloomington: Indiana University Press.

———. 1938. *Tell My Horse.* Philadelphia: Lippincott.

Hymes, D., ed. l969. *Reinventing Anthropology.* New York: Random House.

Inden, R. 1986. Orientalist Constructions of India. *Modern Asian Studies* 20:401–46.

Ingold, T. 1993. The Art of Translation in a Continuous World. In *Beyond Boundaries,* ed. G. Palsson. London: Berg.

Jackson, M. 1983. Knowledge of the Body. *Man* 18:327–45.

———. 1986. *Barawa and the Ways Birds Fly in the Sky.* Washington, D.C.: Smithsonian Institution.

———. 1989. *Paths Towards a Clearing: Radical Empiricism and Ethnographic Inquiry.* Bloomington: Indiana University Press.

Jackson, W. 1986. Melville Herskovits and the Search for Afro-American Culture. In *Malinowski, Rivers, and Others: Essays on Culture and Personality,* ed. G. Stocking. Madison: University of Wisconsin Press.

Jacobs, C., and A. Kaslow. 1991. *The Spiritual Churches of New Orleans.* Memphis: University of Tennessee Press.

Jalloh, A. 1996. The Fula Trading Diaspora in Colonial Sierra Leone. In *The African Diaspora,* ed. A. Jalloh and S. E. Maizlish. Arlington: University of Texas Press.

Johannsen, A. M. 1992. Applied Anthropology and Post-Modernist Ethnography. *Human Organization* 51, no. 1:71–82.

Johnson, J. C. 1994. Anthropological Contributions to the Study of Social Networks: A Review. In *Advances in Social Network Analysis,* ed. S. Wasserman and J. Galaskiewicz. Thousand Oaks, Calif.: Sage.

Joseph, J. 1995. *Remaking America: How the Benevolent Traditions of Many Cultures Are Transforming Our National Life.* San Francisco: Jossey Bass.

Joyner, C. 1987. *A South Carolina Slave Community.* Chicago: University of Illinois Press.

Kearney, M. 1995. The Local and the Global: The Anthropology of Globalization and Transnationalism. *Annual Review of Anthropology* 24:547–65.

Kenyatta, J. 1938. *Facing Mount Kenya.* London: Secker and Warburg.

Keyes, C. 1976. Towards a New Formulation of the Concept of Ethnic Group. *Ethnicity* 3, no. 3:202–13.

Koltyk, J., and N. Foner. 1997. *New Pioneers in the Heartland: Hmong Life in Wisconsin.* New York: Simon and Schuster.

Kopytoff, I. 1981. Aghem Ethnogenesis and the Grassfields Ecumene. In *Contribution de la recherche ethnologique à l'histoire des civilizations du Cameroun,* ed. C. Tardits. Paris: Centre National de la Recherche Scientifique.

———, ed. 1987. *The African Frontier.* Bloomington: Indiana University Press.

———. 1988. Public Culture: A Durkheimian Genealogy. *Public Culture* 1, no. 1:1–16.

Krech, S. 1991. The State of Ethnohistory. Annual Review of Anthropology 20:345–75.

Kroeber, A. L. 1945. The Ancient Oikoumene as an Historic Culture Aggregate. *Journal of the Royal Anthropological Institute* 75:9–20.

Kuhn, T. 1970. *The Structure of Scientific Revolutions.* Chicago: University of Chicago Press. Original edition 1970.

Kuper, A. 1983. *Anthropology and Anthropologists: The Modern British School.* London: Routledge and Kegan Paul. Original edition 1973.

Lamphere, L., ed. 1992. *Structuring Diversity: Ethnographic Perspectives on the New Immigration.* Chicago: Chicago University Press.

Lefkowitz, M. 1997. *No Out of Africa: How Afrocentrism Became an Excuse to Teach Myth as History.* New York: Basic Books.

Leith-Ross, S. 1965. *African Women.* London: Routledge and Kegan Paul.

Lessinger, J., and N. Foner. 1995. *From the Ganges to the Hudson: Indian Immigrants in New York City.* New Immigrant Series. Boston: Allyn and Bacon.

Levine, E. 1977. *Black Culture and Black Consciousness: Afro-American Folk Thought from Slavery to Freedom.* New York: Oxford University Press.

Levitt, P. 1997. Transnationalizing Community Development: The Case of Migration between Boston and the Dominican Republic. *Non-Profit and Voluntary Sector Quarterly* 26, no. 4:509–26.

Levzton, N. 1976. The Early States of Western Sudan to the 1500s. In *History of West Africa,* ed. A. Ajayi and S. Crowder. Vol. 1. 2nd edition. London: Longman.

Lewis, O. 1966. The Culture of Poverty. *Scientific American* 215, no. 4:19–25.

Liebow, E. 1967. *Tally's Corner: A Study of Negro Streetcorner Men.* Boston: Little, Brown.

Linares, O. 1992. *Power, Prayer, and Production: The Jola of Casamance Senegal.* Cambridge: Cambridge University Press.

Little, K. L. 1951. *The Mende of Sierra Leone: A West African People.* London: Routledge and Kegan Paul.

———. 1970. *West African Urbanization: A Study of Voluntary Associations in Social Change.* Cambridge: Cambridge University Press.

Lloyd, P. C. 1962. *Yorùbá Land Law.* Ìbàdàn: Oxford University Press.

———. 1974. *Power and Independence: Urban Africans Perception of Social Inequality.* London: Routledge and Kegan Paul.

Lock, M. 1993. Cultivating the Body: Anthropology and Epistemologies of Bodily Practice and Knowledge. *Annual Review of Anthropology* 22: 133–55.

Lopata, H. Z. 1976. *Polish Americans: Status Competition in an Ethnic Community.* Englewood Cliffs, N.J.: Prentice-Hall.

Lopez, D. 1990. Panethnicity in the University States. *Ethnic and Racial Studies* 13:198–224.

Low, S. M. 1996. The Anthropology of Cities: Imagining and Theorizing the City. *Annual Review of Anthropology* 25:383–409.

Lowie, Robert. 1946. Evolution in Cultural Anthropology: A Reply to Leslie White. *American Anthropologist* 48:223–33.

Bibliography 223

Mahler, S. J., and N. Foner. 1996. *Salvadorans in Suburbia: Symbiosis and Conflict.* New Immigrant Series. Boston: Allyn and Bacon.

Malinowski, B. 1961. *Argonauts of the West Pacific.* London: E. P. Dutton. Original edition 1922.

Maquet, J. 1972. *Civilizations of Black Africa.* New York: Oxford University Press.

Marcus, G., and M. Fisher. 1999. *Anthropology as Cultural Critique: An Experimental Moment in the Social Sciences.* Chicago: University of Chicago Press. Original edition 1986.

Marcus, G. E. 1995. Ethnography in/of the World System: The Emergence of Multi-Site Ethnography. *Annual Review of Anthropology* 24:95–117.

Massefoli, M. 1996. *The Time of the Tribes.* London: Sage.

Matory, J. Lorand. 1994. *Sex and the Empire That Is No More: Gender and the Politics of Metaphor Among the Oyo Yorùbá.* Minneapolis: University of Minnesota Press.

———. 1996. Revisiting the African Diaspora. *American Anthropologist* 98, no. 1:167–70.

Mauss, M. 1973. The Techniques of the Body. *Economy and Society* 2, no. 1:70–85. Original edition 1935.

McDaniel, A. 1995. The Dynamic Racial Composition of the United States. *Daedalus* 1, 124, no. 1:179–98.

McIntosh, S. K., and R. J. McIntosh. 1983. Current Directions in West African Pre-History. *Annual Review of Anthropology* 12:215–58.

McKnight, J. L., and J. P. Kretzmann. 1993. *Building Community from the Inside Out: A Path Toward Finding and Mobilizing Community.* Evanston, Ill.: Center for Urban Affairs and Policy Research/Northwestern University.

Meek, C. K. 1925. *The Northern Tribes of Nigeria.* Oxford: Oxford University Press.

Meillassoux, C., ed. 1971. *The Development of Indigenous Trade and Markets in West Africa.* London: Oxford University Press.

Merleau-Ponty, M. 1962. *Phenomenology of Perception.* Tranlated by Colin Smith. London: Routledge and Kegan Paul.

———. 1964. *The Primacy of Culture.* Translated by James Edie. Evanston, Ill.: Northwestern University Press.

Middleton, J., and R. Cohen. 1970. *From Tribe to Nation in Africa: Studies in Incorporation Processes.* Scranton, Pa.: Chandler Press.

Middleton, John, and D. Tait. 1958. *Tribes Without Rulers.* New York: Humanities Press.

Miers, S., and I. Kopytoff, eds. 1977. *Slavery in Africa: Historical and Anthropological Perspectives.* Madison: University of Wisconsin Press.

Mikell, G. 1997. *African Feminism: The Politics of Survival.* Philadelphia: University of Pennsylvania Press.

Miner, H. 1953. *The Primitive City of Timbuctoo.* Princeton, N.J.: Princeton University Press.

Mintz, S. W. 1970. Foreword. In *Afro-American Anthropology: Contemporary Perspectives,* ed. N. E. Whitten, Jr., and J. F. Szwed, 1–16. New York: Free Press.

———. 1996. *Tasting Food, Tasting Freedom : Excursions into Eating, Culture, and the Past.* Boston: Beacon Press.

Mintz, S.W., and R. Price. 1992. *The Birth of African-American Culture: An Anthropological Perspective.* Boston: Beacon Press. Original edition 1976.

Mitchell, C. 1956. *The Kalela Dance: Aspects of Social Relationships Among Urban Africans in Northern Rhodesia.* Manchester, Eng.: Rhodes-Livingstone Institute by Manchester University Press.

Moffatt, M. 1992. Ethnographic Writing About American Culture. *Annual Review of Anthropology* 21:205–29.

Moore, S. F. 1987. The Production of Cultural Process as a Process. *Intach* no. 11:12–21.

———. 1994. *Anthropology and Africa: Changing Perspectives on a Changing Scene.* Charlottesville: University of Virginia Press.

Morgan, L. H. 1960. In a Letter to Seward on February 2, 1850. In *Lewis Henry Morgan: American Scholar,* ed. C. Resek. Chicago: Chicago University Press.

Morton-Williams, P. 1967. The Yorùbá Kingdom of Oyo. In *West African Kingdoms in the Nineteenth Century,* ed. C. D. Forde and C. Kayberry, 36–39. London: Oxford University Press.

Moses, W. J. 2002. *Afrotopia: The Roots of African American Popular History.* Cambridge: Cambridge University Press.

Mudimbe, V. Y. 1988. *The Invention of Africa.* Bloomington: Indiana University Press.

———. 1994. *The Idea of Africa.* London: James Currey Publishers.

Muller, N. L. 1992. Du Boisian Pragmatism and "the Problem of the Twentieth Century." *Critical Anthropology* 12, no. 3:319–37.

Mullings, L. 1979. Ethnicity and Stratification in the Urban United States. *Annuals of the New York Academy of the Sciences* 318:10–22.

———. 1984. *Therapy, Ideology, and Social Change: Mental Healing in Urban Ghana.* Berkeley: University of California Press.

Murdock, G. P. 1959. *Africa: Its Peoples and Their Culture History.* New York: McGraw-Hill.

Murphy, J. M. 1988. *Santeria: An African religion in America.* Boston: Beacon Press.

———. 1994. *Working the Spirit: Ceremonies of the African Diaspora.* Boston: Beacon Press.

Myrdal, G. 1944. *An America Dilemma.* New York: Harper.

Nadel, S. F. 1942. *A Black Byzantium.* London: Oxford University Press.

Napier, D. 2003. *The Age of Immunology: Conceiving a Future in an Alienating World.* Chicago: Chicago University Press.

———. 1954. *Nupe Religion.* London: Oxford University Press.

News and Views 1996/1997. The Disparity Among the States in Black College Completion Rates: Minnesota Is as Good as It Gets. *Journal of Blacks in Higher Education* 14: 14–17.

Odendahl, T. 1990. *Charity Begins at Home: Generosity and Self-Interest Among the Philanthropic Elite.* New York: Basic Books.

Odendahl, T., and M. O'Neill, eds. 1994. *Women and Power in the Non-Profit Sector.* San Francisco: Jossey Bass.

Ohnuki-Tierney, E., ed. 1990. *Culture Through Time.* Stanford, Calif.: Stanford University Press.

Okri, B. 1991. *The Famished Road.* London: Jonathan Cape.

Omi, M., and H. Winant. 1986. *Racial Formation in the United States: From the 1960s to the 1980s.* New York: Routledge Press.

Oritz, R. 1997. Ògún and the Umbandista Religion. In *Africa's Ògún: Old World and New,* ed. S. T. Barnes. Bloomington: Indiana University Press.

Ortner, S. B. 1988. Theory in Anthropology since the Sixties. *Comparative Studies in Society and History* 26, no. 1:126–66.

———. 1997a. Fieldwork in the Postcommunity. *Anthropology and Humanism* 22 1:61–81.

———. 1997b. Reading America: Preliminary Notes on Class and Culture. In *Recapturing Anthropology,* ed. R. G. Fox. Santa Fe, New Mexico: School of American Research Press.

Owusu, M. 1978. The Ethnography of Africa. The Usefulness of the Useless. *American Anthropologist* 80:310–34.

Padmore, G. 1956. *Pan-Africanism or Communism?* London: Dennis Dobson.

Park, R. E. 1919. The Conflict and Fusion of Cultures with Special Reference to the Negro. *Journal of Negro History* 4:111–33.

———. 1972. *The Crowd and the Public and Other Essays.* Chicago: Chicago University Press.

Peacock, J. L. 1997. The Future of Anthropology. *American Anthropologist* 99, no. 1:9–29.

Peel, J. D. Y. 1968. *Aladura; A Religious Movement Among the Yorùbá.* London: Oxford University Press.

———. 1983. *Ijeshas and Nigerians: The Incorporation of a Yorùbá Kingdom, 1870s to 1970s.* Cambridge, Eng.: Cambridge University Press.

Perez, C. A. 1997. Participatory Research: Implications for Applied Anthropology. In *The Colors of Participation: Practicing Anthropology,* ed. C. A. Perez. Vol. 19, no. 3.

Perlin, F. 1981. Of White Whale and Countrymen in the 18th Century Maratha Deccan: Extended Class Relations, Rights, and the Problem of Rural Automomy Under the Old Regime. *Journal of Peasant Studies*: 172–237.

———. 1985. State Formation Reconsidered. *Modern Asian Studies* 19:415–80.

———. 1988. Disarticulation of the World: Writing India's Economic History. *Comparative Studies in Society and History* 30, no. 2: 379–87.

Pessar, P., and N. Foner. 1995. *A Visa for a Dream: Dominicans in the United States.* New Immigrant Series. Boston: Allyn and Bacon.

Phillipson, D. W. 1992. *African Archaeology.* 2nd ed. Cambridge: Cambridge University Press.

Portes, A., and R. Rumbaut. 1990. *Immigrant America: A Portrait.* Berkeley: University of California Press.

Price, R. 1983. *First Time: The Historical Vision of an Afro-American People.* Baltimore: Johns Hopkins University Press.

Price-Mars, J. 1983. *So Spoke the Uncle.* Translated by M. Shannon. Washington, D.C.: Three Continents. Original edition 1928.

Radcliffe-Brown, A. R. 1952. *Structure and Function in Primitive Society.* London: Cohen and West.

Rahnema, M. 1992. Participation. In *The Development Dictionary,* ed. W. Sachs. London: Zed.

Redfield, R. 1930. *Tepoztlan, A Mexican Village.* Chicago: University of Chicago Press.

Redfield, R., and M. Singer. 1954. The Cultural Role of Cities. *Economic Development and Cultural Change* 3:53–73.

Reed, Michael, ed. 1997. Practicing Anthropology in a Post-modern World. *National Association of Practicing Anthropologists Bulletin,* no. 17. Arlington, Va.: American Anthropological Association.

Reid, I. D. A. 1939. *The Negro Immigrant: His Background Characteristics and Social Adjustment, 1899–1937.* New York: Columbia University Press.

Ridless, R. 1984. *Ideology and Art: Theories of Mass Culture from Walter Benjamin to Umberto Eco.* New York: P. Lang.

Rigby, P. 1985. *Persistent Pastoralists.* London: Zed.

Riesman, P. 1977. *Freedom in Fulani Life: An Introspective Ethnography.* Chicago: Chicago University Press.

Robertson, C. 1974. Economic Women in Africa: Profit-Making Techniques of Accra Market Women. *Journal of Modern African Studies* 12:657–64.

Robertson, G., and M. Mash, eds. 1994. *Travellers' Tales: Narratives of Home and Displacement.* New York: Routledge.

Robertson, R. 1992. *Globalization: Social Theory and Global Culture.* Newbury Park, Calif. and London: Sage.

Rogers, M., et al. 1995. *The Urban Context: Ethnicity, Social Networks and Situational Analysis.* Washington, D.C.: Berg Publishers.

Rosaldo, R. 1980. *Ilongot Headhunting, 1883–1974: A Study in Society and History.* Stanford, Calif.: Stanford University Press.

Rosenau, J. 1990. *Turbulence in World Politics: A Theory of Change and Continuity.* Princeton, N.J.: Princeton University Press.

Rowlands, M. J. 1979. Local and Long Distance Trade and Incipient State Formation on the Bamenda Plateau in the Late 19th Century. *Paideuma* 25:1–19.

Sahlins, M. 1981. *Historical Metaphors and Mythical Realities: Structure in the Early History of the Sandwich Islands Kingdom.* Ann Arbor: University of Michigan Press.

Said, E. 1978. *Orientalism.* New York: Vintage Books.

Salmen, P. 1987. *Listen to the People: Participant Observation of Development Projects.* New York: Oxford University Press for the World Bank.

Sanchez, G. 1997. The Politics of Cape Verdean American Identity. *Transforming Anthropology* 6, nos. 1 and 2: 54–73.

Sanday, P. 1998a. Skeletons in the Anthropological Closet: The Life Work of William S. Willis, Jr. In *Pioneers in African-American Anthropology,* ed. I. E. Harrison and F. V. Harrison. Urbana: University of Illinois Press.

———, ed. 1976. *Anthropology in the Public Interest: Fieldwork and Theory.* New York: Academic Press.

Sanjek, R. 1994. Intermarriage and the Future of Races in the United States. In *Race,* ed. S. Gregory and R. Sanjek. New Brunswick, N.J.: Rutgers University Press.

———. 1996. Race. In *Encyclopedia of Social and Cultural Anthropology,* ed. A. Barnard and J. Spencer. London: Routledge.

Schneider, J. 1999. And How Are We Supposed to Pay for the Health Care? Views of the Poor and Near Poor on Welfare Reform. *American Anthropologist* 101, no. 4:761–82.

Schwab, W. B. 1965. Oshogbo: An Urban Community? In *Urbanization and Migration in West Africa,* ed. H. Kuper. Berkeley: University of California Press.

Senghor, L. 1977. *Liberte III: Negritude et Civilization de l'Universal.* Paris: Seuil.

Shanklin, E. 1994. *Anthropology and Race.* Belmont, Calif.: Wadsworth.

Sharpe, B. 1986. Ethnography and a Regional System: Mental Maps and the Myths of States of Tribe in North-Central Nigeria. *Critique of Anthropology* 6, no. 3:33–65.

Sieber, R. 1973. The Arts and Their Changing Social Function. In *Anthropology and Art: Readings in Cross-Cultural Aesthetics.* Garden City, N.Y.: Natural History Museum.

Silver, H. R. 1981. Calculating Risks: The Socioeconomic Foundations of Aesthetic Innovation in an Ashanti Carving Community. *Ethnology* 2, no. 2:104–14.

Smith, M. F. 1963. *Baba of Karo: A Woman of the Moslem Hausa.* New York: Praeger.

Smith, M. G. 1955. *The Economy of the Hausa Communities of Zaria.* London: H. M. Stationery Office.

———. 1956. On Segmentary Lineage Systems. *Journal of the Royal Anthropological Society* 2:38–90.

———. 1957. The African Heritage in the Caribbean. *Caribbean Studies: A Symposium,* ed. V. Rubin, 34–46. Jamaica: ISER, University College of the West Indies.

———. 1984. The Nature and Variety of Plural Units. In *Prospects for Plural Societies,* ed. D. Maybury-Lewis. Washington, D.C.: American Ethnological Society.

Smith, M. G., and A. Kuper, eds. 1969. *Pluralism in Africa.* Berkeley: University of California Press.

Southall, A. W. 1954. *Alur Society.* Cambridge: Cambridge University Press.

———. 1960. *Social Change in Modern Africa.* London: Oxford University Press.

Soyinka, W. 1976. *Myth, Literature, and the African World.* Cambridge: Cambridge University Press.

———. 1984. The Critic and Society: Bathes, Leftocracy, and Other Mythologies. In *Black Literature and Literary Theory,* ed. H. L. Gates, Jr. New York: Methuen.

Spradley, J. P. 1980. *Participant Observation.* New York: Holt, Rinehart and Winston.

Stack, C. B. 1975. *Our Kin: Strategies for Survival in a Black Community.* New York: Harper and Row.

———. 1996. *Call to Home: African Americans Reclaim the Rural South.* New York: Basic Books.

Stafford, S. B. 1987. The Haitians: The Cultural Meaning of Race and Identity. In *New Immigrants in New York,* ed. N. Foner. New York: Columbia University Press.

Stampp, K. M. 1956. *The Peculiar Institution: Slavery in the Ante-Bellum South.* New York: Vintage Books.

Stenning, D. J. 1959. *Savannah Nomads: A Study of the Wodaabe Pastoral Fulani of Western Bornu Province, Northern Nigeria.* London: Oxford University Press.

Stocking, G. W. 1968. *Race, Culture, and Evolution: Essays in the History of Anthropology.* New York: Free Press.

———. 1987. *Victorian Anthropology.* New York: Free Press.

———, ed. 1973. *The Shaping of American Anthropology, 1883–1911.* New York: Basic Books.

———. 1974. *Malinowski, Rivers, and Others: Essays on Culture and Personality.* Madison: University of Wisconsin Press.

Stoller, P. 1987. *In Sorcery's Shadow: A Memoir of Apprenticeship Among the Songhai of Niger.* Chicago: Chicago University Press.

———. 1989. *The Taste of Ethnographic Things: The Senses in Anthropology.* Philadelphia: University of Pennsylvania Press.

———. 1996. Spaces, Places, and Fields: The Politics of West African Trading in New York's Informal Economy. *American Anthropologist* 98, no. 2:776–88.

———. 1997. *The Taste of Ethnographic Things.* Philadelphia: University of Pennsylvania Press.

———. 2002. *Money Has No Smell: The Africanization of New York City.* Chicago: University of Chicago Press.

Sudarkasa, N. 1973. *Where Women Work: A Study of Yorùbá Women in the Market Place and the Home.* Museum Paper No. 53. Ann Arbor, Mich.

Sullivan, M. 1996. Neighborhood Social Organisation: A Forgotten Object of Ethnographic Study? In *Ethnography and Human Development: Context and Meaning in Social Inquiry,* ed. R. Jessor, A. Colby, and R. Shweder. Chicago: University of Chicago Press.

Susser, I. 1996. The Construction of Poverty and Homelessness in US Cities. *Annual Review of Anthropology* 25:411–35.

Swift, J. 1977. Sahelian Pastoralists: Underdevelopment, Desertification, and Famine. *Annual Review of Anthropology* 6:457–78.

Szwed, J. 1970. Afro-American Musical Adaptation. In *Afro-American Anthropology: Contemporary Perspectives,* ed. N.E. Whitten and J. Szwed. New York: Free Press.

Takagi, D. Y. 1994. Post-Civil Rights Politics and Asian-American Identity: Admissions and Higher Education. In *Race,* ed. S. Gregory and R. Sanjek. New Brunswick, N.J.: Rutgers University Press.

Talbot, D. A. 1923. *Life in a Southern Village.* London: Macmillan.

Taussig, M. T. 1980. *The Devil and Commodity Fetishism in South America.* Chapel Hill: University of North Carolina Press.

Terray, E. 1972. *Marxism and Primitive Societies*. New York: Monthly Review Press.

Thompson, R. F. 1983. *Flash of the Spirit: African and Afro-American Art and Philosophy*. New York: Random House.

Thompson, R. T. 1988. Recapturing Heaven's Glamour: Afro-Caribbean Festivalizing Arts. In *Caribbean Festival Arts*, ed. J. W. Nunley and J. Bettelheim. Seattle: University of Washington Press.

Thornton, J. K. 1992. *Africa and Africans in the Making of the Atlantic World, 1400–1800*. Cambridge: Cambridge University Press.

Tocqueville, Alexis. 1994. *Democracy in America*. New York: Alfred A. Knopf. Original edition 1856.

Tonkin, E. 1990. West African Ethnographic Traditions. In *Localizing Strategies: Regional Traditions of Ethnographic Writing*, ed. R. Fardon, 137–51. Edinburgh and Washington, D.C.: Scottish Academic Press and Smithsonian Institution Press.

Trigger, B. G. 1982. Ethnohistory: Problems and Prospects. *Ethnohistory* 29, no. 1:1–19.

Turner, V. 1957. *Schism and Continuity in an African Society*. Manchester, Eng.: Manchester University Press.

Valentine, C. A. 1968. *Culture and Poverty: Critique and Counterproposals*. Chicago: University of Chicago Press.

Van Mannen, J. 1988. *Tales of the Field: On Writing Ethnography*. Chicago: University of Chicago Press.

Van Willigen, J. 1986. *Applied Anthropology: An Introduction*. New York: Berin and Garvey.

Vansina, J. 1965. *Oral Tradition: A Study in Historical Methodology*. Translated by H. M. Wright. Chicago: Aldine. Original edition 1961.

———. 1985. *Oral Tradition as History*. Madison: University of Wisconsin Press.

Vaughan, J. H. 1977. Environment, Population, and Traditional Society. In *Africa*, ed. P. M. Martin and P. O'Leary, 2nd ed. Bloomington: Indiana University Press.

Vaughan, M. 1991. *Curing their Ills: Colonial Power and African Illness*. Stanford, Calif.: Stanford University Press.

Vlach, J. M. 1976. Affecting Architecture of the Yourba. *African Arts* 10:147–51.

———. 1978. *The Afro-American Tradition in Decorative Arts*. Cleveland, Ohio: Cleveland Museum of Art.

———. 1984. The Brazilian House in Nigeria: Emergence of a Twentieth Century House Type. *Journal of American Folklore* 97, no. 383:3–2.

———. 1986. The Shotgun House: An African Architectural Legacy. In *Common Places: Readings in American Vernacular Architecture*, ed. D. Upton and J. M. Vlach. Athens: University of Georgia Press.

Walker, A. 1993. *Possessing the Secret of Joy*. New York: Simon and Schuster.

Walker, C. E. 2001. *We Can't Go Back Home Again: An Argument About Afrocentrism*. Oxford: Oxford University Press.

Wallace, A. F. C. 1956. Revitalization Movements: Some Theoretical Considerations for Their Comparative Society. *American Anthropologist* 63:264–81.

———. 1980. *Rockdale: The Growth of an American Village in the Early Industrial Revolution*. New York: W. W. Norton.

Wallerstein, I. M. 1974. *The Modern World-System*. New York: Academic Press.

———. 1984. *Politics of the World-Economy : The States, the Movements, and the Civilizations*. New York: Cambridge University Press.

Walters, R. W. 1993. *Panafricanism in the African Diaspora*. Detroit, Mich.: Wayne State University Press.

Waters, M. C. 1990. *Ethnic Options: Choosing Identity in America*. Berkeley: University of California Press.

————. 1994. Ethnic and Racial Identities of Second-Generation Black Immigrants in New York City. *International Migration Review* 28, no. 4:795–821.

Weatherford, J. 1985. *Tribes on the Hill.* New York: Rawson, Wade.

Weisgrau, M. 1997. *Interpreting Development: Local Histories, Local Strategies.* Lanham, Md.: University Press of America.

Werbner, R. P. 1984. The Manchester School. *Annual Review of Anthropology* 13:157–85.

White, H. 1978. *Tropics of Discourse: Essays in Cultural Criticism.* Baltimore: Johns Hopkins University Press.

————. 1987. *The Content of Form: Narrative Discourse and Historical Representation.* Baltimore: Johns Hopkins University Press.

Whitten, N. E., and J. Szwed, eds. 1970. *Afro-American Anthropology: Contemporary Perspectives.* New York: Free Press.

Wikan, U. 1992. Beyond the Words: The Power of Resonance. *American Ethnologist* 19:460–82.

Williams, B. F. 1989. CLASS ACT: Anthropology and the Race to Nation Across Ethnic Terrain. *Annual Review of Anthropology* 18:401–44.

Willis, P. E. 1977. *Learning to Labour: How Working Class Kids Get Working Class.* Farnsborough, Eng.: Saxon House.

Wilson, Tamara D. 1994. *Reconstructing Lives, Recapturing Meaning: Refugee Identity, Gender and Culture Change.* Switzerland: Gordon and Breach.

Winant, H. 1994. *Racial Conditions.* Minneapolis: University of Minnesota Press.

Wirth, L. 1956. *The Ghetto.* Chicago: University of Chicago Press. Original edition 1928.

Wolcott, H. F. 1995. *The Art of Fieldwork.* Walnut Creek, Calif.: Altmira Press.

Woldemikael, T. M. 1989a. A Case Study of Race Consciousness among Haitian Immigrants. *Journal of Black Studies* 20, no. 2:224–39.

————. 1989b. *Becoming Black American: Haitians and American Institutions in Evanston, Illinois.* New York: AMS Press.

Wolf, E. R. 1982. *Europe and the People Without History.* Berkeley: University of California Press.

————. 1998. *Envisioning Power : Ideologies of Dominance and Crisis.* Berkeley: University of California Press.

Woodson, C. G. 1936. *The African Background Outlined.* Washington, D.C.: Association for the Study of Negro Life and History.

Worsley, P. 1984. Three Modes of Nationalism. In *Prospects for Plural Societies,* ed. D. Maybury-Lewis. Washington, D.C.: American Ethnological Society.

Yancey, W. L., et al. 1976. Emergent Ethnicity: Review and Reformulation. *American Sociological Review* 41 (June):391–403.

Zindi, F. 1985. *Roots: Rocking in Zimbabwe.* Gweru: Mambo Press.

Reports and Unpublished Papers

Azzahir, M., and J. Barbee. 1997. *Healthy Powderhorn, Living a Philosophy of Community, Health and Wellness: Final Report.* Minneapolis, Minn.: Healthy Powderhorn.

Copeland-Carson, J. 1984. Religions of the Oppressed? Deprivation and the Origins of Religious Movements: The Cases of the Nigerian African Church and Yorùbá Aladura Movements. Senior Thesis, African Studies Program, Georgetown University.

————. 1990. An Interdisciplinary Method for Planning Culturally Appropriate

Housing: A Case Study of Ilé-Ifẹ, Nigeria. Master's Thesis, City and Regional Planning, University of Pennsylvania.

————. 1991. Beyond the "Traditional" and "Modern": Towards an Ethnoaesthetics of Yorùbá Contemporary Architecture. Master's Thesis, Cultural Anthropology, University of Pennsylvania.

————. 1992. *The Body Politic/The Body Beautiful: The Politics of African Diasporan Aesthetics in the Washington, D.C. Hair Sculpture Industry.* Washington, D.C.: Smithsonian Institution, National Museum of American History, Program in African American Culture.

D'Alisera, J. 1999. Multiple Sites, Virtual Sightings: Ethnography in Transnational Contexts. Chicago, Ill.: Presented paper, 1999 American Anthropological Association Annual Meeting.

Federal Reserve Bank of Minnesota. 1999. *A Profile of the Twin Cities Metropolitan Area.* Minneapolis, Minn.: Federal Reserve Bank.

Harrison, R. J., and D. Weinberg. 1992. *Racial and Ethnic Segregation in 1990.* Washington, D.C.: U.S. Bureau of the Census.

Holtzman, J. 1999. My Commute to Nuerland. Chicago, Ill.: Presented paper, 1999 American Anthropological Association Annual Meeting.

Larson, E., and M. Azzahir. 1995. *Toward a Healthy Powderhorn.* Minneapolis, Minn.: Healthy Powderhorn.

Meter, K. 1995. *Powderhorn Neighborhood: Income Statement and Balance Sheet.* Minneapolis, Minn.: Crossroads Resource Center.

Minnesota Advocates for Human Rights/The Building Immigrant Awareness and Support (B.I.A.S) Project. 1998. *The Changing Nature of U.S. Immigration: Myth and Facts.* Minneapolis, Minn.: Minnesota Advocates for Human Rights.

powell, john. 1999a (Sept.). *Concentrated Poverty: Causes, Effects and Solutions.* Minneapolis, Minn.: Institute on Race and Poverty, University of Minnesota Law School.

————. 1999b (Mar.). *What the Research Shows.* Minneapolis, Minn.: Institute on Race and Poverty, University of Minnesota Law School.

Ronnigen, B. J. 1999 (May). *Estimates of Immigrant Populations in Minnesota/Working Paper 99–16.* St. Paul, Minn.: State Demographic Center.

Sanday, P. R. l998b. *Defining Public Interest Anthropology.* Philadelphia, Pa.: Presented Paper/Opening Statement, Public Interest Anthropology Symposium, 97th Annual Meeting of the American Anthropological Association.

Urban Coalition. 1998. *Getting It All Together: The Health and Well-Being of Minnesota's Youth.* Minneapolis, Minn.: The Urban Coalition.

Urban Coalition and Minnesota Department of Health/Office of Minority Health. 1997 (Spring). *Populations of Color in Minnesota: Health Status Report.* Minneapolis, Minn.: Urban Coalition.

Newspapers, Newsletters, Magazine Articles, and Web Sites

Adams, J. December. 1996. Healthy Powderhorn: The Cultural Wellness Center is Building Community and Respecting Traditional Healing Arts. *The Edge: Exploring the Evolution of Consciousness,* a community newsletter, 25.

Anokye, F. 1998. Ghana's Emancipation Celebration Welcomes Home Africans in the Diapora. *Insight News,* August 26, 1.

Bentley, R., and C. Graves. 1998. Killer Sought as Taxi Driver is Mourned. *Star Tribune,* March 10, A1.

Black, E. 2003. Profile: Omar Jamal, director of Somali Justice Advocacy Center, *Star Tribune*, January 6.

Fukushima, R. 1997. Health with Heritage: A New Neighborhood Wellness Center Takes a Multicultural Approach to Healthy Living. *Vital Signs: Health and Fitness, Well Being and Medicine,* a community newsletter, February.

Great Lake Commercial Center. 1998. *Great Lake Street Stories* 1, no. 1.

Hayes-Taylor, K. 1998a. Working Through a Clash of Cultures: Efforts Made to Ease Tensions Between Somali and African-American Students. *Star Tribune,* March 22, A1.

————. 1998b. Pain of African AIDS Crisis Touches Minnesotans: Groups Take Initiative for Education Overseas. *Star Tribune,* July 4, A1.

————. 1998c. Farming Fulfillment: Cultural Reminders-Songs in Swahili, Smells of Earth-Through a State Outreach Program Help Sudanese Farmers Reconnect. *Star Tribune,* July 30, B1.

————. 1998d. Conference Celebrates States Ties to Africa. *Star Tribune,* October 4, B1.

————. 1999. At Peace in a New Land: African Immigrants are Immigrating to the Twin Cities in Huge Numbers. *Star Tribune,* June 6, A1.

Hoang, V. 1999. Pagans Find a Home on College Campuses. *Star Tribune,* August 14, B8.

Hobbes, D. 1999. When Blacks Hate Blacks: Somali Immigrants Are Bumping Up Against the Twin Cities' Black Community Just as the Irish Once Bumped Up Against the Italians. *Law and Politics,* no. 110.

Ìrìnkòrindò: A Journal of African Migration. 2002. http://www.africamigration.com.

Johnson, D. 1997. Ethnic Change Tests Mettle of Minneapolis Liberalism. *Wall Street Journal,* October 18, A1.

Johnson, S.W. 1998. Letter to the Editor. *Star Tribune,* March 25, A10.

Kumar, K. 2003. Seattle's fledgling Somali Community Takes Heart, Lessons from Minneapolis. *Star Tribune,* January 13, 2003.

Tillotson, K. 1998. Somalis Adapt to Life in a Strange Land. *Star Tribune,* March 22, A12.

Wellness and Culture: Balance in the Mind, Body and Soul. 1998. *Health and Culture: Celebrating Our Health,* A Quarterly Publication by Health Partners (A Minnesota Health Maintenance Company), 1.

Zavoral, N. 1999. Ommmmm in Minnesota: Minnesota's Tibetan Community. *Star Tribune,* September 4, B5.

CWC Program Documents

CWC. 1995. Mission Statement.

————. 1995. People's Theory of Health and Wellness: A Diagram, December.

————. 1995. Spatial Philosophy Statement.

————. 1997. Philosophy Through Imagery. In *Healthy Powderhorn, Living a Philosophy of Community, Health & Wellness: A Program Goal Statement.* Minneapolis, Minn.: Healthy Powderhorn.

————. 1997–99. Program Calendars, Spring, Summer, Fall, Winter.

————. 1998. Statement of Program and Organizational Structure.

————. 1998. An Organic Community Care-Giving System: A Model.

————. 1998. Program Plan Diagram, Winter.

———. 1998. Resource Center for European American Cultural Health, A Program Flyer.

———. 1998. Wellness: Mind, Body, Spirit, Culture, Community Program Brochure, Fall.

———. 1999. Health, Heritage and Harmony: A Briefing for Health Practitioners and Community Residents/Health Care Professionals Acting Alone Can't Do It, Program Announcement, April.

Index